Satmar

*Two Generations of
an Urban Island*

PETER LANG
New York • Washington, D.C./Baltimore
Bern • Frankfurt am Main • Berlin • Vienna • Paris

Satmar

*Two Generations of
an Urban Island*

SECOND EDITION

BY

Israel Rubin

PETER LANG
New York • Washington, D.C./Baltimore
Bern • Frankfurt am Main • Berlin • Vienna • Paris

Library of Congress Cataloging-in-Publication Data

Rubin, Israel.
Satmar: two generations of an urban island/
Israel Rubin. — 2nd ed.
p. cm.
Includes bibliographical references and index.
1. Satmar Hasidim—New York (N.Y.) 2. Jews—New York (N.Y.)—Social
conditions. 3. Judaism—New York (N.Y.) I. Title.
BM198.55.R83 305.6'96074723—dc20 95-51537
ISBN 0-8204-0759-3

Die Deutsche Bibliothek-CIP-Einheitsaufnahme

Rubin, Israel.
Satmar: two generations of an urban island/
Israel Rubin.—2nd. ed.
– New York; Washington, D.C./ Baltimore;
Bern; Frankfurt am Main; Berlin; Vienna; Paris: Lang.
ISBN 0-8204-0759-3

The paper in this book meets the guidelines for permanence and durability
of the Committee on Production Guidelines for Book Longevity
of the Council of Library Resources.

© 1997 Peter Lang Publishing, Inc., New York

Printed in the United States of America.

TO THE MEMORY OF MY FATHER

Menachem Eliezer

AND MY MOTHER

Rochel

WHO WERE MURDERED BY THE NAZIS

ON THE 25TH OF IYAR, 5704

(MAY 18, 1944)

FOR NO SIN OTHER THAN

BEING JEWISH

Acknowledgments

The research for this project was made possible by an Andrew Mellon Fellowship from the University of Pittsburgh. The Conference on Jewish Material Claims Against Germany and the National Foundation for Jewish Culture provided supplementary grants. I sincerely appreciate their help.

I owe a debt of gratitude to the members of the Satmar community, to my informants, and especially to the leader, Rabbi Yoel Teitelbaum, who not only granted permission for my study but cooperated fully during the research and assured the cooperation of all members whose assistance was vital to the project.

I am deeply grateful to Dr. George P. Murdock, Andrew Mellon Professor of Anthropology at the University of Pittsburgh, who spent a generous amount of his time advising and assisting me during various phases of the work.

I wish to thank the members of the faculty of the University of Pittsburgh with whom I studied. I am especially thankful to Professors David Henderson, Roger Nett, James D. Thompson, and C.K. Yang (sociology); Professors Fred Adelman and William P. Lebra (anthropology); and Professor James F. Clarke (history), who not only taught me effectively but went beyond the call of duty, tutoring, advising, and encouraging me in my work.

The editors of Quadrangle Books deserve credit for polishing my style and purifying my often foreign syntax.

My thanks to Mrs. Barbara W. Shirland who typed the manuscript with skill, alertness, and abundant patience.

My wife Anna (Halberstam) has been of immense assistance as critic and especially as a faithful companion who gracefully accepted this study's demands on my time and energy.

Finally, thanks—and apologies—to all friends and colleagues who helped me in various ways but whose names are omitted.

The restudy was made possible by a leave of absence as well as some financial assistance granted to me by Cleveland State University for the Spring of 1988. I am indebted both to our Department of Sociology and the various administrative levels for extending this enabling courtesy to me.

The Satmar community has again cooperated fully with my efforts. I sincerely thank all involved. Special thanks to the leader, Reb Moshe Teitelbaum, who not only granted permission, but also interceded on my behalf, whenever needed, to assure required access to many sensitive areas, especially the school system. His son, Reb Aharon, heir apparent and currently the Rov of Kiryas Yoel, equally helped me in every possible way. Reb Lipe, another of the Rebbe's sons, who serves in a number of advisory and community-relations capacities to his father, spent a tremendous amount of time explaining to me the leadership's official view of controversial issues. He also helped me access various establishments, wherever and whatever I wished to. Reb Moshe's (late) daughter Haya, who was extremely brilliant and a rather extraordinary individual, also donated generously of her time to provide invaluable supplementary insight into the current setup at the top level. To lesser extents, other members of the official family did their share to facilitate my job and to help me navigate within second-generation Satmar. Thanks again to all Teitelbaums, without whose assistance nothing could have been accomplished.

I am also grateful to all my informants, especially educators and school administrators, for their generous help. I owe special gratitude to Rabbi Herz Frankel, one of the veteran administrators of the school-system's secular division, who provided a wealth of information and valuable insight into the immense changes that have occurred, both within the schools and within the community in general, during the three decades since the first study. Incidentally, Rabbi Frankel was also most helpful back in 1960-1961 when I first studied Satmar. Unfortunately, I failed to mention his name the first time around. My sincere apologies.

Mr. Michael Flamini, Senior Acquisitions Editor at Peter Lang, not only lent his skillful editing hand, but took a persistent personal interest in the manuscript, which was extremely helpful and encouraging. Thanks for keeping me at it through difficult times.

Last, certainly not least, I owe a debt of gratitude to Ms. Sheree Thomas, our Sociology Department's capable administrative assistant, whose hard work, advice, and supervision I found indispensable. Many thanks!

Contents

Acknowledgments vii

Introduction to the First Edition 3

Introduction to the Second Edition 11

Part One
The Historical Background

I   How the European Jews Became Culturally
      Diversified 17

II   The History of Satmar 42

Part Two
Religion, the Core of Satmar Life

III The Belief System 54

IV The Rov, Backbone of Satmar 65

V   Social Structure 75

VI Religious Behavior 88

Part Three
Family and Education

VII The Family 122

VIII Education 161

Part Four
Economics, Politics, and Welfare

IX Economic Behavior 190

X   Politics 200

XI Welfare 211

Part Five
Vital Processes

XII   Insulation and Control.. 220
XIII Change and Strain.. 234
XIV   Attraction and Repulsion: A Few Illustrations............ 244

Part Six
Implications and Conclusions

XV   Statics and Dynamics: Some Implications 256
XVI   Conclusion: Some Thoughts on Insular Existence...... 268
XVII Conclusion II 280

Index.. 305

SATMAR

Two Generations of an Urban Island

Introduction to the First Edition

Toward the northwestern corner of Brooklyn, New York City's most populated borough, lies Williamsburg, a typical metropolitan lower-middle and working-class neighborhood. Interspersed among the old two- and three-family houses and medium-sized apartment buildings are a few recently built high-rise projects—each almost touching the next. The area is served by several small shopping centers, the largest of which is on Broadway, in the shadow of the elevated train, which is the chief medium of public transportation to nearby Manhattan. Broadway also bisects Williamsburg north and south; it is in the southern part that the Satmar community is concentrated.

Already between the two world wars, Williamsburg began to attract Orthodox Jews, especially those who meant to perpetuate Orthodoxy on American soil. After World War II, the area received a massive influx of new ultra-Orthodox Jewish immigrants, remnants of eastern Hungarian communities destroyed by the Germans and their allies.[1] Dominant among the postwar immigrants were the Hasidim, bearers of a distinct subculture which originated among eighteenth-century East European Jews.[2]

Contrary to a general impression, Williamsburg Hasidim are far from a homogeneous community. My purpose in this book is not to unravel the complexities of this aggregate, but rather to investigate one core group which is the recognized dominant force in Hasidic Williamsburg. The organizational framework for this core community is the Congregation Yetev Lev D'Satmar. The key word is "Satmar,"[3] the name of the former residence of the community's leader, Reb Yoel Teitelbaum. In Hasidic tradition, the followers of a master "belong" to the latter's place of residence and are identified accordingly. Thus the members of our group are known as Satmarer Hasidim (or simply Satmarer), the leader as the Satmarer Rov or Satmarer

Rebbeh[4] (for his followers he is "the Rebbeh" or, more often, "the Rov"), and the community or the culture as Satmar. These are terms I shall henceforth employ.

In undertaking this study, I had two basic objectives in mind: first, to provide an accurate description of Satmar life, and, second, to attempt to answer, on the basis of the facts, a number of questions about the internal structure of the community as well as its place in the American cultural scene.

Ultra-Orthodoxy and militant anti-Zionism are the two characteristics of Satmar life that are chiefly responsible for the curiosity that outsiders are likely to exhibit toward the community. These same characteristics are also the cause of widespread factual distortions. This is so because those who are most apt to inquire about life in this exotic community are American Jews, most of whom sharply dislike uncompromising Orthodoxy and opposition to the ideal of Jewish statehood. Consequently, reports about Satmar that appear in various American Jewish publications tend to underline aspects that appear ridiculous when measured by Western standards. Occasionally, such reports contain "inventions" when reality fails to substantiate a desired image.

A good example of this sort of reportage is the article "Satmar in Brooklyn" which appeared in *Commentary*,[5] a highly reputable monthly journal of opinion. The editor would, no doubt, have checked more thoroughly the accuracy of the report except that the reported "facts" were in accord with the stereotyped image of Satmar. The authors, for instance, "established" that "the sale of second hand clothing which the men solicIt door to door in the greater New York area" is "a major source of income" for Satmarer Hasidim.[6] The resulting image is that of an aggregate of beggars, a social category of low esteem in most cultures, but especially so in the United States. Yet occupational data on nearly 90 per cent of the population show not only that this occupation is not a major source of income, but that the combined total of individuals of working age who derive their livelihood from sources other than work or business activity is small indeed.

In a similar vein, the authors report as a matter of common knowledge that the Rebbeh "remains inaccessible to the curious outsider," and that he "doesn't grant an audience to one who does not belong to his congregation."[7] To convince oneself of the inaccuracy of this statement, one need only walk into the Rov's residence at 500 Bedford Avenue, Brooklyn, in the late afternoon or evening, wait in the antechamber of his study for one's turn, and then walk in. I did so several times and, while waiting, observed many other outsiders doing the same thing without encountering any obstacles whatsoever. But again, the stereotype of a leader who is inaccessible to the outsider fits well into a negative image. Inaccessibility can easily be interpreted as indication of anti-democratic tendencies within the group, as well as fear of being exposed to critical outsiders who might challenge the Rov's claim to absolute righteousness. Seclusion also connotes a general outdatedness which arouses ridicule in the mind of the "progressive" reader.

One main aim of this study was therefore to investigate the actual ingredients of present-day Satmar culture,[8] accenting facts and minimizing value judgments.

The second major task in this study was to interpret and analyze the processes of control and change in Satmar. On the one hand, we must understand how Satmar has preserved its culture after two decades of living within the heart of the megalopolis where hundreds of thousands of immigrants, Jews and others, have succumbed to the forces of assimilation. On the other hand, we must see what changes have taken place as a result of transplanting the community to its present habitat. The fact that Satmarer have not even attempted to build their own economy but have plunged head-on into New York City's economic life, is a special challenge to the contemporary student. Influenced as we all are, at least to a degree, by Marxian thought on the relationship between the economic base and the cultural "superstructure," we need to answer such questions as: Why has Satmar's participation in the general economy not resulted in acceptance of the general cultural superstructure? Or, are the changes that have occurred in any way related to economic activity? And if so, what is the nature of the relationship?

Larger implication may be found as well. What does Satmar suggest for the understanding of similar problems elsewhere?

Assuming that we can identify the forces that permit Satmar to block undesired change despite its involvement in the outside economy, we may learn something about similar forces at work in similar situation—or about changes that occur in spite of insulating mechanisms.

Finally, while rejecting value judgments, it is difficult to resist formulation of an overall assessment of Satmar's present and future, as well as of its implications for the prospects of Jewish (especially Orthodox) survival in the United States and for the largest question of cultural pluralism in our midst.

During 1960-1961, I made five visits to the Satmar community, each time taking up residence for a period of three to four weeks. While there, I participated in most of the activities that Satmarer engage in as members of their group. Because I had acquired the necessary linguistic and other practical knowledge in the course of my own upbringing, I was able to participate in the life of the community from virtually the first moment of arrival.

When the Rov granted permission for my study, almost all doors opened. This way I had access to such places as the school system, where extensive observation was necessary because the system has undergone basic changes in this country.

Many informants supplied information on aspects of Satmar life which were not readily observable. While subjects such as matchmaking procedures or child-rearing were readily related to me as matters of commonly known fact, more sensitive topics relating to internal conflict and tension required the cooperation of key individuals, access to whom was possible only because of the Rov's nod. A few informants were also informally interviewed for the purpose of eliciting Satmarer's subjective views of their own culture and its relationship to the world without.

Census data gathering was the only quantitative technique I used. It was limited to clearly numerical data such as number of children or age. Information on various items was thus obtained for some 80 to 90 per cent of the population.

My reading of religious literature, both what is currently produced and older writings still read and studied, completes the list of research techniques. Of the older writings, those concerned with religious law were of enormous value; once it became apparent that a given behavior area was strictly guided by religious law, it was possible to consult the codes and interpretations for details.

Since 1961 I have paid numerous short visits to the community—the last one was early in 1971. This way, as well as through correspondence and conversation with other visitors, I watched new developments and filled some gaps in my original data. While I obtained no new census data and, hence, quantitative information, where given, refers to 1961, my recent contact confirms that the main outline corresponds to current reality.

Notes

1 In 1920 the Treaty of Trianon gave most of these provinces to Czechoslovakia and Rumania, and after World War II the Soviet Union claimed a share. I shall nevertheless continue to refer to them as Eastern Hungary, not only for convenience but also because the Jews there shared similar culture patterns and should therefore be treated as a unit.

2 See Chapter 1 for details. Cf. also I. Rubin, "Chassidic Community Behavior," Anthropological Quarterly, 37:3 (July 1964), 138-148.

3 Satmar is the Yiddish name for the Rumanian city of Satu-Mare, the one time Hungarian Szatmarnemeti.

4 In Yiddish, as in German, the suffix er is equivalent to the English "of." The Yiddish form is retained to avoid confusion with actual residence. Thus, Satmarer Hasidim means followers of the Satmarer rebbeh, not Hasidim who are residents of Satmar. The term rov refers to a rabbi of a town (in the United States, of a congregation), a position normally requiring scholarship and leadership ability. Rebbeh (master), on the other hand, designates primarily a Hasidic charismatic leader. As we shall see in Chapter 1, many Hungarian leaders occupied both positions, as did rabbi Teitelbaum. the related term reb has acquired a meaning similar to the English Mister, except that its use is restricted to married men and, in the case of rabbis, it is used somewhat redundantly, as in "the Rebbeh Reb Yoel."

5 H. Gersh and S. Miller, "Satmar in Brooklyn: a Zealot community," Commentary, 28:5 (November 1959), 389-399.

6 Ibid., p.392.

7 Ibid., pp.397-398.

8 Since the main part of my research was completed, two studies of Williamsburg have been published: George Kranzler, Williamsburg: A Jewish Community in Transition (New York: Philip Feldheim, 1961), and Solomon Poll, The Hasidic Community of Williamsburg (New York: Free Press, 1962). Upon examination, I found many similarities between them and the report which follows, but even larger differences. the latter are probably due to two main factors: first, concentration on different problems, and second, the fact that, while the above studies encompass larger aggregates—Kranzler studied Williamsburg as a whole and Poll treats all Hasidim in the district as a unit—the present study is limited to one concrete community. Some differences may be

the result of temporal discrepancies between the studies, but a few seem to be the result of conflicting information. My study was written independently—which accounts for the absence of references to the Kranzler and Poll books in the following chapters. This leaves it to the interested reader to compare and evaluate the partially overlapping reports.

Introduction to the Second Edition

In the Spring of 1988, twenty-seven years after the core data for this book were first assembled, I revisited the Satmar community and spent three months in New York City observing the new scene. I found not merely a new generation, but a vastly changed reality, even though the basic religious culture has been preserved and virtually the entire new, American born-and-bred generation has remained within the fold.

Many areas have been undergoing change. To begin with, the community has grown to about six times the size it was a generation ago, now comprising five to six thousand families. Then, the erstwhile almost exclusively Williamsburg (Brooklyn, New York) community is now subdivided into four geographically separate sub-units, each having a measure of local autonomy. In addition to the flagship unit in Williamsburg, there are Satmar organizations in the Boro Park area of Brooklyn, in Monsey, New York, and, most significantly, in Kiryas Yoel, a new town in the vicinity of Monroe, New York. Organizationally, the most significant transformation has sprung from the demise of Reb Yoel Teitelbaum, the community's founding leader, who was replaced by his nephew Reb Moshe Teitelbaum, a different type of person whose leadership style differs radically from that of his uncle. In conjunction with the passing of the helm, internal strife, occasionally severe, developed for the first time in Satmar's history, a development with potentially significant implications for the community's future. Finally, important transformations have occurred in the econo-technological and associated occupational spheres. This is, of course, not the place for details, which must await their appropriate places. At this moment we merely notice that Satmar today is not the same community it once was and that the changes found have amply justified the restudy effort.

The investigating techniques employed this time were basically the same ones utilized the first time around. Reb Moshe Teitelbaum, the present Satmarer Rebbeh, graciously granted me unqualified permission to observe whatever and wherever I wished. Again, the permission opened appropriate doors. However, this time I frequently encountered resistance on the part of entrenched local administrators who resented what they perceived to be impositions on their authority, thus reflecting the above-mentioned autonomy acquired by local leaders. In such cases it took a call from the Rebbeh to force retreat.

The short research stay, combined with an enlarged and dispersed field, necessitated some compromises. Repeat of the virtually complete census data obtained in 1960-1961 was impossible. Different, less direct information underlies whatever numbers appear in the updates. Consequently, the tables reprinted in the new edition are based on old data and are, hence, out of date. Their significance now lies in reflecting the situation in 1960-1961, illuminating the nature of the reality at that time. However, considerable effort went into checking and rechecking, enabling me to present the newly obtained information with considerable confidence in its accuracy.

The ubiquitous tension between control and change, between insulation and exposure, has remained the conceptual focus of the restudy. At the time of the first investigation the community had been in the United States for little over a decade. Now, after four decades on these shores, the puzzle of Satmar's success in keeping virtually all offspring within the fold is even more intriguing. Similarly, the question regarding the effect of economic behavior takes on new dimensions in light of continuous external and internal changes. The way the latter impact this cultural island (and probably other, similar ones) will be the subject of our theoretical speculations.

Before concluding, it is appropriate to clarify the relationship of what I describe as Satmar culture or behavior and those of other Orthodox or Hassidic Jews. I once thought this to be obvious and thus relegated it to part of a footnote (Ch. VI, n. 12). Alas, I found out a bit too late that both the assumption about its being obvious and the expectation that all readers look at footnotes were ill-founded. Satmarer Hassidim are primarily

Orthodox Jews. Most of their beliefs, thoughts, and actions are shared by most Orthodox Jews. Others are shared by other Hassidim. Uniqueness enters the picture only at certain points (e.g., militant anti-Zionism); in some cases, it is a detail of a larger pattern which sets Satmar apart (e.g., the particular rebbeh they follow). To enumerate in each case whether the pattern in question is Orthodox, Hassidic, or just Satmar, is as unnecessary in our case as it is stylistically prohibitive. While authors of American community-studies (e.g. MIDDLETOWN) successfully assumed it unnecessary to even state that some of the reported details are found throughout the United States, some are a part of small-town society or culture, and only a minority are peculiar to the community in question. In my case, however, a specific statement seems necessary. Let it, therefore, be clear at the outset. A report regarding Satmarer's overt or covert behavior means no more than it says, namely, that Satmarer do this or believe that. By no means does it indicate that it is unique to Satmar.

The original text is reprinted here in its entirety, except for a few corrections and some copy-editing that do not affect content. Also, due to the fact that the Rov died in 1979, all references to him are now in the past tense. The changes which did occur during the last three decades are reported in addenda to relevant chapters. Two reasons underlie the choice of this rather unusual format. First is the already mentioned fact that the basic culture has remained intact. Lengthy repetition of still valid facts seems unnecessary. Then, juxtaposition of the present with the past provides perspective; an opportunity to first examine the way the community was seen a generation ago; to compare-and-contrast that past with the way it appears today; and to draw one's own conclusions in addition to those of the author.

PART ONE

THE HISTORICAL BACKGROUND

I

How the European Jews Became Culturally Diversified

In order to place Satmar in proper historical perspective, it is necessary first to review in broad outline the cultural history of European Jewry, that vastly diversified cultural body from which the Satmarer Hasidim evolved. What concerns us most are those developments that bear most heavily on the emergence of Satmar.[1]

Ashkenazim and Sepharadim

The settlement of large numbers of Jews on the European continent dates to about the beginning of the Christian era. The process of migration gained momentum in the wake of the two unsuccessful revolutionary wars (c.70 and 135 A.D.) waged by the Judeans against Rome.

Gradually, two major Jewish centers developed in Europe, one in Spain and the other in Germany and France. The Spanish Jews became known as Sepharadim, while those of Germany and France came to be called Ashkenazim.

The differences between these two subcultures are difficult to establish, for they vary with the point of view of the historian. What interests us is one cardinal difference about which there seems to be little doubt: whereas the Sepharadim enjoyed for a number of centuries (roughly from 700 to 1200) the free atmosphere of the Arab Golden Age, the Ashkenazim lived in a hostile environment under the Cross. As a result the Sepharadim developed a favorable attitude toward non-Jewish learning, while the Ashkenazim assumed a negative and suspicious posture toward anything not of Jewish origin.

At the end of the fifteenth century, upon the completion of the Christian conquest of Spain, the Jews were ousted from their Iberian homeland. Most of the Sepharadim settled in the Mediterranean basin, especially in North Africa and Turkey, and once again became a part of Near Eastern culture. Thenceforth the history of European Jewry is for all practical purposes synonymous with the history of its Ashkenazic branch.[2]

The Rift Between East and West

In time, the Ashkenazim underwent a cultural subdivision of their own, one between east and west. Following the Crusades, during which a number of Jewish communities in Western Europe were destroyed and others severely shaken, many Jews migrated eastward and settled in the area then occupied by Poland and Lithuania.

Interestingly, before the seventeenth century no marked differences developed between the West and East European Jews,[3] despite centuries of living in different environments. The explanation for this may well be that, at the time, the cultures of Poland and Germany were substantially similar. Thus the "difference" between the two environments may have been more apparent than real.

The Polish-Lithuanian Jews did not respond to their greater freedom in the same fashion as did the Golden Age Sepharadim, that is, by becoming more receptive to outside intellectual currents. Again, all we can do is speculate. A lack of systematic oppression on the part of the host society toward a minority may be a necessary condition for the latter to become receptive to cultural influences of the former, but it may not be a sufficient one. Another ingredient may be necessary, namely, that the borrower perceive the donor culture to be superior to its own. It appears that the Jews found nothing intellectually appealing in either Poland or Lithuania to justify a break with the Ashkenazic tradition of self-imposed isolation in matters pertaining to the spirit or intellect.

In the seventeenth century, events in Europe ignited a chain of cultural changes in Jewish communities—changes that took different courses in the west and the east. The process was completed by the mid-nineteenth century, with a resulting split between Western and Eastern Jews. The gap that developed between theses two segments, even when we narrow our view to the Orthodox subsegments with which we are mainly concerned, appears to have been much wider than the one which had separated the Ashkenazic and Sephardic divisions of European Jewry.

In Western Europe
The Age of Reason opened new vistas for the Jews in the ghetto. For centuries they had been accustomed to regard the world outside the ghetto walls as synonymous with the Christian Church, their arch-enemy. Now that the power of the Church was being openly challenged by king, philosopher, and burgher simultaneously, Jews sensed an opportunity to leave the ghetto and join Western society on a new, secular basis.

Thus, in the eighteenth century, Western European Jews had an Enlightenment movement of their own, which spread rapidly. Spearheaded by the philosopher Moses Mendelssohn (1729-1786), the new movement was characterized by a feverish drive for secular education under the *leitmotif* that knowledge of the local vernacular and secular subject matter was a prerequisite for entering the promised land of the new Western civilization.

Religious leaders were simply not prepared for the sudden turn of events. From their earliest days, Western European Jews had lived in an unfriendly environment and adjusted their attitudes accordingly, having thus no experience dealing with an environment that offered attractive spiritual values not formally connected with Christianity. For nearly a century the rabbis responded with uncompromising reaffirmation of the traditional Ashkenazic refusal to consider any intellectual rapprochement with the non-Jewish world, merely noting with regret the increasing number of those willing to exchange their most valuable spiritual possessions for temporary gratifications.

The absence of effective leadership resulted in a period of chaos, during which a great many Jews left their community altogether in order to join the Christian commonwealth which appeared to offer more comfort and security.[4] Nearly a century elapsed before Jewish leaders tried to create a religious framework for a social reality that seemed to be out of control.

The attempt at religious renascence assumed two polar forms. At one extreme, the Reformers advocated total relaxation of the restrictions imposed by the Jewish religious code. At the same time, they denied the contention that Jews are a nationality and that they hope to return some day to their former homeland. Such hopes, Reformers felt, are incompatible with good citizenship and loyalty to one's country of residence.

What, then, is Judaism? Why should one remain a Jew at all? The Reformers' answer was that the essence of Judaism consists of the moral teachings of the Prophets, and that the Jews have a mission to spread these teachings among the nations—a mission which they can best fulfill when they retain their Jewish identity.

At the opposite pole of the religious rebirth were the Orthodox, who, under the militant leadership of Rabbi Samson Raphael Hirsch (1808-1888), sought to regain the initiative. Instead of a negative response, as in the preceding century, the reorganized German Orthodox set out to redefine their position with an eye on the new reality. Although they reaffirmed traditional beliefs and refused to compromise on any practice for which there was a clear norm in the religious code, they nevertheless allowed for some changes in response to the changed environment. Most important were those involving secular learning, spoken language, and outward appearance. The German Orthodox Jew, not unlike the non-Orthodox, was well educated in the West European sense, spoke German, and was indistinguishable from his non-Jewish neighbor in outward appearance. He also accepted what became Western middle-class standards in areas of behavior that were religiously neutral, such as punctuality, cleanliness, and manner of speech.

Between the Reform and the Orthodox poles were the so-called Historical Jews, the forerunners of today's Conservative Jews in the United States, who tried to steer a middle course between the two extremes. Meanwhile, developments in Eastern Europe also contributed to the chasm within European Jewry.

In Eastern Europe

The prosperity of the Polish-Ukrainian Jews came to a sudden halt in the middle of the seventeenth century. In 1648-1649, the rebelling Cossacks, under the hetmanship of Bogdan Chmielnicki, overran the greater part of southern and central Poland. Wherever they set foot, with almost no exception, the Cossacks exterminated the Jewish population.

Soon thereafter, the survivors of this onslaught underwent another crisis of a different nature. This account will take us back briefly to the Sepharadim, who, we remember, settled in the Near East after being expelled from Spain and Portugal. Some of the migrants, especially the learned element, settled in Palestine and revived, for a while, Jewish life in the Holy Land. The city of Safed (in Hebrew, Zefat), which became the new center of Palestinian Jewish life, rapidly emerged as one of the most prominent seats of the Jewish spiritual world.

In spite of superficial success, the Palestinian Sepharadim remained in a depressed mood, which is reflected in their turn to mysticism. Sixteenth-century Safed was the site of a new mystical movement—Kabalah.

Quest for hidden meanings in sacred writings, the intellectual aspect of Kabalah, did not originate in Safed; it was, as a matter of fact, centuries old by then. But the Safedians developed it into an elaborate system and tried, in addition, to put the findings of their intellectual search to a variety of practical uses. They wrote, for example, Kabalistically meaningful letter combinations on amulets, which were then used for purposes of healing or child delivery or were to be worn as guards to ward off unexpected calamity. More important, they initiated a number of practices which were intended to usher in the Messianic age, the ultimate state of blissful redemption foretold by the Prophets. The Messiah was believed to be detained by sin; to counteract this negative influence, the Kabalists frequently fasted, went into seclusion, meditated certain letter and symbol combinations, and recited special prayers, particularly after midnight.

In the century that followed, Kabalah flourished among the Sepharadim, who, as a result, became increasingly hopeful that the coming of the Messiah was imminent. It is therefore not surprising that when, in the 1650's, Shabatai Zevi, a Turkish Jew, proclaimed himself as the long-awaited Messiah, he soon gathered a sizable following throughout the Mediterranean basin.

From there the Messianic movement spread to Poland, where many of the Jews who had survived the Cossack onslaught in their misery clung to the hope of the approaching redemption. In the light of this hope they were even able to read meaning into the destruction they had just witnessed, for the Messiah is, according to the Talmud, to be preceded by devastating wars and great suffering. The events of the Polish-Cossack war could thus be viewed as the inevitable prelude to the arrival of the Messiah.

The Turkish Sultan, when told of a movement among his Jewish subjects to return to Palestine for the purpose of establishing their own kingdom, summoned Shabatai Zevi to his court and bade him to accept Mohammedanism as a token of loyalty or else be tried as a traitor. The "Messiah" meekly surrendered, accepting the Sultan's demand. Although the Sabbatian movement did not die at this point, it slipped outside the mainstream of Jewish active life and, while leaving traces of influence, gradually faded into oblivion.

With the hope for redemption shattered, the remnants of once-flourishing Polish Jewry were left with despair. Organized community life, the educational system, economic foundations, political security—all lay in shambles. The suddenness of the onslaught, plus the rapid and dramatic collapse of the hope for imminent redemption, seemingly combined to inhibit the disorganized survivors from making a fresh start.

It was in this climate of despair, which lasted for several generations, that a new sociocultural movement, Hasidism, made its appearance among the East European Jews in the first half of the eighteenth century. The father of the movement was Reb Yisroel, commonly known as the Baal Shem Tov, or, in short, the Basht, the Man with a Good Name.[5] His teachings were simple and encouraging. At the foundation of the Hasidic ideology was the principle that, in man's quest for proximity to God, sincerity is a greater asset than scholarship. The latter is only of secondary importance, especially if not accompanied by sincere inner piety. Conversely, sincerity without scholarship may lead to the attainment of the highest level of righteousness.

According to Hasidism, the way to attain this sincere desire to reach God is through joy, not of a vulgar nature but the kind which approaches holy ecstasy, a state in which one rejoices in the privilege of serving the Lord. A maxim attributed to the Basht summarizes this basic idea of Hasidism. There is no *mizvah* (religious command)—the Basht is believed to have said—to be joyous. Yet joy leads to more good than does the execution of any mizvah. Nor is sadness mentioned anywhere as a sin; but being sad leads to more evil than does the worst of sins. These were ideas that the downhearted East European Jew eagerly embraced. He no longer needed to feel inferior on account of his ignorance. All he had to do was to search within himself for the dormant divine spark which every Jewish soul is supposed to contain, rekindle it, and he might reach the same spiritual heights as does the scholar, if not even higher ones. Not only did it become unnecessary to brood over the present state of affairs; optimism and hope actually became virtues. Sadness, on the other hand, was to be avoided.[6] Hasidism amounted to a blueprint for beginning the rebuilding process in a hopeful mood, regardless of the sad reality which confronted the Polish and Ukrainian Jews.

It is no wonder, then, that Hasidism spread rapidly and in a relatively short time became the dominant ideology among the Jews in Ukraine as well as in central and southern Poland—the regions most affected by the Cossack uprising. It is equally understandable that the opponents of the movement, the *Mitnagdim*, had their center in the north, especially in Lithuania, where life was little affected by the Cossacks and where the new teachings were perceived as a threat to the Jewish value of learning.

However, there is more to Hasidism than its teachings of sincerity and joy. Were it only for these, Hasidism should have disappeared after it had succeeded in encouraging the rebuilding of community life. But the movement proved viable long after the East European Jews had restored their basic institutions and when there was no more need to reassure the ignorant of their

acceptability in the eyes of God or to encourage joy in the face
of a depressing reality. Furthermore, the Hasidic movement
spread to a number of outlying regions where the forces that
made for the original attractiveness of its ideas were absent.[7]
Some of Hasidism's other aspects may help us comprehend the
phenomenally durable and widespread success of the movement. Two clusters of behavior patterns are especially interesting: the first concerns community structure, and the second
deals with institutionalized opportunities for expressive behavior, geared to individual need and temperament.

After the death of the Baal Shem Tov (1760), his disciple Reb
Dob Behr took over the leadership of the movement and for
the duration of his life remained the recognized leader of all
Hasidim. However, some disciples of the Basht had accepted
Reb Dob Behr's leadership merely on a *primus inter pares* basis
and already during the latter's lifetime opened new centers of
their own. The pattern of dispersion and decentralization fully
unfolded after Reb Dob Behr died (1773). As no central authority emerged, the local centers which now mushroomed
throughout eastern Europe became fully independent. These
centers developed into a new type of community.

Although it drew the bulk of its membership from the region
within which the leader resided, the Hasidic fellowship was not
a geographical community in the usual sense, for residence—
even in the immediate locality of the leader—did not compel
one to belong.[8] It required a voluntary decision on the part of
the individual to become a Hasid. Further, what drew individuals into the Hasidic community were not those common interests, economic or political, that are usually an outgrowth of
common residence, but a number of apparently rewarding
experiences that awaited those who joined, catering to needs of
a different and more universal nature.

The key to all rewards was the charismatic figure of the
Hasidic leader—the *zadik* (righteous man) or *rebbeh* (master,
teacher)—to whom the followers ascribed all the qualities they
associated with the ideal man and leader. The zadik was
believed to have received at birth a soul of a high order that
made possible his spiritual ascendance. This soul was not crucial to his ascendance, however. In order to realize his poten-

tialities, the zadik had to conquer temptations of Satan, subjugate the impure desires of body and mind, and become thoroughly saturated with love of God and every Jew, even the simplest one.

When one has attained the level of a true zadik, he is able to procure spiritual and even material benefits for others. His prayers carry extra weight, for he prays not on his own behalf but on that of *Kelal Yisrael*, the entire Jewish collectivity. In this capacity he not only begs but also occasionally demands that God accede to the wishes of His people, who, after all, suffer only because of their loyalty to Him and their stubborn refusal to trade this loyalty for a pot of lentils. God must grant this just request, as it is said: "The zadik decrees and God confirms [or fulfills]."

This ideal man, and the atmosphere around him in his "court," constituted the main attraction for the Hasid, who would from time to time leave his routine existence, with its petty worries, and "travel" to see the master. There, a variety of soul-lifting experiences awaited him.

First, all Hasidim present would share certain activities. These usually included praying together with, and often under the leadership of, the rebbeh; participating in the "tables"[9] that the latter "conducted"; listening to him "say Torah," i.e., expound his particular brand of Hasidic teaching; and, finally, mass singing and dancing—the concrete expression of the Hasidic value of joy.

Then each Hasid would have his personal high point of the visit, a few private minutes with the man he admired and trusted and with whom he would now share his problems and anxieties. The zadik would offer both advice and blessing,[10] whereupon the Hasid would leave with feelings of renewed faith and hope, ready to face again the prosaic reality of his material existence. After all, he is not alone in this world. The zadik keeps a protective fatherly eye on him, and with such help the Hasid will somehow manage.[11]

A dynastic pattern of succession gradually emerged in all established Hasidic centers. Though discipleship did not vanish, it became limited to the opening of new territory and to cases in which a weak heir was overshadowed by a lustrous disciple.

The establishment of dynasties facilitated continuity, for loyalty to a zadik could more easily be transferred to his offspring than to a stranger. The ideological basis for the transfer became associated with beliefs about the nature of the zadik—that he possesses a superior soul and that he has succeeded in harnessing all his actions to the service of the Creator. It seemed then reasonable to assume that one born of "holy seed" is more likely to be a potential zadik. For the father, the zadik, no doubt eliminated from the sexual act the element of vulgar carnal pleasure; instead he meant to fulfill a religious command and to bring "worthy sons" to this world. One born of such a pure relation is thus a logical candidate for the kind of soul that enables one to develop into a zadik.[12]

Dynasticism also made for the creation and perpetuation of local traditions, thus completing the process of decentralization and rendering each center fully independent of, and equal to, all others. This, in turn, promoted adaptation to local conditions, or, in case of several systems operating within one area, to the special element to which a system catered.[13]

In sum, then, the Hasidic community was locally adapted and colored, yet not tied to any particular locality and hence highly flexible, while the idealized image of the rebbeh gave it focus and permanence. This floating but stable community was superimposed on the geographical community and provided escape from the latter's irksomeness. It gave its adherents a feeling of belonging to a fellowship, the stability of which could not be shattered by governmental whim. They enjoyed a security they could not know in their community of residence.

The second cluster of Hasidic behavior patterns that provided an outlet for individualized expressive behavior grew out of participation in the community just described, but exceeded its boundaries. Not only was the very belonging a matter of choice, but the extent and mode of participation also were largely unstructured. Each Hasid could therefore suit his own needs and temperament. He "traveled" when, and as frequently as, he felt a need for it. When at the zadik's court, not only did each Hasid have his personal moment that was, in a way, unique in each case, but even the experience he shared with others had a minimum of structure and allowed an almost unlimited range of valid modes of individual participation. At prayer, each congregant had a choice about pace, pitch of voice, and amount, as well as type of bodily movement. This (except pace) was also true for singing and dancing—from which, in addition, one could withdraw altogether. So could one absent himself from the "table" and the "Torah" if he so desired. Thus not only did these experiences provide opportunities for expressive behavior, but they did so in a way that allowed for individual differences.

These norms were then diffused outside the rebbeh's court. In their home towns Hasidim had a *shteebel* (literally, a small room) which they used for prayer and study as well as for community feasts, singing, dancing, and, occasionally, even sleeping. In short, the shteebel was a minor replica of the informal synagogue at the court and thus gave Hasidim an opportunity to practice at home, to some extent, the behavior forms they had learned during their court visits.

As informality and expressiveness were carried into practically all areas of activity, Hasidim became notorious for their vociferousness as well as for their lack of respect for punctuality or any other form of restraint or discipline. One exception was the discipline of the jewish legal code. Hasidim of all times and places remained full and uncompromising Orthodox Jews.[14] When, in the nineteenth century, the Enlightenment movement spread from Germany to eastern Europe, the Hasidim fought zealously against the importers of Western Ideas.[15] Incidentally, in the East the Enlightenment never turned into religious reform but remained a secular movement, largely unorganized. For most of the nineteenth century, it remained a latent, rather than an active, force among East European Jews,[16] whereas the Orthodox Hasidim dominated the scene in the regions affected by Cossack wars and even extended their influence to outlying regions, including Lithuania, the stronghold of their opponents.

Thus while western European Jews drew toward the extreme of Western discipline, the eastern European turned, under the influence of Hasidism, in the opposite direction. Two distinct subcultural types emerged, each maintaining a stereotyped image of the other that left little room for mutual respect. The

East European Jew saw the *Daatsch* (German) as somewhat dull-witted (he does not even appreciate a genuine Jewish joke) and quite comical (who ever heard a Jew become excited about a few minutes or about the crease in one's trousers?). The German Jew, on the other hand, looked at the *Oestjude* (eastern Jew) with a great deal of contempt and suspicion. He regarded him as noisy, filthy, shrewd, and hence untrustworthy.

The mutual stereotyping of Daatsch-Oestjude often overrode the division between Orthodox and non-Orthodox that existed in both the West and the East. The Orthodox case is particularly interesting. Each continued to grant the other the status of a bona fide Orthodox Jew, for, in reality, neither the Westernized Frankfurt am Main Orthodox nor the Hasid tampered with religious law. Yet each party saw the other's behavior as strange, with the result that for more than a century there was little intercourse between eastern and western Orthodox Jews.[17]

Table 1 is a paradigmatic presentation of the East-West cultural poles in the late nineteenth century, before Zionism and other movements altered the scene. Of course, these are ideal types. In actuality the distinction was not so neat, as we may see in the case of Hungary.

Hungary

During the period in which the split between East and West occurred, Hungary emerged as an important and distinct center of Jewish Orthodox life. Unlike that in Germany, Orthodoxy in Hungary persisted in the traditional Ashkenazic pattern, with but minor changes.

The community was revitalized under the direction of Reb Mosheh Sofer, or the Hatam Sofer,[18] who came from Germany in 1807 to occupy the rabbinic chair of Pressburg[19] and soon became the recognized leader of Hungary's Orthodox Jews. He was a fierce opponent of any innovation whatever. *"Hadash asur min hatorah,"*[20] "The new is forbidden by the Torah!" was the slogan launched by the Hatam Sofer and adopted by Hungarian Orthodox Jews. To this day they are quick to cite it in arguments against proposed innovations.

Table 1

The East-West Cultural Poles of Ashkenazic Jewry in the Late Nineteenth Century

	East (except Lithuania)	West
A. Orthodoxy		
1. General framework	Predominantly Hasidic	Westernized Ashkenazic
2. Leadership	a. Hasidic community: charismatic-traditional; important qualities are: pedigree and piety; scholarship is of secondary importance b. Residential community: of primary importance are the qualities of scholarship and leadership ability, both rationally evaluated; oratorical skill is an asset but not a "must"; is, as a rule, secondary in importance to the Hasidic rebbeth	Accent on achieved qualities of scholarship and rhetorical skill which are subject to rational evaluation; mastery of local vernacular is essential
3. Synagogue behavior	Informal, vociferous, individualized, and includes various unconventional activities	Formal, quiet, and orderly; sermons in vernacular
4. Community	Potent Hasidic community superimposed on weak residential community	Good local organization
5. Attitude toward secular learning	Negative	Permissive
6. Spoken language	Yiddish	Local vernacular
7. Outward appearance	Jewish: beard, dark long coat buttoned right side on top of left, and white shirt	Western urban
8. Occupations	Middle-class occupations except liberal professions and white-collar work	All middle-class occupations

Table 1 (continued)

	East (except Lithuania)	West
B. Non-Orthodox Elements		
1. General nature	Enlightenment; accent on value of secular knowledge; attempt to create secular literature in Yiddish and Hebrew; no endeavor to create religious reform	Thorough and partial reform; the latter (Historical Judaism) became main force behind study of Jewish history and archaeology
2. Community	No separate community; loose local community permitted their existence without organizational chasm	Weak congregational organization; no true community to speak of
3. Spoken language	Mixture of Yiddish and vernacular	Local vernacular
C. General Characteristics (cutting across split between Orthodox and non-Orthodox)		
1. Attitude toward time	"No sense in hurrying"	Western respect for punctuality
2. Economic aspects		
a. general picture	Shaky	Sound
b. business practices	Shrewdness; bargaining	Western-style orderly practices
3. Cleanliness	No particular emphasis	Meticulous
4. Manners	Vociferousness; gesticulation; free display of emotions	Restrained mode of speech; general "good manners" as defined in the West

The Hatam Sofer considered the emancipation a mixed blessing. He saw a danger in the new freedom that lured the Jew into the comforts of the world. He expressed his concern in a well-known parable:

A king once punished his son by confining him to a life of misery on a distant island. After the prince had suffered for many years, architects arrived on the island and began to build him a palace. Soon thereafter servants arrived with luxurious furniture, as well as an abundance of fine food—all dispatched by his father in order to make the prince comfortable. At first the prince rejoiced at the prospect of beginning again to live a decent life. But a little reflection turned his joy to tears. Until now, he cried, I had hoped that my father would soon recall me from exile, but now that he goes to such expense to provide me here with all the comforts, it seems that he has in mind to keep me here for a long time yet!

The implication is clear. A Jew should not be misled by the emancipation. The new freedom should not make one lose sight of his true mission and ultimate hope that the Messiah will one day take all Jews back home.

Yet the very emancipation they distrusted also provided Orthodox Jews with opportunities to build their strength. The Hungarian state supported religious communities and invested them with considerable power over their membership. When the Jews were emancipated, the state extended these privileges to include the Jewish community. The Orthodox leadership lost no time in securing permission from the government to form a community of their own. They then proceeded to enforce discipline. Not only did they sever all associations with the reformed, or Neologues, as they were called in Hungary, but they also dissociated themselves even from the so-called Status Quo, who actually abided by all religious laws but refused to become part of the Orthodox community. The Orthodox leaders employed all available Jewish legal structures against those who refused community discipline and placed the Status Quo outside the fold. This way, Hungarian Orthodoxy became one of the best-disciplined communities ever to exist among Jews.

At about the same time the Hatam Sofer came to Pressburg, Hasidism intruded in eastern and northeastern Hungary and gradually became a force. Two Hasidic leaders pioneered the "invasion": Reb Levi Yitzchok Taub, who settled in Nagykallo in the province of Szabolcs, and Reb Mosheh Teitelbaum, the Yismah Mosheh, who established himself in the town of Ujhely (full name: Satoraljujhely) in Zempleny province. While the former did not succeed in establishing a dynasty of any importance, the latter did establish the House of Teitelbaum, which was transferred two generations later to the town of Sighet,[21] where it remained till the deportation of Hungarian Jewry in 1944.[22]

In addition to the two pioneers, another Hasidic dynasty, the House of Halberstam, exerted a lasting influence in the same general area. The influence came from across the border, in western Galicia, which was part of the same political body, the Austro-Hungarian Empire. The founder of the Halberstam dynasty, Reb Hayim of Sanz, the Dibrey Hayim, had a wide reputation, not only as a zadik but also as a rabbinic scholar. After his death in 1877, his son Reb Yehezkel Shraga of Shinyeveh, the Dibrey Yehezkel, attracted most of the followers. Although the son was not well known as a scholar, he seems to have had an enormous sway over his Hasidim, who accorded him a degree of reverence not far removed from their sentiments for his father.

After Reb Yehezekel's death in 1899, no single individual Halberstam seems to have been able to assume the leadership over the body of followers who used to travel to Sanz and Shinyeveh. Smaller centers did form around several scions of Sanz-Shinyeveh, but each attracted only a fragment of the former Sanzer and Shinyever fellowship, and none of the minor leaders ever even pretended to be the prime successor to the throne. Thus a considerable number of Hasidim in Galicia, and particularly in Hungary, remained "orphans" after 1899.[23]

The two subdivisions of Hungarian Orthodoxy—the Ashkenazim[24] of the Pressburg school and the Hasidim—were, with minor exceptions, on friendly terms and cooperated closely within the framework of the central Orthodox organization. The common enemy was reform in all its variations, and they would not let minor differences detract them from what they all defined as their central aim, namely the preservation of unaltered Orthodoxy.[25]

Cooperation naturally led to mutual diffusion of culture traits. The most noticeable Hasidic influence on the Ashkenazim was in the area of dynastic succession. Not only did the Hatam Sofer's descendants continue in the rabbinic position at Pressburg,[26] but throughout Hungary, if an individual was appointed as rabbi in a town and thought the position worthwhile, he would make every effort to have his son, or even son-in-law, inherit it. The Talmudic legal concept of *hazakah*, claim to ownership on the ground of present possession, was invoked to substantiate a rabbi's claim to ownership of his position and his subsequent right to leave it to his heir, if the latter had minimum qualifications. Both the central Orthodox office in Budapest and the influential rabbis of the country would normally support the claim. This pattern of position inheritance spread to minor clerical positions as well, especially to the one of *shohet* (ritual slaughterer).

The Ashkenazim, on the other hand, modified somewhat the Eastern pattern of Hasidism. The principal Hasidic leaders of Hungary held the double position of rebbeh and rov (town rabbi). The latter position entailed responsibilities that forced the rebbeh to leave his secluded court and interact with community leaders—not necessarily his followers—concerning local affairs, as well as with other spiritual leaders—Hasidim as well as Ashkenazim—in matters of national scope.[27] The "clientele" was not quite the same as in the East. The Hungarian Hasidim were mostly sober middle-class people whose source of livelihood was fairly secure, as was their political status. The Hungarian Hasidic courts were therefore considerably less "Dionysian" than were their counterparts further east.

Figure 1 summarizes graphically the developments we have described to this point.[28] The end of the nineteenth century is a convenient break-off point. It brings us to within a few years of the beginning of the history of Satmar proper—our actual objective. And it marks the emergence of Zionism, the Jewish nationalist movement that brought about radical changes in the cultural map of Jewry in general and of European Jewry in par

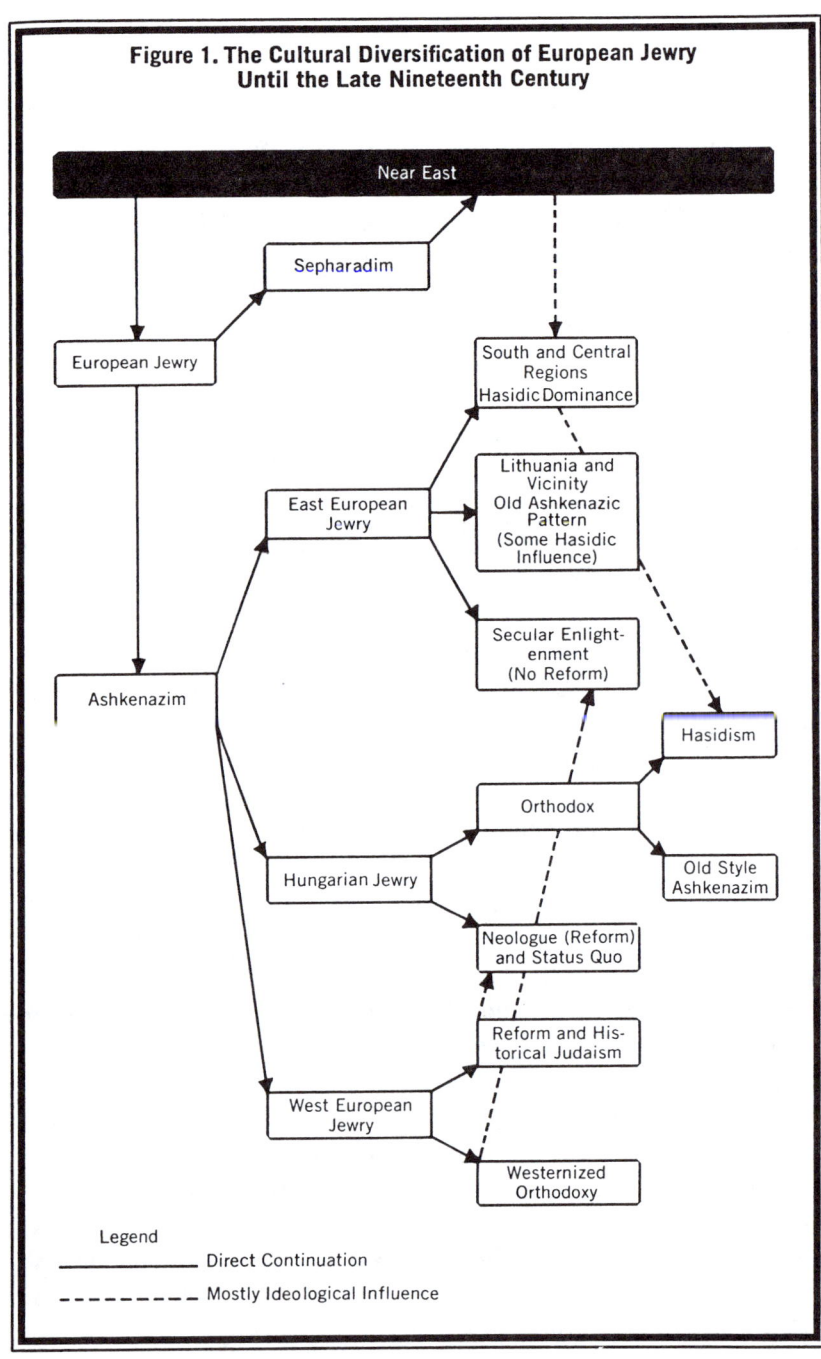

Figure 1. The Cultural Diversification of European Jewry Until the Late Nineteenth Century

ticular. Some implications of the rise of Zionism are significant in view of Satmar's fierce opposition to it.

The non-Orthodox element of the Jews in Eastern Europe became the main social basis for Zionism. This element, as we have seen, had no positive ideology to speak of, and Zionism therefore moved easily into the ideological vacuum.

Another element—again a non-Orthodox one—that played a secondary, though important, role in the movement came from Western Europe. It consisted of educated men and professionals who were disappointed with their status in Western Society. After nearly a century of official emancipation—and despite their extensive Western education[29]—they still felt discriminated against and, perhaps even more important, socially rejected by the Gentiles.

Opposition to Zionism came from several directions. In the East, socialism became a powerful rival, appealing essentially to the same secularized element as did Zionism, concentrating perhaps more, but not exclusively, on the working class.

In Western Europe, rejection of Zionism was the rule rather than the exception. The majority of Western European Jewry saw in Jewish nationalism a threat to the status won by Jews since the French Revolution. The sentiment prevailed that economic and political rights had been obtained on the premise that Jews were, despite their different religion, an organic part of the respective nation within which they lived. It therefore seemed incongruous to embrace openly an ideology that declared Jews to be a distinct nationality whose true homeland is Palestine.

The Orthodox reaction to Zionism was mixed. In order to understand this reaction we must recognize two basic factors which made Zionism attractive. First was the deep-rooted hope of returning to Zion, the hope that Jews had nurtured for nearly two millennia. Second, anti-Jewish sentiments provided an added incentive for wishing to become "like all the nations" and to once and forever abandon the status of a minority that is at the mercy of the ruling majority. This reaction to anti-semitism naturally affected the Orthodox no less than it did other Jews. It was different with regard to the idea of returning to the homeland. On the one hand, the Orthodox should logically have been most enthusiastic for this idea, since it was they who cultivated it. On the other hand, they believed the return would be accomplished by a God-sent Messiah, and human effort in this direction could therefore be interpreted as a denial of the Messianic belief. In the light of this ambiguity, we may read some sense into the variegated Orthodox response to Zionism, which ran the gamut from strong sympathy and involvement, through mild passive sympathy and indifference, to sharp, active opposition.[30]

Without going into complicating details, let us merely note that the militantly Zionist party of religious Jews, *Mizrahi*, recruited its ranks mostly from Eastern Europe, then dominated by tzarist Russia, where anti-Jewish policy sharply underscored the status of the Jew as an alien. But Mizrahi did not attract any significant portion of the recognized religious leadership, and the party was often viewed as embracing elements that were only marginally Orthodox. Later, the middle-of-the-road, sympathetic, but critical Agudath Israel drew into its ranks a significant portion of both recognized Orthodox leaders and the solidly Orthodox laity. Agudath Israel also centered in Eastern Europe but managed, between the two world wars, when anti-Jewish activity reassumed threatening proportions, to gain considerable influence in Western and Central Europe.

Zionists encountered the staunchest resistance among the fairly secure and well-organized Hungarian Orthodox Jews. Especially the Hasidic courts in East Hungary and in West Galicia became bulwarks of resistance to anything that smacked of even mild sympathy for Zionism. This included the Beth Jacob school network for girls, which otherwise enjoyed wide popularity among Orthodox Jews. Satmar has been one of these anti-Zionist bastions. We now turn to the history of this community in which we are mainly interested.

Notes

1 The account which follows is based on well-known facts of Jewish history. I gathered the information from a variety of sources—primary source material, histories, living lore, etc. The interpretation is occasionally original, but by no means revolutionary. Thus, notes indicating sources seem both superfluous and impractical.

2 Amsterdam had, after the exodus from Spain-Portugal, the only major Sephardic community in Europe (several Balkan cities that were under Turkish rule are not considered here as part of Europe). Several less important communities existed in southern France and in England. These exceptions, however, do not alter the general picture described above.

3 Rabbinic traffic provides a clue to the extent of cultural difference between the communities under consideration. In our case, it seems that a rabbi from Poland would have had no difficulty obtaining a position in Germany, or vice versa.

4 Moses Mendelssohn's son the composer Felix Mendelssohn's father, was among the baptized. Perhaps an exaggerated but nonetheless characteristic example of the then-prevailing mood is the famous comment by the poet Heinrich Heine, upon his acceptance of Christianity: "I purchased an entrance ticket to Western society."

5 Some translate Baal Shem Tob as "Master of the Good Name," suggesting that the title refers to an ability to master and manipulate the name of the Lord. It seems to me that "Man with a Good Name" conveys more accurately what Hasidim have understood the term to mean. For a more detailed statement, as well as for an argument against the above suggestion concerning the intended meaning *cf.* Israel Rubin, "Chassidic Community Behavior," *Anthropological Quarterly*, 37:3 (July 1964), n. 4 and 146-148.

6 One of the Basht's disciples, Reb Nahum Tshernobler, pointed out that the Hebrew root *ozeb* means both "sadness" and "idol," concluding hence that the two are related.

7 One example was Hungary, discussed later in this chapter. Even Lithuania, the perennial stronghold of the Mitnagdim, became in various ways influenced by Hasidic ideas. And, as our case illustrates, Hasidism shows signs of viability even now in the United States, Israel, several other Western European countries, and in South America.

8   Occasionally individuals who depended for their livelihood on Hasidim, or who could not endure the strains of social isolation in an all-Hasidic locality, joined involuntarily. But our concern here is with the movement's widespread and long-lasting success, which can logically be explained only in terms of its appeal to voluntary enthusiasts.

9   A sort of public feast. Further details of this and other Hasidic patterns will be discussed at the appropriate moment in the description of the Satmarer Hasidism, who have largely preserved the main elements of Hasidic behavior.

10 In most courts, the private visits have also been the occasion for the Hasid to hand the rebbeh a sum of money, a so-called *pidyon* (literally "redemption"). On the basis of this, as well as of the Hasid's requests that the rebbeh assist him in solving his problems, many historians have portrayed the Hasidic rebbeh as a sort of magician or faith healer, who exploited the Hasid's trust to enrich himself by selling his services to the latter. Careful scrutiny lends little support to this view. Hasidic lore and behavior suggest that the quest for miracles was primarily the domain of the simple-minded Hasidim and that the more sophisticated regarded miracle-seeking as a sign of inability to comprehend the true nature of the Hasidic experience. As for the pidyon, in some courts (e.g., Radomsk) it did not exist at all, while in others (e.g., Sanz, Satmar) pidyon money was used mostly for charitable purposes, and support of the rebbeh's household would come from income from the rebbeh's position of town rabbi and/or from special contributions by Hasidim for this purpose. Then, the amount that the Hasid gave was, with few exceptions, not specified and often amounted to a mere token. Finally, giving (again with some exceptions) was not dependent upon whether one had a special request. Hence the distance between this pattern and the service-for-fee exchange between faith healer and client seems obvious.

11 At this point it may be of interest to trace the semantic transformations of the term *Hasid* that reflect the social developments I have been discussing. Since biblical times, the term had been used as an adjective to connote piety beyond formal requirement. (For a relatively short period in the second century B.C.E., the anti-Hellenists were called Hasidim.) With the advent of the Hasidic movement, the term acquired the specialized meaning of one who belongs to this particular culture (hence my use of capitals). After decentralization and the emergence of independent communities, it became necessary to add an adjective consisting of the name of the rebbeh's locality and the suffix *er* which in Yiddish means "of," as noted. For example, a Gehrer Hasid was not a Hasid who lived in Gehr, as the term literally suggests, but one who was a follower of the rebbeh in Gehr; thus the individual's community membership, rather than his residence, was emphasized. The next step was one of the generalization: "Hasid" came into wide colloquial use as a synonym for "follower," reflecting the personal Hasid-rebbeh relationship in addition to community membership and cultural type.

12 The Hasidim were obviously influenced by Kabalah, the mystical movement briefly discussed above. This can be seen in the former's preoccupation with types of souls (see Chapter 3); in the notion that one's thoughts during a particular act influence the result of that act; in the search for hidden scriptural meaning in Hasidic writings, some of which are outright Kabalistic; and in the adaptation of Sephardic style of the prayer book throughout the area of Hasidic conquest.

13 A good example is provided by the Hasidic system of Lubavitsh, which was situated in the north in the vicinity of the critical and scholarly Lithuanian Mitnagdim. In response, the Lubavitsher developed an intellectualized brand of Hasidism and an elaborate philosophical literature that deals with their interpretation of Hasidism.

14 My use of the term *Hasidim* is thus limited to those who share the culture traits I have enumerated, including Orthodoxy. The limitation is needed in view of certain pseudo-Hasidisms which have recently become fashionable in a number of Jewish circles and which are otherwise little, if at all, related to the bearers of Hasidic culture.

15 In many regions, especially Hungary, the term *Hasid* became coterminous with "ultra-Orthodox." A Hungarian Jew would, for example, typically evaluate someone's behavior as "Yossel's conduct is not only *Yiddish* [Orthodox] but actually *Hasidic* [extremely so]". We should keep this point in mind in connection with the zealous Orthodoxy of our group.

16 The situation changed radically toward the end of the century, with the emergence of the Zionist and several Jewish socialist movements. To the degree that these later developments concern us, they will be discussed later in the chapter.

17 In the hundred years between the mid-nineteenth and mid-twentieth centuries, we find practically no cases of rabbis from Eastern Europe taking positions in the West, or vice versa. (*cf.* n.3 of this chapter. See also Table 1 for the difference between Eastern and Western Orthodox leadership.) In the twentieth century, an organization by the name of Agudath Israel was founded with the aim of bringing Orthodox Jews and leaders from everywhere within the scope of a single organization. But this development ought to be viewed against the background of Zionism, which had become by then a major factor in Jewish life. We shall discuss these developments to the extent that we need to understand the behavior of the Satmarer Hasidim, who, we recall, are widely known for their fierce opposition to Zionism, as well as to everything in some way connected with it.

18 Since the Middle Ages (*c.* ninth or tenth century), a tradition developed among Jews, both Ashkenazim and Sepharadim, to refer to most scholars not by name but by the title of their writings.

19 This is the German and Jewish name (though many Jews pronounce it Preshborg) for the Slovakian capital Bratislava, the onetime Hungarian Pozsony.

20 This is a play on words. The Hebrew term *Hadash,* "new," also refers to the yearly new crop which the Torah forbids to be eaten before the second day of Passover.

21 This is the Rumanian spelling, which, because of its phonetic quality, is preferred in the text over the Hungarian Maramarossziget.

22 See figure 2. We shall return to this dynasty in the next chapter when we arrive at the history of our group. The leader, you may have noticed, is a Teitelbaum—of the same family.

23 The writer's father was one of these orphans. Interestingly, he never knew even the Shinyever Rebbeh, yet he identified himself as a Shinyever Hasid. When mentioning the father or the son, he would refer to them, respectively, as "the holy Sanzer Rov" and the "holy Shinyever Rov."

24 The Hungarian Orthodox Jews who were not Hasidim were know as Ashkenazim, a designation which is historically justified, for they were culturally closest to the original Ashkenazim (with the Lithuanian Mitnagdim a close second).

25 To be sure, some changes, mostly in the areas described above as religiously neutral, were eventually adopted by a great many Hungarian Ashkenazim, and Hasidim began to apply to them the Daatsch epithet. Yet a noticeable distinction remained between a Daatsch from Frankfurt am Main and one from Pressburg. The latter remained basically loyal—at least this seems to have been so at the end of the nineteenth century—to the Hatam Sofar's rejection of basic innovations.

26 The last occupant of the post fled in 1939.

27 This was true of the Yismah Mosheh in Ujhely and later of his descendants in Sighet. The Halberstams in Galicia were also, in most cases, both rov and rebbeh. Farther east, however, the pattern was almost nonexistent.

28 It should, of course, be understood that Figure 1, like the preceding discussion, is intended to highlight the aspects we are interested in rather than to give a complete picture. For example, Hungary is more prominently represented than its proportionate importance would warrant.

29 The expectation that education will render the Jew acceptable to Westerners was, as we recall, a main theme of the Mendelssohnian Enlightenment.

30 The fact that Zionist leadership was largely in non-Orthodox hands naturally constituted an additional obstacle for the Orthodox Jew. A more detailed discussion of both these objections will be presented at appropriate points in the description of present-day Satmar, where these issues are very much alive.

II

The History of Satmar

SATMAR is a Hasidic community of the kind we have described—one which is focused around a Hasidic leader and his court, not around a residential area. Its history dates back to about 1904-1905. During this entire period of more than six decades, it has been led by one rebbeh, Reb Yoel Teitelbaum. The history of this community can therefore more accurately be conceived of as the history of the leader, who has actually molded the members of varied origin into a distinct community.

Origin

Reb Yoel Teitelbaum was born in Sighet in 1887, the second son of Reb Hananya Yom-Tov Lipa Teitelbaum, who was at the time the rov of the town and the rebbeh of the Sigheter Hasidim (see Figure 2). In 1904, at the age of seventeen, he married the daughter of the rebbeh of Plantsheh, of the House of Horovitz, a Hasidic dynasty that was on close terms with the Teitelbaums and Halberstams.

Shortly after his marriage, Reb Yoel's father died. Although no strict system of primogeniture was operating in Sighet, Reb Hayim Hersch, Reb Yoel's older brother, was the logical heir to the vacated rov-rebbeh position. First, Reb Hayim Hersch was no less capable than his brother, and in such a case there was certainly no reason to prefer the younger brother. Second, the seven-year difference in age was a factor, considering that the sons' respective ages at the time were twenty-four and seventeen. When a rebbeh dies and a son must take his place, the followers must adjust to the fact that one who has been their equal has now been elevated to a lofty position. Yesterday's informal-

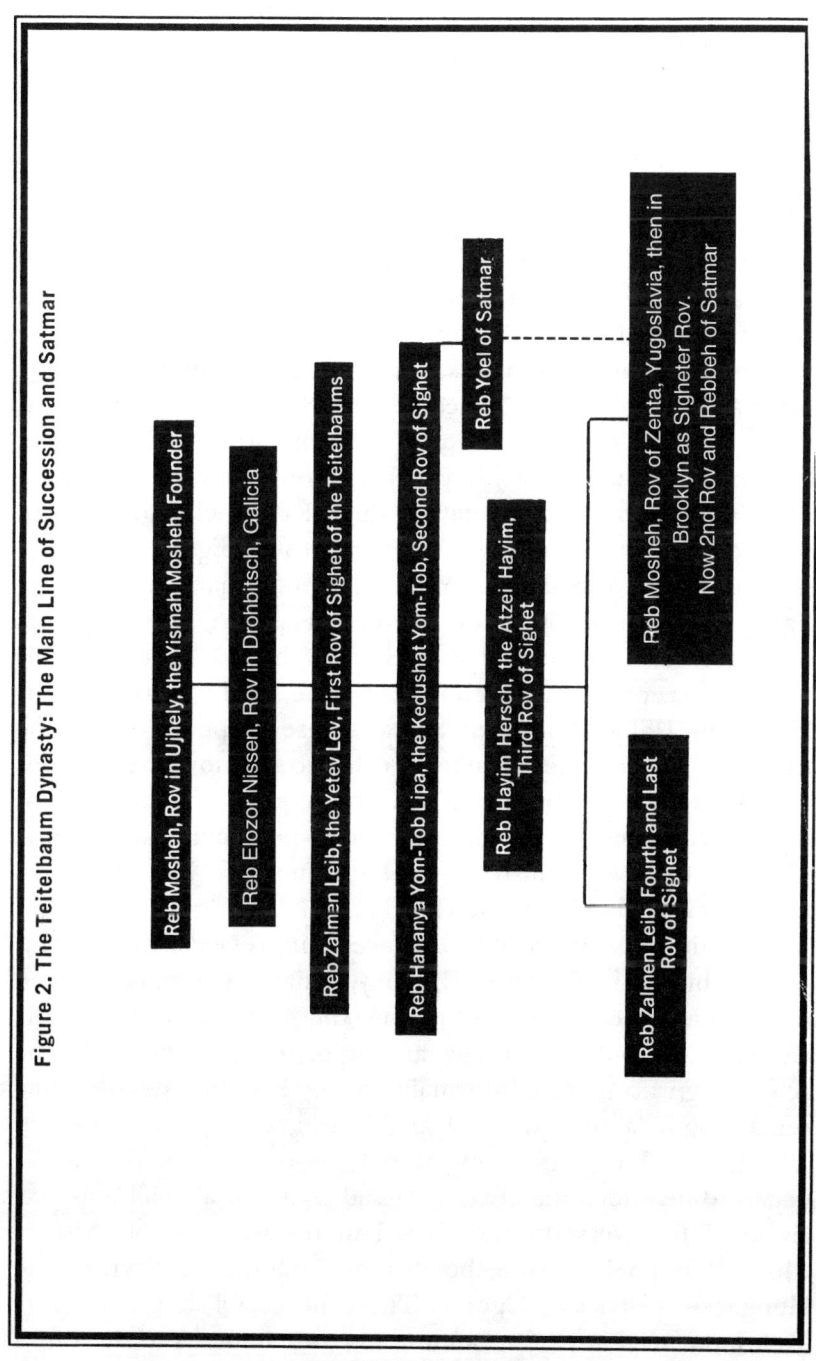

Figure 2. The Teitelbaum Dynasty: The Main Line of Succession and Satmar

Reb Mosheh, Rov in Ujhely, the Yismah Mosheh, Founder

Reb Elozor Nissen, Rov in Drohbitsch, Galicia

Reb Zalmen Leib, the Yetev Lev, First Rov of Sighet of the Teitelbaums

Reb Hananya Yom-Tob Lipa, the Kedushat Yom-Tob, Second Rov of Sighet

Reb Hayim Hersch, the Atzei Hayim, Third Rov of Sighet

Reb Zalmen Leib Fourth and Last Rov of Sighet

Reb Yoel of Satmar

Reb Mosheh, Rov of Zenta, Yugoslavia, then in Brooklyn as Sigheter Rov. Now 2nd Rov and Rebbeh of Satmar

ity must be promptly replaced by unqualified reverence and subordination. Such an adjustment is easier to make with respect to one who has reached the mature age of twenty-four than it is to a teenager. Finally, Reb Hayim Hersch's personality was more attractive to the town and the Hasidic community than that of his younger brother. He was more calm, reserved, organized, and tactful, all of which made him appear closer to the traditional mood of Sighet. The choice was hence inevitable, and Reb Yoel was, as a result, confronted with an uphill struggle for recognition.

Hasidic tradition demands, and so does common sense, that once a successor to the deceased rebbeh has been chosen, the other married sons move out of town in order to begin their careers in a place where they will not compete with the official heir. Thus, soon after his father died, Reb Yoel moved to the town of Satmar, a hundred kilometers west of Sighet.

At the time, the Jewish community in Satmar was predominantly Ashkenazic with a few scattered Hasidim, most of whom were former followers of Sanz-Shinyeveh and were not able fully to accept as their rebbeh any one of the scions of the House of Halberstam then living. These "orphans" were the first ones to become attracted to the young novice Reb Yoel. His diligent study of Torah and subsequent scholarship, his uncompromising piety, and his radiant personality were reminiscent of the two illustrious Halberstams who had embodied for them the ideal image of a zadik.

In addition, some Ashkenazim were impressed with both his scholarship and militant Orthodoxy, traits that ranked high in their value system. Through joining the newly forming Hasidic circle, many individuals saw an opportunity to embrace the rewarding warmth and informality of the Hasidic shteebel while remaining loyal to traditional Ashkenazic values.

Within a few years young Reb Yoel—or Reb Yoelish, as he began to be affectionately called—had acquired a small but loyal circle of followers that competed mildly with Sighet. After a while, Reb Yoel became the Rov of Orshovah, a town in the Hungarian district of Ugocsa. There he established a *yeshivah* (Talmudic academy), thus adding his own students to the ranks of his following. It was in Orshovah that Reb Yoel's group began its active opposition to Zionism. At that time, Mizrahi, the party of religious Zionists, began its activity in the area. The newly forming Mizrahi clubs were especially singled out for attack by Reb Yoel and his students. Zionism, they argued, was even more dangerous when it operated under a religious guise, for it might appeal to religious youngsters who would otherwise refuse to associate with outspoken atheists.

Despite its militant character, until 1926 Reb Yoel's group was, in all, a relatively insignificant force in Eastern Hungary, being overshadowed by such established Hasidic fellowships as Sighet and Moonkatsh.

Growth

In 1926, Reb Hayim Hersch, the rov-rebbeh of Sighet, died unexpectedly. His oldest, rather mediocre, son was only fourteen at the time. Thus, logically, Reb Yoel should have received the call to occupy the chair of Sighet. But town politics prevented such a move, and Zalmen Leib, the fourteen-year-old boy, became the heir-designate. As far as the position of town rabbi was concerned, the decision went into effect. Established residents do not, as a rule, leave their homes just because someone not to their liking is chosen as leader. Four years later, Zalmen Leib married and assumed the position of Sigheter Rov, which he held until the destruction of Hungarian Jewry in 1944.

It was different with respect to the community of Sigheter Hasidim. Hasidic communities are voluntary in nature; an individual Hasid visits a rebbeh only when feeling a need to do so. Thus, unlike in the case of the residential community, participation is necessarily an active process in which the rebbeh plays an essential role as activator. Young Reb Zalmen Leib was simply too colorless a person for this role, especially in view of the fact that a plausible alternative was at hand. Reb Yoel was, by then, at the mature age of thirty-nine, a recognized scholar, and, above all, a dynamic person with a reputation of undisputed piety and saintly conduct. And, after all, the Rov of Orshovah was not altogether a stranger, so that accepting him as rebbeh did not involve a serious adjustment for former followers of his father or brother. Most of the Sigheter Hasidim now began to travel to Reb Yoel instead of to Sighet.

Thus the year 1926 was a crucial one in the history of the Rov and his community. Almost overnight, Reb Yoel and his followers became a leading force among Jews of the area that was once Greater Hungary. In the fall of the same year, Reb Yoel became the Rov of the town of Krooleh.[1] In accordance with Hasidic tradition, his followers now became known as Krooler Hasidim.

Eight years later, in 1934, after a long and bitter struggle, his original and new followers who resided in Satmar succeeded in bringing Reb Yoel back to the city where he had begun his career. But this time he came to be the rov of this once predominantly Ashkenazic community, a position he was to occupy till the deportation of the entire community in 1944.

The eighteen years in Krooleh and Satmar were marked by continuous growth and ever increasing militancy of the community. Increase in numbers came partially through the yeshivah, which attracted new students, and partially through the familiar process of "nothing succeeds like success." A certain glamour about the person of the Rov combined with the aura of success to attract new followers both from the above-mentioned stock of hitherto uncommitted Hasidim that abounded in Eastern Hungary and from Ashkenazim who had no previous history of Hasidic affiliation. As for militancy, Satmar was active in practically every sphere of Jewish life in the area, whether it was a question of filling a vacant rabbinic position for which there was no clearly legitimate heir or the persisting problem of Zionism. Fighting against Zionism and, in general, against any ideological deviance became an earmark of Satmar, an earmark retained to this day.

Destruction

In March 1944 the Nazis occupied Hungary, unseated the wavering Horthy regime, and replaced it with a government that could be relied on to cooperate fully. One of the first tasks of the new regime was to rid Hungary of its Jews. Within a few months the Hungarian Jews were herded into ghettos and—with the exception of some who lived in the city of Budapest—hurriedly deported to Birkenau-Auschwitz, where the majority were immediately murdered. A minority, consisting of those whom Dr. Mengele, the chief German selector, judged to be capable of hard work, were sent to concentration camps.

Between May 1944 and late 1945 Jewish life in Hungary, outside Budapest, was totally extinct. Of the Satmarer Hasidim, a great many were dead and those alive were scattered in concentration camps. A few were in the ghetto of Budapest and still another few lived a normal organized life in the southern part of Transylvania—mostly in the two cities of Arad and Temeshvahr[2]—which remained in Rumanian hands throughout the war.

The Rov, however, was saved, ironically through the efforts of Zionist leaders who were able to bribe a few key German officials and to transport a number of Jews to Switzerland. The Rov was in this transport. After a short stay in Switzerland he went to Jerusalem, where he resided until 1946.

Reorganization

When the Germans surrendered in 1945, many concentration camp inmates still lived, among whom were Satmarer Hasidim. As soon as the latter heard that their rebbeh was alive, they immediately began to think of reunion with their beloved leader. When, in the fall of 1946, the Rov left Jerusalem to establish his residence in the Williamsburg section of Brooklyn, New York, his Hasidim knew at once in which direction to aim. As soon as possible, most of them left their temporary places of residence and came to Brooklyn.

The Congregation Yetev Lev D'Satmar, founded in 1948 with a few dozen members, experienced spectacular growth in a relatively short time, reaching a membership of 860 household heads in 1961.[3] Not only did old members return, but a great many new ones joined. Background data on some 90 per cent of the members revealed that not more than half belonged to the Hasidic fellowship of Satmar before the Second World War, another 9 per cent either vacillated between Satmar and the related fellowship of Sighet or completely belonged to the latter, while a full 40 per cent were newcomers.

This core community in Brooklyn by no means indicates the actual strength of Satmar, which exceeds by far the boundaries suggested by these figures. First, a number of smaller groups of Satmarer Hasidim are to be found outside the United States in such places as Jerusalem and Bnai Brak in Israel; Antwerp, Belgium; London; Montreal; and, in South America, Montevideo, Sao Paulo, and Buenos Aires. Being located in key cities, these groups maintain a kind of "global" organization. Second, in Williamsburg proper there are a host of satellite organizations of various sizes that follow the leadership of Satmar. Third, the *Neturey Karta*,[4] the ultra-Orthodox organization of several hundred Jerusalemians, mostly descendants of pre-Zionist inhabitants of the Holy Land, who have been the most persistent enemies of Zionism and the State of Israel, have accepted the Satmarer Rov as their spiritual leader. Finally, Satmar has influenced practically all Orthodox Jews[5] in the United States, including elements that have nothing to do with Hasidim. Satmar has shown that Orthodox Jewish life is possible on American soil. Altogether it appears that the Satmarer Rov has not only managed to reconstruct his pre-war community but has actually built a much more influential following than the one he had before the destruction.

Hasidic custom would normally have dictated that the community's designation be changed to the leader's new place of residence. But the name Satmar was retained because many Hasidic rebbehs had settled in the same section of New York City, and there would have been no way of distinguishing among them had it not been for the retention of the European designations.

In 1968 the Rov suffered a paralyzing stroke. Although he partially recovered and resumed some of his activities on a limited scale, it seemed clear that Satmar life would never be the same again. At this point, the community must be viewed as having entered a new and critical stage from which it would emerge partially transformed. The description of Satmar life in this book, especially the parts that involve the Rov and his relationship with the community, refers to life as it was lived before the crisis of 1968.

In August 1979 Reb Yoel Teitelbaum died at the age of 92. He was rebbeh of the community he founded for a period of seventy-five years, which, I think, is unprecedented in the entire two-and-a-half-century history of Hasidism. He was succeeded by his nephew Reb Moshe Teitelbaum, the former Sigheter Rov (see Figure 2). The succession was accompanied by dissent and controversy. Aside from problems inherent in any succession to an extraordinary individual, who, furthermore, reigned for three quarters of a century, the situation was complicated by the facts that 1) Reb Moshe had his own community and was not part of Satmar during Reb Yoel's lifetime, 2) his uncle did not publicly designate him as his heir, and 3) no will was found that could have settled the succession issue. However, a delegation of community leaders beseeched him to accept the helm, which he did. After the customary year-of-mourning, Reb Moshe was crowned with great fanfare as the new Satmarer Rebbeh. While dissent and conflict continues, he is, no doubt, the Rov and Rebbeh of Satmar.

Notes

1 The Rumanian *Carei*; in Hungarian, *Nagykaroly*.

2 In Rumanian, *Timisoara*.

3 As indicated in the first chapter, 1961 was the year in which I gathered most of my data and, in fact, the only time I received whatever quantitative data I have. For this purpose, 1961 figures are more revealing than similar data of a decade later, since growth in the second decade was internal, i.e., created by children who grew up and married here. Figures including the latter would have considerably blurred the picture.

4 Literally "Guardians of the City," better known as "Guardians of the Walls," a translation of their less frequently used Hebrew designation, *Shomerey Hahomot.*

5 The term "Orthodox Jews" is used to designate the category of Jews who observe the basic Jewish religious laws set forth in the standard codes of Maimonides, Karo, and others. It should not be confused with members of synagogues that operate under the Orthodox label.

PART TWO

RELIGION, THE CORE OF SATMAR LIFE

Parts Two through Four describe the sociocultural system of Satmar by dissecting the culture into its institutional components. As used here, "institution" denotes a broad cultural area which centers on a set of individual and collective needs. Such dissection obviously involves a degree of artificiality since institutions overlap, and of arbitrariness, for numerous behavior patterns legitimately belong to more than one institution. Yet it is logical to regard food consumption, for example, as basically an economic rather than a religious activity (except, of course, in cases where religion dictates the consumptive act itself), even though religion may prescribe the avoidance of certain foods or ceremonial procedure before or after eating.

The religious institution is our logical starting point, since religion is at the root of the Satmarer Hasidim's effort to preserve their culture. Part Two, then, considers the basic belief system, the Rov and his central role, the social relationships that involve religion generally and directly, and behavior that is primarily religious, not an adjunct to nor an adornment of a secular act.

III

The Belief System

No formal theology exists among the Satmarer[1]—no systematically compiled set of dogmas which would be available to someone who might wish to learn exactly what a Satmarer Hasid is required to believe. Theology, as a distinct subject, is not offered at any level of the school system, nor do adults study it directly. In fact, the Satmarer decidedly shun discussion or inquiries in matters of belief.[2]

Yet religious belief, simple and without reservation or intellectualization, is one of the most explicitly cherished values in Satmar, a value that is an absolute requisite for anyone who wishes to consider himself a member of the community. The reluctance to probe into the logic of religious belief stems from fear that, in the process, one may contaminate his pure belief. Furthermore, the act of inquiry or debate is in itself viewed as testimony of doubt; sincere believers should feel no need for analysis or discussion.

God, Torah, and Israel

The three concepts of God, Torah, and Israel are closely interwoven. Together they constitute the foundation of the Satmar belief complex.

God is believed to be one, timeless,[3] and incorporeal. He is also everywhere, though his essence is not equally distributed throughout space.[4]

The second concept, Torah, has two closely related and complementary meanings. In its narrow definite sense—*the* Torah—it refers to the Five Books that God is believed to have composed, even before He created the world, and then revealed to Moses at Sinai. In its broader meaning Torah used as a collective noun—it includes, in addition to the Pentateuch, all Jewish religious writings, from the Prophets to the most recent publication of Jewish religious content written by an Orthodox Jew, as well as unpublished utterances of the same nature.

Various degrees of holiness are attributed to the numerous segments of the vast Torah literature. The Pentateuch, the core and essence of Torah, has a unique holiness. Its contents—both the manifest meaning and, particularly, the higher-order secrets which are believed to be coded in symbolic terms and letter combinations—represent the unalterable divine will and purpose. Because of its supreme sacredness, scribes of all ages are believed to have exercised utmost care not to alter even a single letter, as a result of which the text available today is taken to be the very same that God revealed to Moses on Sinai. The Prophets and Writings—the two sets of books that, together with the Pentateuch, make up the Jewish Bible—likewise believed to have been revealed, are but slightly inferior in sacredness to the Pentateuch. The Talmudic books are a step removed from the Bible. Talmudic sages are believed to have been aided in their labors by *ruah-hakodesh*, the presence of the Lord's holy spirit, an experience somewhat inferior to revelation. They are also believed to have been in receipt of an oral tradition which was passed on from Moses alongside the written text, containing actual details of laws that the Torah mentions in general terms only (e.g., Sabbath), as well as rules by which to deduce the unwritten from the written. Strictly authoritative Torah comes to an end with the closing of the Talmud (c. 500 A.D.). Thenceforth, importance gradually decreases with the passage of time,[5] and some of the latter-day rabbinic decisions, though definitely considered Torah, are recognized to have been of temporary nature or for local consumption.

While the Torah is taken to represent the divine purpose, Israel is the people chosen to live according to the Torah. To be capable of carrying out this weighty responsibility, a Jew is believed to have been endowed with a soul of a higher type than that of a non-Jew. Consequently, no Jew can renounce his/her affiliation with the Jewish people.[6]

These three concepts and the relationship between them are used to interpret all that has happened since the beginning of time, as well as for predicting the future. Before examining the Satmarer's historical outlook, we must look briefly into their perception of the nature of man and his relationship to the deity.

Body, Soul, Life, and the Thereafter

Some ambiguity is discernible in the Satmar belief system with respect to the nature of the human body. On the one hand, we find there the familiar dichotomy between the evil nature of the flesh and the divine character of the soul.[7] On the other hand, it would be a grave error to label the Satmar culture as basically ascetic, for Satmarer definitely do not regard the satisfaction of bodily needs as an evil, not even of the necessary variety.[8] A closer examination of the literature, as well as of behavior, yields the following synthetic formulation that reconciles most[9] elements of these seemingly contradictory notions.

God is believed to have instilled in the human body desires that are basically good. The satisfaction of these desires is, in fact, made mandatory, either through direct command (sex, some food consumption) or through the indirect mandate to stay alive.[10] But God also wanted humans to choose freely between good and bad, and hence He made their bodily needs such that, in the process of satisfying them, human beings are tempted to transgress the prescribed boundaries. This affords Satan a foothold in the body, in the form of the so-called *Yezer-Hara*, the bad inclination. And it is the task of the *Yezer-Tov*, the good inclination that exists simultaneously, to fight the evil temptations and direct humans to follow the divine Torah.

Consequently, life is basically good and worthwhile. When separated from the body, the soul is not tempted to sin, and without temptation obedience is no virtue. It follows that the few years during which the soul is permitted to stay in the body, though dangerous because of the possibility of Satan's prevailing, also provide opportunities for doing good. Since one is alive against one's will, one may as well concentrate on the positive side of the gamble. Even if one sinned, he can, while alive, repent, finish with a favorable balance, and enable his soul to occupy its deserved place under His Throne of Honor, where it may enjoy the light of His blissful presence forever after.[11] But if one falls prey to temptation, then, depending on the severity of the sins, one's soul may be (1) sent to hell for a period of time to be purged, (2) condemned to wander aimlessly in space, (3) sent back to earth into another body, or (4) exterminated.

In this general picture there is no basic difference between Jew and Gentile, except that the Jew is believed to have a better chance to withstand Satan because of his superior soul and because of *zekut-abot* (literally, merit of fathers; credit one claims on the basis of descending from worthy ancestry). Also, since Jews received more *mizvot* than did Gentiles—613, instead of seven[12]—Jews claim greater reward for living properly. To be sure, the heavier load of mizvot also increases the opportunity for transgression. Furthermore, the Jew is expected to exemplify the ideal man, and, hence, failure on his part to live up to his status may result in *hilul hashem*, profanation of the Lord's name, which is considered to be the severest of all sins.[13]

Cosmology, History, and Teleology

Satmarer are, in general, not history-oriented. Rather, they display a static world view in which change over time is not especially important. They believe that events have always revolved and will continue to revolve around the God-Torah-Israel relationship and His plan to endow humans with free will in order to make them responsible for their actions. Only those past events are important that clarify the nature of these relationships and provide a rationale for them. The following cosmological, historical, and teleological elements constitute an important part of the Satmar belief system.[14]

God is believed to have created this world some six thousand years ago. The disclosed objective of creation was the human race, that He created "in His image," and endowed with abilities to speak, think, and choose between alternatives, qualities that render humans capable of both perceiving the divine teachings and accepting responsibility for one's deeds.

God wanted man to always do good, but He wanted him to do so on a completely voluntary basis. For this purpose, He created Satan and placed him in charge of the forces of evil which were to challenge the forces of good by tempting humans to disobey their Maker and thus bring on their own doom.

By eliminating predestination, the Lord is seen to have injected an unpredictable factor into history, with the result that what has happened since creation is primarily the outcome of human actions and only secondarily the work of God. The Lord has done nothing more than respond to human deeds, rewarding the good ones and punishing the wrong ones. [15]

While humanity was the general goal of creation, the more specific aim was to eventually select the people of Israel who were to accept the obligation to live according to the Torah. Giving of the Torah on Sinai is thus considered, in a sense, as the final act of creation. Human history is consequently subdivided into two major eras, referred to, respectively, as "Before the Giving of the Torah" and "Since the Giving of the Torah."

The first era is believed to have involved twenty-six generations from Adam to Moses. It was a preliminary age, during which man gradually found God, and He gradually discovered of what His unpredictable creature was capable. At first the Creator placed Adam and Eve in paradise, hoping they would obey the single commandment not to eat from the Tree of Knowledge. When they disobeyed, their leisurely existence was replaced by one of toil and sweat. The Lord also imposed finiteness on human existence, reserving immortality for the souls of those who choose to obey Him. [16] But this proved to be no solution either, and the Lord brought a flood to destroy all mankind, with the exception of Noah and his family who remained loyal to Him. A few generations later, humans openly rebelled, building the Tower of Babel in an attempt to strike a balance of power between God and mankind. In response, God diversified mankind linguistically in order to prevent communication that might lead to a new rebellion.

The last six generations of this preliminary era are believed to have witnessed the gradual emergence of Israel as a separate entity. Abraham is taken as the first man to have resolved to break with the ways of his ancestors and, furthermore, to try to make his family a permanent carrier of the new God-oriented way of living. In recognition, God is believed to have promised Abraham that his children would be chosen to receive the Torah, and the Holy Land. As a symbol of the covenant, He bade Abraham to circumcise himself and all males in his household. This is taken as the first mizvah intended to obligate Abraham and his descendants, but not the rest of mankind.

Of Abraham's children, Isaac was the only one to follow the new creed and hence to be suited to assume leadership after his father's death. In the case of Isaac's sons, the choice narrowed down to two, Jacob and Esau. From the point of view of continuing Abraham's way of life, Jacob was thought to be more suited to head the clan. Crucial here is the agreement the twin brothers are believed to have reached concerning the proper sphere of each, an agreement intended not only to guide their own relationship but also, perhaps mainly, to regulate the future relationships between Jew and Gentile, whom Jacob and Esau respectively symbolize.[17] Jacob's sphere is the spiritual: Torah in this world and consequent higher status in the thereafter. When he clings to his legacy he is also entitled to share of "the fat of the land." Esau's lot, on the other hand, was to be full mundane enjoyment, reliance on the sword, and a claim to some share in the next world, provided he obeys the modest number of mizvot given him and is not excessively hostile to his brother. This is considered as the final stage of physical separation, for "Jacob's bed was flawless," and all of his twelve sons followed in the footsteps of their father.[18]

When Jacob and his sons settled in Egypt, where they later became enslaved, their identity as bearers of a distinct tradition is believed to have been strong enough to enable even the enslaved generations to resist assimilation. Thus, when God sent Moses to redeem His people, Moses is believed to have found a distinct ethnic unit, in which he succeeded to rekindle the hope for freedom and which he eventually led out of slavery into the desert. Shortly thereafter, Jews accepted the Torah at Mount Sinai. This marks the end of what is viewed as the first historical era and the beginning of the second major period, the one "Since the Giving of the Torah."

Sinai is considered a timeless event. The Pentateuch is believed not only to contain in a concealed way all of the Torah of future generations, but also to have legitimized the latter by the command: "And you shall come to the Levite priests and to the Judge of those days . . . and you shall do according to what they tell you . . . you shall not deviate from what they tell you, right or left . . ."[19] (Deuteronomy 17:9-11). This is interpreted as an authorization for legitimate leaders of all ages both to interpret the Torah and occasionally to add decrees of their own that might become binding for observant Jews. All souls of all generations are believed to have been present at Sinai and thus placed under the obligation to keep the Torah.[20] In combination, these two beliefs are at the root of the basically ahistorical world view of the Satmarer,[21] in which the concept of uninterrupted legitimate leadership—from Moses through Joshua, the Prophets, the Talmudic sages, the post-Talmudic recognized scholars of subsequent generations, the Baal Shem Tov and his disciples, to the Satmarer Rov and a few others in our day—is of central importance. History "Since the Giving of the Torah" is perceived as consisting of variations on the same single theme, namely, the unrenounceable covenant between God and Israel concluded in the desert, in which the Lord promised the Holy Land, general welfare in this world, and eternal life in the next—all in return for the Israelites' promise to obey the Torah. The Lord has kept His side of the agreement, providing continuous leadership so that there can be no doubt about the proper way of behaving. However, the Jews have behaved unevenly and, as a result, their fortunes have fluctuated. Their periodic disobedience has brought upon them plagues, famine, wars, and, ultimately, destruction of their land and exile.

The Lord's promises nonetheless stand and are believed to be unconditional: as a people the Jews will never be destroyed. Ultimately He will send the Messiah to return the Jews to the Holy Land, ushering in the era of everlasting universal peace and happiness toward which all history has been leading. One of the central themes of contemporary Satmar—extremely militant anti-Zionism—has been associated with an aspect of the Messianic belief. Based on a passage in the *Babylonian Talmud,*

Ketubot 111:1, the Satmarer believe that the Lord imposed an oath on the Jews never to attempt seizure of the Holy Land by physical force without the guidance of the God-sent redeemer. Violation of this oath, they believe, will bring about a major disaster, affecting even those who do not participate in the crime, for, "once released, the Angel of Destruction does not discriminate between guilty and innocent."[22] The murder of six million Jews during World War II is thus interpreted as punishment for the Zionists' violation of the oath.[23] Bemoaning the fact that the glory of an independent state has misled a majority of even Orthodox Jews, Satmarer are determined to resist the Zionist heresy and to continue what they consider to be the genuine tradition of "old Israel," on their own if need be. The fact that, even counting their allies, the faithful are still a small minority, does not discourage them. This accords with the retrogressive aspect of their historical view, their belief that each successive generation is of a lower quality than its predecessor. Furthermore, the Talmudic sages have foretold extreme darkness immediately before the coming of the Messiah. Thus the Satmarer take the very bleakness of the present age as a sign that the coming of the Messiah is imminent. Meanwhile, they persist in their allegiance to what they believe to be the only authentic version of Jewish belief and practice.[24]

In sum, the active ingredients of the Satmar belief system appear to be: a timeless and incorporeal God; an eternal-truth-containing Torah; an equally eternal people of Israel, committed to obey the Torah, around whose obedience or disobedience the drama of history revolves; an image of human beings as creatures endowed with free will and hence with responsibility; a concept of the desires of the human body and of earthly life as basically good but also risky; Messianic hope; and, finally, a collective self-image of an elite community which represents the contemporary link in the uninterrupted chain of authentic Jewry. Together these beliefs constitute the heart of the Satmar ethos.

Notes

1 The widely known thirteen articles of faith that the medieval Jewish philosopher Maimonides had formulated, though accepted by the Satmarer, are far too inadequate for our purpose. An abbreviated version of the articles is included in all standard Jewish Orthodox prayer books. For an excellent English translation of the shorter version, cf. Philip Birnbaum, trans., *Ha-Siddur Ha-Shalem* (New York: Hebrew Publishing Company, 1949), pp. 154-156.

2 I once discussed with a Satmarer Hasid the meaning of a phrase in one of Maimonides' principles. After several minutes, the Hasid suddenly interrupted, "Anyhow, we should not discuss these things!" and, somewhat annoyed at himself, walked off.

3 The fact that the human mind does not conceive the full meaning of the "beginning of time" or the "end of time" is seen as a reflection on our human limitation, not on God's. Incidentally, when confronted with apparent inconsistencies among various beliefs and attitudes, Satmarer frequently get out of the dilemma by recourse to the limitation of the human mind. This implies to them that God's ways and commands ought to be trusted, even though we humans fail to comprehend them in full.

4 Difference in degree of divine concentration is used to explain the contradiction between the belief in God's omnipresence and numerous biblical passages that refer to his residence in Heaven or the various sanctuaries (cf., for example, Exodus 25:8).

5 Exceptions to the "the older—the holier" rule do exist. The writings of highly revered Kabalists, Hasidic rebbehs, and others to whom holiness is attributed, are treated with extreme reverence, regardless of the period of their authorship.

6 While it is not possible to "resign" from being a Jew, it is possible to take on this obligation. The proselyte is conceived to have owned a "lost soul" (i.e., to have descended from Jews) that has yearned to return to its source, thus activating a desire on the part of its bearer to embrace the Jewish faith.

7 The view of the body as evil is found in the literature and is also reflected in numerous behavior patterns designed to "purify" one's body after one has taken care of such bodily needs as sleep, sex, or elimination.

8 Satmarer make it a point to emphasize that, all things considered, they end up with greater physical satisfaction than do the pleasure-hunters—except that they are not enslaved to the body and are therefore capable of postponing gratification when necessary.

9 Most, but not all. The purifying acts following legitimate sexual intercourse or elimination are difficult to explain by our formula. So is the occasional valuation of asceticism revealed in frequent remarks about the Rov: that he does not enjoy the consumption of food, or sex as such, but that he does indulge in sex (only minimally), and that whatever enjoyment he derives from these activities is due to his regarding them as divine commandments. Similar appraisals of various highly esteemed persons of both past and present are likewise commonplace. These notwithstanding, the culture is, in the writer's view, basically nonascetic.

10 Even neutral acts are rendered desirable by the fact that the Jewish religion prescribes the manner in which one ought to take care of one's needs, and following the Torah's prescription is a desideratum.

11 Though some reward for good deeds is believed to be forthcoming in this life.

12 The seven mizvot considered to be binding for all men (known as the Seven Commandments of the Sons of Noah) are (1) not to eat flesh that was cut from living animals; (2) not to curse God; (3) not to steal or rob; (4) to have laws, and agencies to enforce them; (5) not to kill; (6) not to commit adultery; and (7) not to worship idols.

13 What transgression constitutes hilul-hashem varies with the status of the transgressor. For a detailed discussion, see *Babylonian Talmud, Yoma,* pp.84-86.

14 It is assumed that the reader has a cursory familiarity with the main outline of the biblical narrative. The account which follows aims neither at paraphrasing the entire biblical story nor at separating the biblical material from the various supplementary commentaries—mostly of the Talmudic period—that in Satmar were found to be inextricably fused with the biblical core. Our interest, we should remember, lies in those parts that relate significantly to the perceived nature of things which, in turn, relate to the self-image of the Satmarer.

15 One qualification is in order. God is believed to have foreordained long-range occurrences. Thus, the Jews are believed to have been destined to become slaves in Egypt and then to be redeemed. Likewise, God is believed to have guaranteed that the Jews as a people shall not perish and that the Messiah will ultimately return them to the Holy Land. Specifically, however, who will escape persecution and which generation will be the one to be redeemed depend mainly on human action.

16 Although Jewish traditional belief contains the notion of original sin, which is believed to be responsible for man's mortality and his need to toil for a living, no connection is seen (unlike some Christian theologies) between original sin and predestination with respect to salvation.

17 The belief about this agreement is tied to the biblical account of the different blessings Jacob and Esau received from their dying father (Genesis 27). The Satmarer's view of Jew and Gentile in our time is considerably colored by this belief.

18 The above is used for explaining the origin of the name "Sons of Israel" —Israel being the other name by which Jacob is known—thus leaving no room for ambiguity. On the other hand, the sons of Abraham or Isaac would have had to include Isaac's descendants who tore away from the main branch of the clan.

19 Unless otherwise indicated, all translations of Hebrew and Aramaic in this report are my own.

20 The careful reader will note the connection between this belief and the one concerning the special soul of the Jew, and the consequent theoretical impossibility of abdicating one's Jewishness.

21 An informant once remarked to me, "You see us here. We are essentially the same Jews who stood at Mount Sinai!" By "same" he did not refer to the belief that their souls were present at Sinai, but rather to his conviction that, since Sinai, no basic culture change has taken place among legitimate Jews.

22 *Babylonian Talmud, Tractate of Baba-Kama,* 60:1

23 The Rov has elaborated this theme in his book *Vayoel Mosheh* (New York: "Jerusalem" Publishing, 1959), especially in the Introduction.

24 The history of other peoples is beyond the scope of the Satmarer's interest, except for parts connected with Jews. The Gentiles are seen to follow a similar reward-punishment pattern in the spirit of the Jacob-Esau agreement.

IV

The Rov, Backbone of Satmar

Satmar is a personal community *par excellence*. This much we know by following the history of the community via the history of its leader (Chapter II). Before we try to comprehend life as it is lived in today's Satmar, it would be useful to scrutinize the individual who was the heart and soul of the community; the man whose presence made all the difference to the existence of Satmar in its present form. We must see both his personal attributes, particularly the way these attributes were (and still are) perceived by his followers, and the role he played in the social fabric of Satmar.

Personal Attributes

Reb Yoel Teitelbaum was a truly remarkable individual, even when stripped of the halo with which his followers endowed him. He was, first, a most intelligent man with almost boundless mental energy. As a young man he used to sit and study Torah some sixteen hours each day, according to some informants. It is said that in his younger years he rarely went to bed during weekdays. Instead he acquired the habit, which he still had at the time of the study, of taking catnaps in his chair when overcome by fatigue. When I last saw him (before his stroke) he was in his late seventies and still put in a long and enormously active day: studying during morning hours, praying around midday, and spending the afternoon and evening in an unbelievable multitude of activities. Reception of callers of all varieties—Hasidim seeking personal audiences, community leaders requesting decisions, outside visitors—was a daily phenomenon which absorbed an enormous amount of time. On top of this, he presided over congregational executive meetings, attended official affairs, officiated at weddings, examined students at the school, and still managed to save time for afternoon-and-evening prayers and for writing. In all, his schedule called for a continuous active period of some ten hours, interrupted only by an occasional catnap, in addition to several hours of study in the morning—a truly remarkable day for a man who was at that time close to eighty.

His apparently high native intelligence, combined with his almost legendary diligence, enabled Reb Yoel to reach a high level of scholarship quite early in life. At twenty years of age he already began to be known as a scholar, and his reputation grew with time. By the time he established his postwar position in the United States, he was respected among the great Torah scholars the world over. The fact that recognition in this respect came even from those who disagreed with his religious philosophy is important, as we shall see later.

Although scholarship is very important, in itself it is hardly sufficient for the exercise of the role occupied by Rabbi Teitelbaum. Unquestionable piety of the Orthodox Jewish variety, piety that includes both strict adherence to written religious law and reaching beyond it when necessary, is absolutely vital. Again, it appears beyond doubt that the Rov met this requirement. Not even his fiercest critics—and they are numerous—have ever accused him of violating any religious law, of having used his position for purposes of personal enrichment, or of hedonistic indulgence. His austere, disciplined life was an open book, available to all who wished to inspect it. His followers had done so to their satisfaction.

Persistence was another obvious trait in the Rov's character, one that his followers admired. Satmarer are quick to point out that not only was the Rov a saint and scholar during his life, but that he had been "saintly from the womb"[1] and scholarly since his childhood. They emphasize the same with regard to his philosophy, especially his anti-Zionism. One informant reminisced: "After the war [World War II], we were temporarily back in Satmar and the Rov was in Jerusalem, with no communication at all. The general atmosphere in town was, as a consequence of the holocaust, highly pro-Zionist, since people were disgusted with the Gentiles. Once a messenger came from the Holy Land

and told us that the Rov was reconsidering his anti-Zionist stand. We refused to believe. We had absolute confidence in the Rov's steadfastness, for he never gives in to popular vogues. When communications were re-established, we were awfully glad to hear that we were justified in our belief."[2]

Finally, such mundane qualities as common sense, a sense of humor, a pleasant voice, a strikingly handsome and imposing countenance, and oratorical skill enabled Reb Yoel to discharge his multiple duties not only authoritatively and forcefully but with a high measure of sensitivity and in a distinctly pleasant manner.

Did the Rov have no weaknesses? It would be senseless to suggest such a proposition. Things that followers regarded as strong attributes, might be deemed weaknesses when evaluated with critical eyes. Persistence might be viewed as obstinacy, piety can be revised to have been fanaticism, and even the Rov's scholarship might be considered narrow rather than generally applicable. Further, for example, during one of my visits, the Rov once declined an invitation to an affair on the ground that one of his long-time opponents was expected to be present. The host felt hurt and saw it as part of the Rov's weakness to keep long-term personal accounts; but followers judged it a desirable trait not to seek proximity to a critic, who, they felt, was almost an enemy. From our perspective these considerations are beside the point. We will not sit in judgment over the individual; we are merely trying to understand the basis for the tremendous sway he had over his followers. To this end, what is important is the way he was perceived by the members of the community, rather than the way he was seen by critical outsiders.

Rov and Rebbeh

As we have mentioned, originally the two leadership roles were distinct, even in those cases where one individual simultaneously occupied both posts. But in the case of the American phase of Rabbi Teitelbaum's leadership, the two components largely merged. Here he was no town rabbi, and the congregation he led consisted of his own Hasidim, exclusively. Consequently, all facets of his leadership were affected by the charisma that separated him from his followers.

Decision Maker

Satmarer are, as a rule, loathe to make decisions. This is so even in personal matters. On the community level, decision-making via participatory democracy is completely alien to Satmar. Consequently, the burden of deciding vital matters falls entirely upon the leader's shoulders. Not only did the Rov shape the overall goal orientation of his community (this was virtually unavoidable in view of the fact that he created rather than inherited his following), but through all the years of his life he rendered strategic and tactical decisions on new problems that resulted from changing circumstances.

After World War II, the Rov made the momentous decision to establish his headquarters in the United States rather than remaining in the Holy Land, and to continue the fight against Zionism on a larger scale than ever before. Once in the United States he decided to build his own school system and, furthermore, to include in that system a girls' school, despite the lack of precedence for such a school in the community.[3] This was part of the larger decision to try to preserve Satmar culture on American soil, disregarding the experience of earlier immigrants. The Rov was convinced that those immigrants had surrendered to American culture out of sheer lack of will; that they would have survived culturally had they been willing to invest the necessary effort and finances. He was determined not to let Satmarer repeat the error.

Once the necessary structures were established, the burden of deciding a myriad of tactical matters in the new environment lay squarely on Rabbi Teitelbaum's shoulders. A school in the United States must have a secular division—where does one recruit staff? What should be the curriculum for the religious division of the girls' school? What policy should be adopted with regard to the public library that has on its shelves literature considered undesirable in Satmar? Should Satmarer take advantage of the free political climate in the United States to organize demonstrations against Israel and Zionists? If so, how far should such tactics be carried? Such questions were decided almost daily by the only man in the Satmar community who was both institutionally invested with the necessary power and personally equipped to assume the responsibility for whatever consequences it may bring.

Ultimate Torah Authority

Among the many decision-making areas, the one involving application of religious law is especially noteworthy. True, authority in this sphere is vested in all individuals who have been properly ordained, so that small daily problems (e.g., whether a given product is kosher) are handled by ordained clergy. But when larger questions with community-wide implications arise, the Rov is called upon to render a verdict. No lesser figure will take it upon himself to decide, for example, whether or not it is in accordance with Torah law for Satmarer Hasidim who live in Israel to participate in elections, or whether or not to practice birth control. The effectiveness of the Rov in this area can only be appreciated when we consider that his Torah scholarship is beyond question. In addition, the Hasidim have the absolute trust that, as a saintly individual, their master has divine assistance which prevents him from erring in any matters, let alone those involving what they see as his main mission in life, namely, to lead his flock on the only right path as prescribed by the Torah.

Source of Comfort and Security

Finally, providing comfort and security to members of Satmar through a variety of public and private activities—the Hasidic rebbeh element—was probably the most important component of Rabbi Teitelbaum's social role. Publicly he discharged this part of his role at synagogue services, at the Hasidic "tables," and at occasions such as banquets or weddings at which he was invited to officiate.

At the synagogue the Rov's presence was in itself a noteworthy event. He assumed leadership in the services quite often on Sabbaths and virtually always on major holidays. He also delivered lengthy sermons several times a year, especially during the Days of Awe, when the talks reached a high emotional pitch as he called on the congregants to repent and resolve to improve their behavior.

On the Sabbath and on major holidays the Rov conducted tables, i.e., he ate his meals publicly several hours after his followers' mealtime, so that everyone had an opportunity to attend. At these semi-formal occasions, which often lasted for hours, he recited sanctification prayers, handed out food, wished *"lehayim!"* (to life!) to anyone who approached him with the same wish, delivered Torah talks, and occasionally participated in community dancing—all highly welcomed and eagerly sought by the Hasidim, who not only visited the tables frequently but often brought their wives and children along in order that they too could experience the subtle joy of these occasions.

The desirability of having the Rov officiate at one's wedding was so great that in the 1960's, as the post-World War II children grew up and began marrying at the rate of several a day, a canopy was set up in front of the Rov's house. Each couple came to be married by the Rov and then returned to the catering hall for the reception. No banquet in Satmar or in satellite communities was quite complete without the Satmarer Rov's presence and his few words of Torah-exposition and encouragement.

Perhaps most important and certainly most time-consuming in matters of comfort and security are the private visits of Hasidim who come with their personal problems and requests to the only individual they trusted and adored. Not being used to making important decisions, Satmarer came for consultation on just about any matter of importance.[4]

By all objective measures, the Satmarer Rov seemed to have been a giant of a man, having performed a huge role in the social fabric of the Satmar community. Of course, the community's great reliance on this one man had its detrimental side, which we shall treat in a later chapter.

In order to appreciate the structural changes related to the change of leadership, we must return to the conflict that surrounded the succession, a conflict that has not been settled; at best it has been contained, even that not completely. During

Reb Yoel's lifetime, Reb Moshe was not part of Satmar, but was known as Sigheter Rov, heading a congregation of modest size. He was also a Hasidic rebbeh with a modest following. Suddenly, he inherited a virtual empire which included a massive body of Hasidim, as well as a huge network of educational organizations. Even though Hasidic successions have often been marred by controversy and conflict, it rarely happened that a former outsider was asked to assume the top position. Questions were thus raised: Was he really an outsider? Isn't he a brother's son who, in the absence of any other claimant, is the logical, in fact the only heir? Why, then, did Reb Moshe choose to head his own small community, rather than being part of Satmar as the recognized crown prince? Why did Reb Yoel, realizing that the community is without an heir apparent, fail to designate him as heir, either publicly while he was alive or in a written last testament?

As expected, when seeking answers to these questions, one receives different scenarios, depending on which side of the argument the respondent stands. First, however, we need to introduce here the old Rebbetzen, Reb Yoel's widow, who is the symbolic (to a degree also the real) head of the dissenters and who actually attempted to block Reb Moshe's accession, an attempt that, we know, failed. Presently, she lives in a house near the central Satmar synagogue in Kiryas Yoel. The house includes a small synagogue where a few dozen of Reb Moshe's opponents worship regularly. In the house she holds court and maintains a shadow Satmar organization.

Returning now to the questions posed above, supporters of the present rebbeh blame the Rebetzen for all the trouble. She, they claim, disliked Reb Moshe from the very beginning and pressured her husband to keep him at arm's length. This is allegedly the reason for Reb Moshe's failure to stay within the Satmar community and for creating, instead, one of his own. What the Rebbetzen wanted and still wants, they further claim, is to step into her late husband's shoes, to become an unprecedented female rebbeh. For those who could not quite accept the concept, she would serve as an intermediary to her late husband and would take their written requests and read them at his grave that she visits every night. Some of the "old believers" supposedly took her up on this and treat her as a quasi rebbeh. Finally, Reb Moshe's supporters are convinced that while pressure from his wife prevented Reb Yoel from publicly declaring his nephew as the successor designate, he did so in a will he left, but which the Rebbetzen destroyed.

Opponents, on the other hand, offer a different story. According to their version, it was Reb Yoel himself who disapproved of his nephew, because the latter has invested a lot of effort (going into a variety of business ventures, by himself and with partners) into acquisition of material possessions. They see this pursuit as being in sharp contrast to Reb Yoel's lifelong effort to climb the spiritual ladder, an effort responsible for his reaching the heights he did. The Rebbetzen and her close associates categorically deny the existence of any will (a thing viewed by loyalists as highly unlikely, not only because of the crying need for the old Rebbeh's guidance in this case, but also in view of the high value accorded in Jewish religious tradition to the writing of a will).

The internal division refuses to disappear and periodically surfaces whenever an issue arises. Some issues involved are trivial, mostly symbolic rather than substantive in nature.

In the late Eighties, however, the opposition became more aggressive, moving from symbolic to substantive action, the most serious of which revolves around the school system. We shall return to details of the educational strife later. Of interest here is the structural effects of the conflict, specifically on the Rov-Rebbeh role. Is our earlier designation of "the backbone of Satmar" still valid?

Reb Moshe occupies the position his uncle did, namely, Rov and Rebbeh of Satmar. He does so not only *de jure* (we recall that he was publicly inaugurated as such), but also *de facto*, as he performs all the myriad activities embedded in the dual role. Yet, there are differences. For example, officially Reb Moshe is the ultimate authority, the same way his uncle was; the provision in the bylaws (see Chapter V under "Formal Organization") regarding the absolute authority of the Rov-Rebbeh in matters spiritual, has been transferred to Reb Moshe without modification. We noted that in case of internal disagreement, the Rov-Rebbeh's pronouncement used to settle it all. This is still so to a large degree. In the Fall of 1988, for example, a problem developed around a principal of one of the Satmar schools' general studies division, as a result of which the principal resigned. When the matter was brought to the Rov's attention, he ordered reinstatement, an order which was executed without further ado. Incidentally, this incident evoked favorable reaction mixed with some envy on the part of non-Hasidic Orthodox Jews. "I wish we had leaders whose decisions are unquestionably heeded" commented one. I also mentioned my own case when attempted obstruction by a local administrator was quickly and effectively resolved by the Rebbeh's phone call.

However, due to lingering dissent, there are exceptions. Perhaps the most significant example of the latter may be seen in the fact that despite the Rebbeh's vehement reaction to the creation of rival schools which we shall discuss later, he failed to deal effectively with this issue and the strife around it continues. However, full appreciation of the change that occurred requires a brief comment about changes in leadership style that are independent of the tense internal situation.

Due to a variety of factors—huge numerical growth, geographic dispersion, changed economic factors resulting in more outside contact, self cognition—Reb Moshe introduced a substantial administrative component into his role, instituting some radical, potentially far reaching, organizational changes in the various Satmar branches which, supporters plausibly claim, have saved the system from collapsing under its own weight.

This said, we may now return to the question whether the Rov-Rebbeh is still the backbone of Satmar. The answer seems to be a clear "yes!" but with a difference in the nature of the cement provided. Reb Yoel utilized his radiant personality which generated such deep sentiments that opposition to decisions he pronounced was unthinkable. Reb Moshe, on the other hand, provides administrative glue. Acting as caretaker of the estate, he has been channelling his efforts into holding together the huge, dispersed, and diversified structure. Speculation on the effectiveness of the newly organized leadership must be deferred to later chapters where it will be discussed in several different contexts.

Notes

1 The phrase "saintly [or sacred] from the womb" connotes both lifelong saintly conduct and belief that conception and birth resulted from saintly parental conduct. See Chapter 1.

2 The positive valuation of persistence in the leader's behavior is part of a general emphasis on this trait in Satmar culture. For example, converts to the community are trusted to the degree to which their prior ideas approximated those of Satmar. I was told of at least one case in which a teaching position in the school system was denied to an applicant because of his prior Zionist leanings.

3 More about the girls' school, its significance and its problems, in later chapters.

4 For more details on these private meetings and on other types of Hasid-rebbeh communion, especially how these affect the Hasid's behavior, see Chapter 6, "Maintenance of a State of Spiritual Well-Being." After the Rov suffered a stroke in 1968, the visits ceased. As he gradually recovered, they began again but in radically different form. The Rov's residence has been moved to a Long Island suburb. Each visitor had to make an appointment and someone close to the Rov usually accompanied him. Otherwise he would have had difficulty communicating, for the Rov did not hear well and relied a great deal on his intimates, with whom he learned to communicate as he recovered from his illness. It all adds up to contacts on a much more limited scale, consonant with the restrictions placed on him by his condition. Other aspects of his role had been similarly curtailed.

V

Social Structure

BEFORE considering the formal and informal relationships within the religious institution, let us see how the structure is composed and hierarchically arranged in terms of prestige, though not necessarily of power. Again, the elements described here are important not only in the religious structure but in other institutionalized relationships as well.

The Hierarchy of Social Elements

The Rov

Without repeating the details of the Rov's dual role of "rov," derived from the European town rabbi, and of Hasidic "rebbeh," we need only note that as a result of the magnitude and multifariousness of his activities, Reb Yoel Teitelbaum was in a class by himself, separated by a wide gulf from the rest of the community, even its upper layer.

The Sheyneh Yidden

By virtue of occupation, pedigree, or self-definition, some individuals occupy positions that are in varying degrees superior to those of the overwhelming majority of the membership. For lack of a better term we shall refer to the upper layer as *sheyneh yidden*.[1] This category consists of several aggregates. Those who belong here because of occupation are known as *keley-kodesh*,[2] holy accessories, indicating that their occupations are necessary for the smooth flow of religious life. Such are *shohatim*, or ritual slaughterers; *soferim* (singular: *sofer*), or scribes; rabbis (some prefer the title "rov," and others "rebbeh"), who head satellite congregations[3] and are at the same time members of the larger

Satmar congregation; and educators of Torah, especially those at higher than elementary levels.[4]

The second subcategory of sheyneh yidden consists of *eineklach* (singular: *eyenekel*), pedigreed individuals whose claim to elevation above common status rests on being descendants of "holy seed," i.e., Hasidic rebbehs. A few, who come not from rebbeyic family background but from that of Hungarian Ashkenazic clergy, have rather easily become assimilated into this aggregate, a fact that is probably attributable to the proximity between the two segments of Hungarian Orthodoxy. Many eineklach are also keley-kodesh, especially in the capacity of congregation heads. Others have entered business or have accepted jobs as industrial operatives but retain to some degree their identity as eineklach as well as their claim to above-average status.

A third aggregate of sheyneh yidden, which overlaps both the first and the second aggregates, consists of a modest number of scholars, some of whom are ordained,[5] who enjoy a large measure of respect. Several are employed as educators, mostly in the upper division of the school system. Others are among the congregation heads, and a few are scattered in a variety of positions. Finally, there are individuals I have dubbed "McCarthyites," holier-than-thou zealots, self-appointed community watchdogs, who keep an eye on what they consider to be transgressions of Satmar religious standards and who also spearhead militant anti-Zionist actions.[6]

Besides these three groups, a few scattered individuals aspire to higher status because they are either close to the Rov or active on behalf of the community. In some cases the aspiration is due merely to self-image.

The Rank and File

Because Satmar as a whole is an elite group,[7] the self-image of even the average man is one of above-average distinction. Further, equality as a value has made deep inroads in contemporary Satmar, so that many average men refuse to recognize a firm line of demarcation between themselves and the sheyneh yidden, especially those whose claim to membership in the latter category rests on ascription rather than on achievement.[8]

Owing to the equality ideology, the borderline between the sheyneh yidden and the rank and file is considerably blurred.

The Lower Stratum
The lowest stratum in the religious sphere consists of two kinds of individuals. First, there are those who, though definitely a part of the community, exhibit conduct considered substandard and hence damaging to the image that Satmar strives to maintain both to its own followers and vis-à-vis the outside world. Second, some individuals actually belong to other communities but maintain formal membership in Satmar, usually out of sympathy with some aspects of Satmar ideology. They occupy a permanent position of marginality.

Formal Organization

Formal organization in the realm of religion is of limited import in contemporary Satmar. Nevertheless, several aspects of the religious structure are accurately reflected in formal rules and regulation.

First, the absolute authority of the Rov is formalized in Article 8 of the congregation's bylaws[9] which reads:

> His honorable holiness, our lord, teacher and master, the scholar and saint Reb Yoel Teitelbaum—may he live for long and good years, Amen!—is our rov, may he be thus for long years to come. No one may replace him without his consent. He is the sole authority in all spiritual matters. No religious functionary may be appointed without his approval. His decision is binding for every member.

Second, the requirement of abidance by the community's religious standards as a prerequisite for membership in the congregation is also spelled out in Article 3 of the bylaws:

> The following may be accepted as members of the congregation:
> a) He who observes the Sabbath properly and does not willfully violate any proscription of our holy Torah.
> b) He who in general conducts himself according to the Torah and brings up his children likewise and his wife does not wear her own hair.
> c) When one is 18 years old and married.[10]

Third, dominance of the adult male in anything having to do with religion is both formally instituted[11] and actually enforced.

Finally, Satmarer abide by the formal rule that only an ordained man may be consulted in questions involving religious law. An unordained scholar renders an occasional decision for himself or his family, but not for someone else.

The formal religious structure consists of two major overlapping organizations, the Congregation Yetev-Lev D'Satmar (hereafter referred to as the Congregation) and the Central Rabbinical Congress of the United States and Canada (hereafter Rabbinical Congress or the Congress).

The Congregation is the basic organizational framework of the community. All Satmarer, even those who do not regularly worship in the main synagogue, belong to it. In addition to the Rov, the Congregation's governing body includes an elected council of twenty-one elders, presided over by a president and vice-president, several secretaries, and *gabaim* (singular: *gabai*), or officers in charge of distributing congregational honors. All these serve without pay, including the Rov, who has refused to accept a salary, claiming that he does not perform in the United States the duties he had performed abroad as town rabbi, for which alone he was paid.[12] The only salaried individual is the sexton, who is in charge of the central synagogue's daily operation.

The activities of the Congregation are oriented toward the satisfaction of the daily religious needs of the membership. Running the central place of worship is one of its tasks. Another is the administration and supervision of the cemetery, as well as of funerals and burials, accomplished by one of the Congregation's suborganizations, the *Hevra-Kadisha* or Holy Association. Still another task is the operation of the two ritual baths, one for men and one for women.[13] Aside from a few routine matters[14] and some enterprises such as education which are only officially under its jurisdiction, these activities exhaust the scope of the Congregation's authority.

The membership of the second major organization, the Rabbinical Congress, consists of individuals who have a claim to rabbinic title because of ordination, pedigree, or occupation, and who also wish to retain their clerical identity. The Congress is governed by a permanent president—the Rov—an elected executive committee, and a full-time salaried secretary, who is a layman.

Only a portion of the members of the Congress belong to the Satmar Congregation. The majority consists of sympathizers. A few are there because they feel for some reason compelled to follow the lead of Satmar. Among the outsiders are rabbis who lead sizable congregations and enjoy considerable esteem in their own right.

Officially the Congress is charged with safeguarding religious standards of economic and political behavior—for example, checking whether a product is kosher, or seeing that a conflict is settled according to Jewish religious law. It also serves as a setting within which one may legitimize his claim to higher status.

These formal organizations do not tell the entire story of Satmar religious structure. Occasionally they may even be misleading. For example, it would be inaccurate to assume that membership in, or even presidency of, the Congregation's elected governing body invests one with power in the religious structure. Actually this body has no power either to render or to implement important decisions. As a result, the community takes little interest in the Congregations's elections. The proposed slate is invariably elected, with few members voting or exercising write-in privileges. Correspondingly, few desire to run for office, and those who do enjoy long tenure. There are, to be sure, a few powerful individuals among the elders, but their power derives from attributes other than council membership. Similarly, it would be erroneous to confine the significance of the Rabbinical Congress to its official role or to assume that high prestige, let alone power, comes with membership in the rabbinic organization. Several fundamental aspects of religious organization are nowhere recorded officially but are nonetheless of vital importance.

Informal Structural Aspects

Four factors are central to the informal side of religious organization. First, Satmar is primarily a Hasidic fellowship and Rabbi

Teitelbaum a Hasidic rebbeh whose power and influence derive from his followers' belief in his virtual infallibility. Second, Satmar has become a synonym for an ideology, the earmarks of which are ultra-Orthodoxy and anti-Zionism. Third, Satmar is situated in the midst of a dynamic urban civilization which compels a degree of change, ideology notwithstanding. Fourth, the community claims that its ideology represents authentic Judaism rather than a position peculiar to Satmar.

The first factor rules out any possibility of critical evaluation of the Rov's decisions by an elected body, or of investing such a body with decision-making powers. Whatever power exists outside the person of the Rov is derived from having access to the powerful leader, from enjoying his trust and from being able to influence his decisions.

The second and third factors—the fact that the community is committed to a conservative ideology and at the same time is confronted with the demands of a dynamic reality—are at the foundation of the main split between the conservatives and the moderates within the Congregation. At the conservative end are the "McCarthyites" who fight any sign of innovation. The moderates, on the other hand, are represented chiefly by individuals who occupy official and semi-official positions which force them to confront demands of reality.

Friction between these two factions is one of the ongoing processes in Satmar. Both sides vie for power mainly by trying to influence the Rov. On the surface it may appear odd that one should attempt to influence a person for whom one has admiration that borders on worship. Yet it occurs daily, and the two attitudes seem to be quite compatible. The Hasid justifies his action by saying that the Rov lacks direct contact with the outside world and must therefore rely on information fed to him by those who are in touch with daily events. Therefore, it is one's duty to bring to the attention of the Rov any important event he should know. Consequently, all capable of exerting such influence—and only they—possess a degree of power. This way militancy and courage to initiate action for the Rov are greater correlates of power[15] than is membership in, say, the Rabbinical Congress.

The influencing process comes into play on issues involving some change perceived by the conservatives as dangerous deviation and by the moderates as harmless or even necessary. The issue may involve the entire community or may be such a seemingly private act as borrowing a book from the library, but which may, nonetheless, be seen as breach of discipline with community-wide repercussions.

Another important issue is the extent of anti-Zionist militancy. Conservatives often organize their own anti-Israel protest marches; some have on occasion painted swastikas on the Israeli consulate in New York City, while others have placed anonymous anti-Israel ads in the newspapers. Frequently these acts have been misinterpreted by outsiders as representative of Satmar as a whole. Actually the militants are a minority. The majority watches these extreme acts with a great deal of consternation; many frequently voice dissociation from and disapproval of the extremists.

The Rov has sharply criticized the zealots' excesses, occasionally even ordering mild sanctions.[16] But while his opinion was accepted by all concerned, the Rov had not managed to heal the basic split within the community. To a large degree this was no doubt due to the fact that, basically, the Rov was committed to a conservative line; his anti-extremist pronouncements have thus been not altogether convincing. Furthermore, in issues other than those involving anti-Zionist excesses, the Rov, while sometimes resenting the watchdogs,[17] on other occasions had thrown his weight on their side, thus adding considerable legitimacy to the right-wing aggregate as a whole. Residues of dissatisfaction and mutual distrust thus linger within the community. One day they may threaten its unity.

For the time being it is difficult to determine the relative strength of the two camps. On the one hand, some changes—the establishment of a girls' school, for example—simply had to be made, whether the zealots liked it or not. On the other hand, the conservative position frequently prevails. The very nature of extremist activity seems to provide some advantage, as moderates can match neither their emotional appeal nor their militancy.[18] This would appear to be so even when the ideology of the extremists is opposed to that of the official regime. It is even more so in a case like Satmar, where the zealots are in accord with the official "line." In such a situation the moderates are in the difficult position of trying to make a convincing case against enthusiasts for the ideas they themselves profess.

We can best understand the significance of the Rabbinical Congress in terms of Satmar's claim to represent authentic Judaism, the fourth of the factors listed above. The Congress serves as the instrument of Satmar's "foreign policy," the mechanism through which the community extends its leadership beyond its boundaries. Undertakings such as anti-Zionist rallies are more conveniently staged under the sponsorship of the broad-based Congress than under the explicit banner of Satmar. The Congress can more plausibly appeal in the name of all Torah-true Jewry than can Satmar. Hence power in this organization is in large measure based on ability to rally the necessary support for the Rov's line. For, unlike that in the Congregation, such support is not always automatic, and it often takes political acumen to enlist the support of reluctant members who may have to contend with countervailing forces within their own congregations. [19]

Satmar religious structure thus has both formal and informal aspects. The formal side, while indicating some reality, may occasionally also mislead, especially when power depends upon informal aspects. Finally, we should note that Satmar is in the midst of a transitional stage in which vestiges of a highly valued but extinct past are confronted with new realities, not the least of which is a high regard for social equality.

At the time I revisited the Satmar community in 1988, the hierarchy of social elements was basically the same with just a couple of changes worth mentioning. At the top of the pyramid, the Rov-Rebbeh shares, to a degree, the social summit with at least some members of his immediate family. It is a natural outgrowth of two factors. First, unlike his uncle, he does have a large family, four sons and three daughters, and it is to be expected that some prestige and power of a leader will "rub off" on primary kin, especially those considered to be in the line of succession. (In fact, one of the sons has already been installed in a position which marks him as at least one of the heirs to the throne and a second is considered by numerous members I interviewed as a possible future leader of a segment of the next generation's Satmar.) The second factor is the already-mentioned altered character of the Rebbeh's role. The reduced emotional ties between rebbeh and hasid allow for the entry of others into a role once occupied by a single individual whose commanding presence excluded the possibility of sharing the spot with someone else.

The second significant development is the entry of the dissidents, a category we discussed at length in the update to Chapter IV. They constitute a new type of marginal element, one unimaginable under the leadership of Reb Yoel. To be sure, some zealots (as pointed out in the original text in this chapter) operated on the margin, engaging in activities not approved by the Rebbeh. However, they were far from a full-fledged opposition. The Rebbeh had the last word, without anyone daring to claim superiority. In contrast, today's dissidents see themselves as an elite representing the true Satmar of yesteryear and regard the establishment and its supporters as the real deviants. From the establishment's perspective, however, insubordination to the Rov-Rebbeh *is* deviant. In support of their position they cite numerous precedents among Hungarian Jews, which have always served as a model for Satmar, as well as a corroborating body of literature. The fact that the dissidents are a minority out of power, renders them marginal by definition, although in a different sense than the two varieties listed previously. What we have here is an element which exhibits a mixture of characteristics associated with both the uppermost (not counting the Rov and his family) and the lowest strata; an element the presence of which is significant both for understanding present-day Satmar and for projecting future developments.

In the area of formal organization, a change, apparently not unrelated to the rise of internal dissention, occurred in the way congregational elders rise to their position. In the previous generation, as we have seen, they were elected and, due to the existing internal harmony emanating from the Rov's absolute authority, interested individuals agreeable to the Rov were invariably elected and once elected, had virtually no power, even formally. Now, however, they are appointed by the Rov and have a much more important role to play. Officially it is justified by the fact that in the past, elections were mere formalities; why waste time and resources on unimportant processes? Informally, it is plausible to argue, the change enables tighter control at the top. It, first, prevents opponents to challenge the official slate. This possibility was manifested in 1991. For a while, Kiryas Yoel was authorized by the state to have for handicapped children its own school district (later ruled by the courts as unconstitutional). As such it needed an elected school board, for which dissidents ran a candidate. The election took place in January, 1991 and the opposition candidate embarrassed the establishment by drawing about 40% of the vote. By eliminating elections, similar periodic occurrences are avoided. Also, the elders, acting in the name of the formal congregation, are the ones who administer when necessary punitive reprisals against opponents, thus enabling the leaders to claim that the acts in question are a result of the organized community's rules. In the latter capacity, the lay leaders perform an important function for the established leaders.

Finally, as a combined result of demographic growth and changed leadership, maintenance of ties with outsiders has grown beyond its modest beginnings via the Rabbinical Congress. Satmar representatives now sit on executive bodies of a variety of organizations with activities—e.g., first aid of medical and welfare character—that reach out to many Orthodox Jewish circles, Hasidic as well as non-Hasidic ones. Furthermore, unlike in the case of the Congress, participation in these organizations is a two-way street. Here, Satmar, although important, due to sheer size, does not play a dominant role. In many of these, namely, the ones providing specialized services requiring college-trained personnel, Satmar's culture, which opposes college education, actually prevents its members from even aspiring to positions of leadership.

Notes

1 Singular: *sheyner yid,* "nice [or beautiful] Jew." However, neither "nice" nor "beautiful" conveys the correct meaning of the Yiddish *sheyn* in this phrase.

2 The Satmarer use this form for both the singular and the plural.

3 The membership of the satellite congregations usually consists of both Satmarer Hasidim and outsiders.

4 Abroad, another type of keley-kodesh existed, a *dayan* (literally, "judge"), who was a sort of assistant rabbi. He had two major duties: to answer inquiries concerning religious law, mostly about defects found in cattle and fowl and whether these defects rendered the animal nonkosher; and to adjudicate interpersonal disputes (whence came his title). In the United States, the dayan has disappeared along with his duties. The character of meat marketing in this country has greatly reduced the number of inquiries about animal diseases. Whatever questions remain, as well as the not too numerous inquiries in other areas of religious life, are answered by ordained individuals who are not, however, doing this as an occupation. Adjudications are also performed by ordained individuals and by qualified laymen on a fee-for-service basis, but again not as full-time occupations. *Cf.* Chapter 10, which deals with political behavior.

5 Ordination among Orthodox Jews amounts to certification, by one or several ordained scholars, that the person ordained has sufficient knowledge of Torah-based law to be consulted on religious problems.

6 Many of these extremists are young, and those of the older generation who are in this category are mostly newcomers to Satmar—a fact which should not surprise us, as the tendency toward extremism among converts has been observed through the ages. The "McCarthyite" label suggested itself to the writer because the position of these zealots is similar in several respects to that of the followers of the late Wisconsin Senator in the early years of the first Eisenhower administration: They watch for deviance from orthodoxy; they do so in a self-appointed capacity; and they operate within a system basically committed to the general direction in which they aim, but not to such an extreme degree. The latter fact, as we shall see later in the chapter, gives more power to the militants than their not too large number would suggest.

7 It is, for example, a fact that Satmar is the recognized leader of a host of satellite communities. Then (and this was, to a degree, the case abroad also) Satmar attracted people who have been considered above

average by the prevailing standards of scholarship and piety. This may be related to the fact (see Chapter 2) that Satmar is in a sense a newly formed community, which means that whoever wishes to join must abandon a previous pattern. This ability to change behavior may be characteristic of above-average individuals.

8 The quest for equality and the concomitant resentment against the claimed superiority of many sheyneh yidden are frequently verbalized by commoners and are also reflected in many behavior patterns. The researcher was particularly impressed by one recent innovation. A number of rank-and-filers—especially younger ones—have adopted modes of dress that, abroad, were reserved for the sheyneh, actually the most distinguished persons among them. All this does not, however, affect their attitude toward the Rov.

9 The bylaws are in Yiddish, and the excerpts were translated by the writer.

10 The listed requirements ought, of course, to be understood as additive; i.e., only those who meet all of them are eligible for membership.

11 The formal rules in this case are dispersed in various relevant religious codes. Note also that the foregoing quotation from the bylaws refers to a member's wife, thus taking it for granted that membership in the congregation is restricted to males.

12 A separate organization, the Union of Satmar Students, exists for the sole purpose of supporting the Rov's household. Membership is open not only to former students of the Rov but to anyone willing to contribute an amount he feels he can afford. The Union has no other significance.

13 Behavior connected with the use of the baths will be discussed elsewhere.

14 An example is the annual cooperative completion of the *Babylonian Talmud* by members of the *Hevra-Shas,* the Talmud Association, also a part of the Congregation. Several business operations, such as baking *mazah* and meat marketing, though also under the Congregation's auspices, are actually connected with the school system for which the benefits of these enterprises are used.

15 Naturally, militancy alone is not enough. It is necessary that the Rov take one seriously, for which additional attributes—such as unquestionable religiosity, active participation in community affairs, and a reputation for common sense—take on importance. In the case of the zealots, however, an ample dose of the first two qualities seems to compensate for the absence of the third.

16 In 1964 a few youngsters were arrested by the police for painting swastikas on Israeli consular property. When community leaders came

to the Rov to plan their release, the Rov counseled, "Let them spend a night in jail. It will do them good!" In 1970, after an ad appeared in the *Times*, the Rov ordered that those responsible be barred temporarily from admittance to the main synagogue.

17 The Rov once remarked jokingly, "I have about me people who watch that I shall not, God forbid, become deviant."

18 The watchdogs do not confine their activity to direct attempts at influencing the leader. They typically begin with admonishing the "culprit" and threatening to tell the Rov. If the individual fails to heed, they not only carry out the threat but occasionally also launch a rumor campaign in order to enlist public opinion, which appears to be a factor even in a hierarchical society like ours. An incident that occurred during one of my visits may illustrate the zealots' immediate reaction to a "deviant" act, as well as the way minor conflicts are frequently settled. The principal of the girls' school—not a Satmarer—was preparing the graduating class for the graduation exercises. A zealot passed by and mistook the activity for a physical education lesson. Without questioning, he lashed out at the principal: "You so-and-so, who gave you permission to teach gymnastics to our girls?" Indignant at the false accusation, the principal, instead of answering, called his attacker before the boys' school administrators and told them the story. Realizing his error, the zealot apologized and fined himself ten dollars for charity, thus settling the incident.

19 The lay secretary, for example, has a great deal of power. He communicates frequently with the Congress' key members and generally controls the organization's machinery. At the time of my visit, a characteristic incident occurred. The Congress organized a rally for which it sought support from all members, who were expected to lend their own names and those of their congregations. A prominent member hesitated. The secretary promptly issued a proclamation announcing the rally, which bore the signatures of all its hundred or so members but from which the wavering rabbi's name was conspicuously absent. The rabbi quickly requested that his name be added. The request was, of course, granted and the proclamation was reissued with his name inserted. The incident was widely noticed and discussed in Williamsburg; it had the desired effect of impressing on potential challengers the means available to the Congress for eliciting compliance.

VI

Religious Behavior

The Pentateuch contains 613 basic religious laws—248 prescriptions and 365 proscriptions—and each of these has a great number of minutiae. In addition there are numerous latter-day rabbinic decrees—some meant as "fences" to preserve the original laws, others decreed in response to new situations—which are now almost indistinguishable from the Pentateuchal core. Although Satmarer subscribe to this entire vast and complicated code, to enumerate it all would not only be impossible within our limits but would actually be unnecessary for our purpose. Many of these laws, such as those dealing with sacrifices and priesthood, are inapplicable today, and others—regulation of food consumption and family behavior, for example—we shall treat in connection with their respective institutions. In general, strictly religious behavior in Satmar can be said to center on six substantive, though overlapping, themes: prayer, study of Torah, observance of holidays, retention of a state of spiritual purity, symbolization of identity, and maintenance of spiritual well-being.

Prayer

The elements that comprise the so-called covert aspect of Satmar prayer include those found in most major religions, namely, attempts to express one's innermost wishes and feelings; hope of enlisting divine help in fulfilling one's desires; and plea for the forgiveness of sin. But there is an added element of legal obligation as well, since the religious code prescribes when, what, and occasionally even how to pray. This legal factor is responsible for the formal aspect of Satmar worship, whereas Hasidic culture accounts for most informal patterns.

Hardly anything of the formal aspect is peculiar to Satmar. The prayer book used is the standard so-called *Nusah Sepharad*, or "Sephardic Style," which is actually a combination of the Ashkenazic and the Sephardic versions.[1] The equipment used in conjunction with prayer—phylacteries (*tefilin*) worn by males over thirteen[2] during weekday morning services; the prayer-shawl (*talit* or *taalis*) worn at morning prayer by all married males; the scroll containing the Pentateuch (*sefer-Torah*), kept in the holy ark, located in the eastern wall of the synagogue and read from on numerous occasions; and articles of an ornamental nature—all are of the standard variety used by Orthodox Jews everywhere. Likewise, the formal structure required for public worship is the standard Jewish *minyan*, consisting minimally of ten males over thirteen, six of whom must participate fully while the other four may merely stand by and occasionally respond "Amen" or recite a few lines when required to do so. One of the ten, the *baal-tefilah*, leads the congregation, an easy task which practically every individual performs on occasion. Finally, the time is the usual twice-a-day, morning and evening,[3] when all Orthodox Jews pray. The details in these formal matters need not concern us here, since the interested reader may easily locate them in any standard Nussah Sepharad prayer book and in the codes that deal with the subject. All we need to observe is that, unless prevented by an emergency, Satmarer Hasidim attend synagogue twice each day, that they recite the entire services as prescribed, and that they are extremely discriminating in their purchase of such religious articles as phylacteries, for which they spend rather large amounts of money, in order to assure themselves full compliance with prescribed details.

It is a different story with the informal aspect of worship. Here we find an unusual Satmar pattern. details of which provide important clues to the less tangible aspects of the group's existence. To begin with, there are no strict schedules for services either in the main *bet-midrash*[4] or in the satellite *shteeblach* (plural of shteebel).[5] Instead there are time limits imposed by legal prescription as well as by practical considerations. According to the rules, one should pray in the morning sometime between dawn and midday, whereas in the evening the combining of afternoon and evening prayers necessitates starting when it is still officially daytime. The practical considerations stem from the need to be gainfully occupied during the hours usually reserved for work and business. These limitations leave wide latitudes, especially since the legal limits are rather loosely interpreted.[6] Thus on weekday mornings, from about five o'clock on, there is a constant flow of *minyanim* (plural of minyan). At any point during the first hours, not one but several minyanim are simultaneously in progress, each in a different corner or anteroom. A few individuals walk in and find that the ongoing minyanim are too far advanced for them to join, so they walk over to the next corner and in a few minutes they usually have a quorum to start a service of their own. The amount of time one spends in the synagogue in the morning—and, to a lesser degree, this is equally the case in the evening—is rarely the minimum thirty to forty minutes that the actual service requires. Rather, most Satmarer spend additional time—a few hours in some extreme cases—before and/or after prayer for a variety of activities.

Informality is especially noticeable in the typically Hasidic manner of Satmar prayer—the high degree of individuation in this basically collective activity. First there is the matter of pace, which varies not only with each minyan but also between individuals participating in the same service; participation does, with few exceptions, not require simultaneous recital of prayers. Then we find a wide array of expressive acts—shaking one's body, raising one's voice, closing of eyes, contracting one's forehead, and occasional shedding of tears—employed to keep away outside thoughts and to intensify one's concentration on the meaning of prayer.[7] In all these, the extent and exact manner are not strictly prescribed and I found no status to be associated with a particular manner of praying.

The architectural features of the Satmar bet-midrash, with its numerous corners, columns, open corridors, and anterooms, as well as the large size of Satmarer's *taaleysim*,[8] fit admirably into the pattern. An individual may seek out one of the niches, envelop himself in his talit, and pray the way he wishes with only occasional regard for the rest of the congregation, of which he nevertheless remains a part.

Finally, rounding out the informal atmosphere in the Satmar bet-midrash are the numerous nonprayer activities permitted in various parts of the sanctuary while services are in progress just a few steps away. Some of these activities—reciting of psalms and study of Torah—are of a religious nature. Others are secular acts with only an occasional religious tinge. An example would be eating. Satmarer take turns in sponsoring coffee each morning for the benefit of those who spend extended periods of time in the synagogue. On the death anniversary of a close relative, one usually distributes *tikun*,[9] consisting of liquor and cake, to the congregants. And, if one is in a hurry to leave for work, one may bring along food and eat it in a corner. Still other activities, gossiping and politicking, even border on the profane. In combination these are likely to suggest to the uninitiated a lack of dignity (if not outright sacrilege) or a complete absence of regulations. One could hardly be more wrong. Satmarer have profound respect for their place of worship, except that, unlike those of Western society, Satmar norms of respect allow for a wide range of valid behavior and leave ample room for improvisation within limits. In line with Hasidic tradition, a measure of deviation even from these highly permissive norms is tolerated, whereas sanctions are reserved for the rare cases of gross improprieties.

Study of Torah[10]

Ideally one should study Torah with two—and only these two—purposes in mind: to comply with the biblical command ". . . and you shall teach them to your children" (Deuteronomy 6:7), which is interpreted to include studying, and to acquire knowledge for proper living. But other, rarely admitted motives no doubt underlie Satmar Torah study. First, prestige depends greatly on scholastic reputation. Second, the collective self-image of Satmarer as an elite community includes a respectable level of Torah literacy. Finally, Torah study has, as we shall see, acquired several latent recreational and social functions.

Practically every male in Satmar devotes some time to "learning Torah," though the amount of time naturally varies according to knowledge, capability, motivation, and occupation. But even jobholders and storekeepers find time for study in the morning, in the evenings, during services in the synagogue, at lunch, during subway rides, and especially on holy days, when one is free from the yoke of labor and thus able to turn his attention to what the Satmarer consider the essential aim of creation—Torah.

Satmarer study in solitude as well as in a variety of social settings, including partnerships of two, larger study groups, or while helping one's sons in their school studies, thus complying with the literal meaning of the biblical command. The subject matter studied includes the range of literature that comprises Torah in the broad sense, a sufficiently wide selection to suit everyone. Scholars delve into complicated Talmudic and latter-day rabbinic discourse. The more humble are limited to simplified behavior codes, books of morals, and the "softer" parts of the Talmudic and related literature. Even the scholar familiarizes himself with this easier literature, knowledge of which is essential for a scholarly reputation.

The nature of study in Satmar needs clarification, for it differs radically from much of what is called study in the West. Acceptance beliefs of the Torah's divine origin and the legitimate leaders' divine assistance in their interpretation of the Torah preclude the possibility of anything resembling free inquiry in the Western sense. Yet, within confines of acceptability there is room for a great deal of creative effort. While average individuals merely try to understand what has already been said, scholars strive to "innovate" in the form of new syntheses derived from traditional methods of hermeneutics and logical argumentation, the purpose being either exposition for its own sake or application of Torah to new problems.

Also differing from the Western is the Satmar technique of studying. Preferably, one should pronounce the words one studies, for verbalization is believed to facilitate retention. When difficult subject matter is involved, Satmarer chant the words in an effort to concentrate fully and to eliminate competing stimuli.[11] Silent reading—or "looking into a *sefer*— (a religious book; plural: *sefarim*)—is practiced when in the company of strangers or in the case of light material that does not require intensive concentration. Writing—note-taking or underlining—does not enter the process, except for the scholar's recording of contributions.

Festivals and Festivities

The monotony of the weekday routine is frequently interrupted in Satmar as the community observes numerous festive occasions. These are of three general types: major holidays, minor holidays, and occasions peculiar to this community.[12]

A few details about the Jewish calendar, especially the one used outside the Holy Land, are helpful: First, day follows night; thus any mention of a particular day refers to the one that began the previous evening. Second, the calendar is a lunar-solar one. The month is equivalent to the moon's revolution around the earth. Because twelve moon-months add up to twelve or so days less than the solar year, an extra month is added every two or three years (seven times in a nineteen-year cycle). Thus any given Jewish month comes in the same solar season but varies up to some twenty days from one year to another. Third, the year begins in the fall, as *Tishrey*, the first month, begins at some point during September or in the beginning of October. Finally, Jews living outside the Holy Land add an extra day in the celebration of the three Pilgrim Holidays (Tabernacles, Passover, and *Shabuot*). This addition dates back to the time before the establishment of a fixed calendar, when the authorities in Jerusalem determined the beginning of each month upon the receipt of testimony that the new moon had been seen. The decision had then to be communicated to those living outside Jerusalem, but it was not possible to reach the Diaspora before the holiday's arrival. Therefore, Jews outside the land, not knowing when the month began, had to observe two days instead of one. When the calendar was fixed, the rabbis decreed that the "second Diaspora day" continue to be observed, a decree that continues in force today.

The weekly Sabbath and the five once-a-year holidays are all mentioned in the Pentateuch as days on which work must cease and on which special sacrifices are to be offered. In Satmar, observance of these days (minus sacrifices, of course) is among the minimal requirements for community membership and for being considered an Orthodox Jew at all.[13]

Most important is the weekly *Shabat*, observed on Saturday.[14] Sabbath observance calls for refraining from work, honoring the day, symbolizing its distinct nature, and enjoying oneself physically as well as spiritually. In addition, a few minor themes appear here and there, the most prominent of which is the commemoration of the manna that the Israelites had received in the desert.[15]

Work is defined on two general levels. First, there is a legal definition of thirty-nine major, and several minor, work categories. Here individual judgment is of no avail, and everything depends on authoritative interpretation, which, for example, renders the writing of two alphabet letters a capital violation but defines the moving of furniture within one's house as not constituting a serious offense. Then, there is the considerably less precise principle of avoiding doing, touching, or even talking about anything not pertaining to Sabbath activities, This leaves occasional room for individual judgment. Together the two sets of proscriptions render the Shabat a day of nearly complete rest from what is normally called work.

The positive aspect of Sabbath observance may be seen as a quest for an ideal identity. This quest is best expressed in the belief that one receives for this day an "extra soul." During the week the need to earn a living forces one to be a slave to one's occupation, to spend most of the time in activities not essentially different from those engaged in by other people, thus providing no justification for the elevated self-image that Satmarer seek to maintain. Shabat, however, provides an opportunity for eradicating all the inequities and limitations of the work-a-day reality and for concentrating one's efforts on spiritual matters. It is a chance to assume the higher identity one would like to consider his true one.

The distinctive character of the day is symbolized, first, in the outward appearance of people as well as environment. While all individuals wear better and cleaner clothes, most males have special types of garments not worn on weekdays.[16] Similarly, home and synagogue are given a recognizably holiday appearance by covering all tables and by removing from sight all implements that are not to be used on the Sabbath. Even the streets look different, rendered so both by people's holiday attire and by the closed business establishments. The prayers contain added portions in honor of the day, and the atmosphere during Sabbath prayer is one of relaxation and festivity. The weekday hastiness reflected in the multiple simultaneous minyanim largely disappears; the Rov participates in and often leads the only minyan in the main betmidrash; and the slow-moving services include many portions of singing—something absent on weekdays. Finally, the atmosphere during meals leaves no doubt about which day it is. The white tablecloth, the candlesticks, the special Shabat white bread, *halah,* and the other special dishes not served during the week tell the participant that it is Shabat. Distinctiveness thus permeates every area of the environment, so that an individual cannot avoid feeling different during virtually every minute of the Sabbath.

Distinctiveness and the quest for the ideal are also—perhaps mainly—reflected in what the Satmarer do during their Shabat, as well as in the way they do it. To begin with, of the roughly twenty-five hours between Friday's sunset and Saturday after dark,[17] some five to ten hours are spent in the synagogue and a few more at home in study and prayer, those highly valued activities for which one has not enough time during the work week.

Even the mundane activities one engages in during Shabat shed their neutral character. Not only is eating a required part of the day's celebration, but behavior during meals incorporates many Satmar ideals with regard to eating, as well as to family life, ideals that cannot very well be approximated on ordinary days. First, the entire household is present and family status is strictly observed, both in the seating arrangement and in the order of serving. All meals begin with short services that set a solemn, religious-service-like tone that is, in some measure, retained for the duration of the meal. Informal talk is kept to a minimum; instead, eating is interspersed with hymn-singing and Torah discussion which males carry on while females are busy clearing away and serving. Neutrality is eliminated—though to a much lesser degree than in the case of eating—from sleeping and legitimate sexual intercourse, since both are religiously sanctioned as part of the positively valued enjoyment of the day.

Finally, special acts are prescribed for both the reception of the Sabbath and for marking its departure, acts that seal off the day at both ends in unmistakable fashion. Actually, a sequence of several acts is involved in each case. It begins at home on Friday evening with the candle-lighting, performed by the woman of the house and normally attended by her unmarried daughters. Men personally accept the Sabbath with their participation in the "Reception of the Sabbath" service—especially by reciting Psalm 92—which precedes the evening service. The climax of this series of acts occurs upon the males' return from the synagogue when, preceding the evening meal, the head of the household recites (usually over a cup of wine) the *kidush* (the day's sanctification), while the rest of the household listens solemnly. On Saturday evening males begin to shed the Shabat by inserting in the evening service a paragraph that refers to the separation between the sacred and the profane. Females, when noticing that it is time for the Sabbath to end, recite a short prayer in Yiddish, asking the Lord for a healthy and prosperous week. The culmination comes again in a family ceremony at home called *habdalah*, or separation. Again, the family head recites over a cup of wine or beer and the other members listen reverently, except for blessings over the smelling of spices and the enjoyment of light, in which all participate. The last one is important, since it is done in front of a candle just lit, an act forbidden on the Sabbath. It is testimony that one is again permitted to engage in weekday activities.[18] These boundary-marking ceremonies provide virtually every individual with concrete experiences that help him feel that he/she became a different person when the holy day entered and that the "extra soul" was shed when the Sabbath departed.[19]

Table 2 summarizes the notable once-a-year days on the religious calendar. The major holidays are of two kinds: the Days of Awe highlight the extended fall holiday season, emphasizing piety and repentance, whereas the three Pilgrim Holidays, with joy as their main theme, are scattered throughout the year. Sukot is at the end of a long fall season. Passover, on the other

Table 2
The Annual Religious Calendar

Month	Day	Day of Significance	Reason for Observance	Level of Significance	Behavior Involved in Observance
Tishrey	1 & 2	*Rosh Hashanah* (Head of the Year—)first of two holidays comprising "Days of Awe"	Creation of the world; yearly time for judgment of all men	Major	Sabbath-like behavior (except for permission to do work connected with food preparation); longer and more fervent prayers in synagogue, lasting most of the day; blowing of shofar is central part of services; symbolization of wish for good year and favorable judgment in foods and greetings; toning-down of joy theme (including recommendation for abstention from, though not outright prohibition of, sexual relations); general heightened emphasis on piety and penitence
	3–9	Days of Penitence	Middle days of "Ten Days of Penitence"	Minor	Addition of litanies to synagogue services; continuation of emphasis on repentance
	10	*Yom Kipur* (Day of Atonement)—second and final holiday in "Days of Awe" series—climax of penitence season	Sealing of verdict in judgment begun on Rosh Hashanah	Major	All evening and day in synagogue, mostly engaged in prayer; wearing of white gown (*kittel*) by all married males in synagogue as reminder of shrouds and thus man's finite nature; total prohibition of food and drink; also, prohibition of sexual relations, wearing of leather shoes, and washing or anointing of the body; Sabbath-like behavior in dress and refrain from work; climaxing of emphases on pious and penitential behavior

Table 2 _(continued)

Month	Day	Day of Significance	Reason for Observance	Level of Significance	Behavior Involved in Observance
Tisney (cont.)	15 & 16	First two days of *Sukot* (Tabernacles)—first of three Pilgrim Holidays (these were occasions for pilgrimage to the Temple in Jerusalem)	Ingathering of harvest; commemoration of living in huts during desert journey to promised and; symbolization of temporary transient existence in Diaspora	Major	Sabbath-like behavior (except for permission to prepare food); all meals eaten in *Sukah* (hut) erected before the holiday; ritual handling of the "four kinds"—*etrog* (citrus medica), palm branch, myrtle, and willow—to symbolize (1) the harvest theme and (2) the unity of the Jewish people, as the four kinds represent four basic types in terms of piety and scholarship; general emphasis on joy, especially within family context
	17–21	Intermediate days of Sukot	Same, except for last of these, *Hoshenah Rabah*, believed to be occasion for Yom-Kipur-like fate-sealing	Intermediate	Preferred, but not mandatory, refrain from major work; continuation of eating in Sukah, utilization of "four kinds," and emphasis on joy; slightly lengthened synagogue services; festive atmosphere maintained at home by leaving tables covered and serving more elaborate meals than usual; fifth day (*Hoshana Rabah*) assumes major significance as services similar in character to the ones of the Days of Awe last almost the whole day
	22 & 23	*Shemini Azeret* and *Simhat Torah*—last two days of Sukot	Same	Major	Same as first two days, except for discontinuation of eating in Sukah and handling of "four kinds"; climaxing of joyous behavior through lengthy dancing and singing during service of *hakafot* which involves holding Torah scrolls, expressing joy in the possession of the Torah

Month	Day	Name	Event	Type	Observance
Heshvan	No days of note during entire month				
Kislev	21	Twenty-first of Kislev	Escape of the Rov from Nazis	Community	Feast of thanksgiving in synagogue
	25 through 2 or 3*	Hanukah	Commemoration of (1) Jewish victory over Syrian Greeks (2nd Century B.C.E.) and miracle of oil found at end of that war, containing one day's supply for Temple candelabra, but lasted eight days (hence, eight-day holiday)		
Tebet	10	Tenth of Tebet	Beginning of Babylonians' siege of Jerusalem leading to destruction of first Temple	Minor	Fasting; addition of litanies and Bible-reading in synagogue services
Shebat	6	Sixth of Shebat	*Yoortzaat* (death anniversary) of Rov's brother	Community	Lighting of memorial candles during services in synagogue
	15	Fifteenth of Shebat	Head of the Year for Trees (sealing of fate of tree crops)	Minor	Inclusion in major meal of varieties of fruit, especially of the type grown in the Holy Land
	29	Twenty-ninth of Shebat	Yoortzaat of Rov's father	Community	Lighting of memorial candles in synagogue; festive meal conducted by the Rov; Rov also leads synagogue services

* Variation is due to the fact that *Kislev* sometimes has 29, and at other times 30 days.

Table 2 (continued)

Month	Day	Day of Significance	Reason for Observance	Level of Significance	Behavior Involved in Observance
Adar	13	Fast of Esther	Commemoration of fasting by Mordecai and Esther (told in Book of Esther 4: 15–17)	Minor	Fasting; addition of litanies and Bible-reading in synagogue services
	14	*Purim* (Festival of Lots)	Commemoration of delivery of Jews from extermination planned by Haman (Book of Esther)	Intermediate	Reading of *Megilah* (scroll containing Book of Esther); some extension of synagogue services; sending of gifts (especially food) to one another; giving money to poor individuals and needy organizations; all kinds of merrymaking activities, especially by children (including masquerading and amateur dramatization); major feast and some heavier-than-usual alcohol consumption; voluntary refrain from major work
	15	*Shushan Purim*	Commemoration of celebration of Purim by Jews of Susa (Esther 9:18)	Minor	Some modification of synagogue services; leaving tables at home covered to maintain festive atmosphere
Nisan	14	*Erev Pesah* (Passover Eve)	Final preparation for Passover; commemoration of pascal sacrifice	Intermediate	Thorough inspection in the evening by the head of the household to assure no *hamaz* (leaven) or products containing hamez are left, followed in the morning by burning of anything that is left; fasting of males or (in most cases) absolution from obligation through participation

Month	Date	Holiday	Historical Significance	Category	Description
					in minor feast on occasion of completing study of a book in the Talmud; changeover to dishes reserved for Passover and extensive preparation for major feast of the following evening
	15 & 16	First Two Days of *Pesah* (Passover)—second of three Pilgrim Holidays	Exodus from Egypt	Major	Sabbath-like behavior in dress and refrain from work (except food preparation); no hamez eaten, used, or even kept in the house; substitution of *mazah* (unleavened bread) for leavened bread; *seder*, major and unique service-feast at home on both evenings (details in text); beginning on second day of forty-nine days counting of *Omer* (see details below)
	17–21	Intermediate days of Passover	Same	Intermediate	Preferred, but not mandatory, refrain from major work; continued restriction on eating or using hamez; slightly lengthened synagogue services; covered tables and elaborate meals maintain festive atmosphere at home
	22 & 23	Second days of Passover	Crossing of the Red Sea by Jews leaving Egyptian slavery	Major	Same as first two days, except absence of seder; some attend after evening meals the Rov's "table," during which dancing in water poured on floor commemorates Red Sea crossing
Iyar *Sivan*	16–30 plus entire month plus 1–5	*Sefirah*, forty-nine days of counting of the *Omer* (offer of produce on second day of Passover in days of Temple)	Prescription for counting in Bible (Leviticus 23:15–16); mourning of students of Rabbi Akiba (famous Talmudic scholar), believed to have perished	Minor	Addition of short counting service after evening prayer; mourning expressed through refrain from haircuts and from arranging or participating in celebrations other than those prescribed for a given day (holiday celebrations at end of Passover, circumcision which

Table 2 (continued)

Month	Day	Day of Significance	Reason for Observance	Level of Significance	Behavior Involved in Observance
Sivan (cont.)			during these days in revolt against Rome (second century C.E.)		is mandatory on eighth day from birth); mourning is interrupted on thirty-third day of counting (eighteenth of Iyar or *Lag Baomer*) when the fallen rebels were permitted to be buried
	6 & 7	*Shabuot*—third of three Pilgrim Holidays	Giving of Ten Commandments on Mt. Sinai; harvest	Major	Sabbath-like behavior (except for food preparation); extended synagogue service includes solemn reading of Ten Commandments; decoration of both home and synagogue with tree branches and flowers recalling the outdoor surroundings at Sinai; males spend whole or part of first night studying Torah in synagogue; eating of dairy food, which has multiple symbolic significance relating to the giving of the Torah at Sinai (e.g., milk is white, a color that signifies grace, the quality bestowed at Sinai)
Tamuz	17	Seventeenth of Tamuz—beginning of season of mourning known as the Three Weeks	Beginning of last phases leading to destruction of both Jerusalem temples (especially the second)	Minor	Fasting; addition of litanies and Bible-reading in synagogue services

Month	Day				
	18–29	First and milder part of Three Weeks	Same	Minor	Mild mourning, similar to that observed during the Sefirah (counting) period between Passover and Shabout
Ab (Ov)	1–8	Beginning of more severe part of Three Weeks known as the Nine Days	Same	Minor	Same as first part, plus abstention from eating meat (except on the Sabbath)
	9	Ninth of Ab—climax of Three Weeks	Destruction of both Jerusalem temples	Inter-mediate (almost major)	Fasting and abstention from all pleasures forbidden on Yom Kipur; abstention from major work activity, at least until noon; reading of Lamentations and addition of lamenting litanies as well as Bible-reading in synagogue
Elul	Entire month	Preparation for forthcoming Days of Awe		Minor	Blowing of *shofar* (ram's horn) following services in synagogue; beginning of general emphasis on repentance and piety in daily behavior; addition of litanies to morning synagogue services during last week
	6	Sixth of Elul	Yoortzaat of Rov's grandfather	Com-munity	Same as 29th of Shebat

hand, despite its relatively short duration, constitutes by itself a spring holiday season which is really more extensive and more intensive than it appears. Quantitatively, the requirement to rid the house of all traces of leaven requires an almost month-long thorough cleaning process in preparation for the holiday proper. Qualitatively, Passover observance may well be the most personally rewarding of all holiday experiences. In large measure this is due to the unique event of the *seder*, the meal-service observed in practically every household on the first and second evenings of Passover, in commemoration of the liberation from Egypt which, according to the Bible, occurred during the night of the 15th of Nisan. No single characterization is likely to do it justice, for the seder is a combination of a religious service, a royal feast, an ethnic celebration, and a family affair which includes even a measure of fun, especially for children. Similarly, the underlying ethos comprises, in addition to the core themes of Egyptian slavery and the ensuing exodus, several additional themes accumulated through the ages, such as commemoration of the Passover celebration at the Jerusalem Temple, survival of the Jews in the face of persistent attempts at their annihilation, and the continuous hope for the ultimate Messianic redemption (which, according to one version, should materialize at just this time of the year)—all of which are appropriately symbolized by the presence of objects (equipment, food, and so forth), as well as acts (reciting, eating certain foods, and others).[20]

Despite the variety of the seder's moods, it is not a conglomeration of unrelated small events but a united whole. The unity is achieved by the standardized, orderly (seder means order) procedure, as well as by the figure of the father, who, dressed in his kittel[21] and seated in Eastern royal fashion on a bed in which he can occasionally lean back while eating and drinking, presides over the affair, thus combining the roles of king, priest, teacher, and master of ceremonies with that of family head. An air of mystery is present on the Passover evening, the result of the whole long history of the Jews which many of the Satmarer, who do not care about history, have forgotten.[22] The mysterious nature of the evening is elaborated in the literature (often discussed at the seder) and woven around the biblical designation of this night as a *leyl shimurim (Exodus 12:42)*, a phrase which lends itself to several interpretations: "night of watching," "of expectation," or "of observance." Furthermore, numerous meanings are read into each of these interpretations. At the seder, mysteriousness reaches a high point during the few seconds toward the end at what may be considered the climax of the evening. After the completion of after-meal grace, Elijah's Cup, which has been on the table all the while, is filled with wine and the door is opened for the Prophet, who is believed to be visiting every seder. Everyone greets the invisible guest with the traditional "Blessed be the comer!" The door remains open for a few seconds during which the participants utter a traditional curse at their enemies of all ages: "Pour Thy wrath at the peoples that do not know Thee . . . for they have consumed Jacob and devastated his dwelling . . .," after which the door is closed. The feeling of being in the presence of the Prophet who, more than any other, has lived in the heart of the Jews as the messenger of good news and who occasionally appears to help one in need; the sweet hope of redemption, awakened by the believed presence of the one who will eventually bring news of the Messiah's coming, plus the darkness and the unknown intruding from without—all render these few moments extremely exciting and memorable. Add to this the special emphasis on family togetherness and even such a small matter as the custom that every member of the family buy something new for the liberation festival, and it becomes understandable why Passover generates more excitement than any other holiday, despite the hard work of preparing for it.

Shabuot, finally, follows Passover by six weeks. Despite its connection with Passover through the seven weeks of the Sefirah, it is sufficiently removed in time to constitute a small but separate entity.

The minor holidays are also of two basic types, one commemorating happy events in which the basic theme is joy and thanksgiving, and the other being in memory of calamities in which the observance is of a sad nature. Yet, with two notable exceptions (one, Purim, in the happy category and the other, Tishah Beab, of the sorrowful kind), neither joy nor sorrow seems to be essential to actual behavior. Rather, these occasions have assumed a character of moderate festivity, which elevates them above ordinary eventless days.

Of the minor days described in the chart, all but one are of Talmudic, not biblical, origin. Hence their "minor" character. The exception, Purim, even though of biblical origin (the Book of Esther), requires no cessation of work as part of its observance, which is the reason for its relegation to basically minor status.

The chart omits the monthly *Rosh Hodesh* (Head of the Month), celebrated each month (with the exception of Tishrey, when Rosh Hashanah takes its place). Extended synagogue services and quasi-holiday meals are all that its observance involves, thus not upsetting the weekday routine significantly.

In all, the Satmar year is packed with public festive occasions, spread over the entire calendar, to which one must add a few that have no fixed date (the annual fund-raising dinner for the various branches of the school, for example) and the numerous private celebrations (weddings, bar-mizvahs, and the like)[23] that one must attend because of multiple personal ties maintained in a closely knit community such as Satmar. It is an eventful year which shields the individual from becoming lost in the gray working days and the impersonal social atmosphere of New York City.

Symbolization of Identity

Belief has it that the main virtue of the Hebrew slaves in Egypt, on account of which they merited redemption, was their retention of distinctiveness in dress, names, and language. Commitment to identity maintenance has been a major value among Jews of all ages and varieties and is, as we have seen, central to Satmar. Accompanied by their claim that their way represents genuine Jewishness, Satmarer regard it as a commitment to retain Jewishness, rather than as an effort to safeguard Satmar as such. Consequently, the boundary which a given pattern helps to maintain may vary from one instance to the next; in one case, it may establish common territory with all Orthodox Jews; in a second, with Hasidim; in a third, with Hungarian Orthodox Jews; in a fourth, with Hungarian Hasidim, and so on. The combined effect of these patterns is to retain boundaries that are quite clearly those of the community proper.

We have noted the Satmarer's emphasis on the theme of identity in their observance of the Sabbath. We may add that the Sabbath is called in the Bible a "sign" (Exodus 31:17) between the Lord and the Jews, and Sabbath observance is thus manifestly interpreted as one of the identity marks of a Jew. Similarly, putting on phylacteries is a sign (Exodus 13:9 and 16; Deuteronomy 6:9 and 11:18) which is similarly interpreted. The most important of the Biblical mizvot, so termed and oriented, is the "sign of the covenant" concluded between God and Abraham (Genesis 17), namely, circumcision of males, which must be performed in a prescribed manner on the eighth day after birth. Satmarer trust its performance only to highly respected individuals in whose knowledge, skill, and integrity they have complete faith.[24] Finally, this category includes the *mezuzah*[25] affixed to every door, which, even though not called a sign in the Bible, is still regarded as marking a Jewish home.

The triad of dress, names, and language continues to be important in Satmar. Outward appearance, particularly of the male, is highly significant. From the age of three, all males have their heads shaved periodically, except for the sideburns which they grow into long dangling curls that are to mark them for the rest of their lives. To this they eventually add a beard which, ideally, ought to remain uncut and untrimmed.[26] On top of their shirts they wear a *talit-katan*, a miniature prayer shawl that has a hole in its center so that it can be pulled over the head. Hungarian and Galician Hasidim may be recognized by the large-size woolen talit-katan that is visible underneath their coats. Finally, men wear Hasidic long coats and Hungarian Hasidic hats.

For females, long sleeves, full stockings, and dresses reaching below the knee are required over the age of three. Married woman must, in addition, shave their heads and wear a wig or other type of headdress.

In Jewish religious life first names are the ones that count, as surnames are recognized to have been imposed from without, fairly recently. Satmarer make it a point not to add any new first names to those commonly used by their forebears.[27] In fact, this pattern has been intensified on American soil, for Hungarian law demanded civil registration under a common Hungarian name, thus forcing many Jews to have separate Jewish and civil names. In the absence of such a law in the United States, this duality in naming children was discarded by most strictly-Orthodox Jews. Consequently, many American-born children are, curiously, less assimilated in their names than are their immigrant parents.

Ashkenazic Jews have customarily used two languages, the Holy Tongue for prayer and study, and Yiddish for daily communication. Satmarer continue to cling tenaciously to both, refusing to modify even their pronunciation.

Besides these characteristics of appearance and speech, Satmarer have developed a set of common attitudes which accentuate their identity. Foremost among these is allegiance to the group and to the Rov.[28] The religious nature of this loyalty lies in the central importance of the concept of legitimate leadership in the Satmar belief system and Satmarer's absolute conviction that the Rov is today's legitimate leader. Hence, committing oneself to accepting the Rov's guidance is considered tantamount to joining the ranks of authentic Jewry.

Satmar in the United States has also become the leading symbol of a renewed quest in Jewish Orthodox circles for purism in kosher food and a variety of other practices. Actually, more than attitude is involved here, for within a few short years after the arrival of the core group to the United States, Satmarer have managed to develop their own brands of all foodstuffs that fall in some way under religious regulation, brands that have found sizable markets outside their community. Satmarer and their satellites have also taken the initiative in building ritual baths throughout the United States according to the strictest specifications. Underlying such activity is a suspicion that the standards of other Orthodox groups, especially those who came to the United States earlier, are inadequate, and a corresponding conviction that in these matters only Satmarer have the required know-how and integrity. These beliefs form part of the collective self-image of an elite group. It is an image that has characterized Satmarer all along, but which in the

United States has been considerably reinforced by the sizable following they have acquired.

The last feature of Satmar identity to be noted is its intense opposition to Zionism and the State of Israel, as well as its complete dissociation from everything and everyone in any way related to the Jewish nationalist movement. As we have noted several times, Zionism has been declared a heresy, a denial of the fundamental Messianic belief, and a breach of the God-imposed oath never to attempt seizure of the Holy Land without the Heaven-sent Redeemer. Again, Satmar has always been anti-Zionist, but in the postwar United States phase of the group's history, anti-Zionism has been elevated to one of the most distinguishing earmarks of Satmar culture and is one of the chief rallying points for those satellites that have accepted its leadership.

Maintenance of Purity

Although most of the vast number of Pentateuchal-Talmudic laws for maintaining spiritual purity are considered inapplicable today, those still in force, combined with others that Satmarer practice voluntarily, are elaborate enough to give us a taste of this important element of Jewish culture. The ambiguity in the attitude toward the human body noted in our discussion of the belief system comes to light here, for, even though "impure thoughts" (in connection with illicit sexual desires) are occasionally mentioned, practically all instances of impurity requiring acts of purification involve the body or some bodily function.

There are degrees of impurity and corresponding degrees of acts required for the return to a pure state. Severest of all is the unclean state of the menstruating woman, a state which lasts for a minimum of twelve days at the end of which she must submerge herself in a *mikveh* (ritual bath) that meets a number of specifications.[29] Men also consider it important to submerge in the mikveh on the morning following sexual intercourse, before prayer or Torah study. Although recognized as not actually mandatory, mikveh-going for men, even without intercourse, is highly valued and hence widespread.[30] The men's mikveh is open for business (a few cents is charged for its use) every day from about five in the morning. It is especially crowded on Fridays and other pre-holiday afternoons, as no healthy male would wish to enter a holy day without purifying himself.

In the course of daily life, many occasions call for handwashing. In some instances, such as after sleeping, defecating, or cutting fingernails, one must pour water on each hand three times. In other cases, such as after urination, once on each hand is sufficient. In still others, for example, touching a normally covered part of the body or a shoe, only wetting of hands is required. These norms are highly internalized, to a degree that before the required handwashing one experiences a definite uncomfortable feeling of being impure, a feeling that comes to the surface in the almost instinctive withdrawal of "unclean hands" from a proffered handshake.

The frequency of occasions requiring purification, the pride shown by Satmarer in their mikvehs, the verbal emphasis on purity in a variety of contexts—all attest to the importance in Satmar culture of retaining a state of spiritual cleanliness in the face of the frequent descents to impurity that are an inevitable outcome of having a body that functions in animal-like fashion and that requires animal-like gratification.

Maintenance of a State of Spiritual Well-Being

All religious behavior leads, of course, to some degree of spiritual well-being (as it also helps maintain identity, especially in the case of traditional Orthodox Judaism in which religion and peoplehood are inextricably blended). Some acts, however, are explicitly oriented toward this purpose, especially those Hasidic elements in Satmar behavior not based on any formal rules which are nevertheless universally followed by Satmarer Hasidim. We have noted some Hasidic patterns in the informality of the synagogue. Here we shall concentrate on the quest for communion with the Rov.

Typically, a Hasid regards his rebbeh as the embodiment of the ideal man, as the greatest scholar, as the most pious and the wisest of men who has a great deal to offer as teacher, adviser, model of ideal behavior, as one who can intervene in Heaven on one's behalf, and, generally, as a holy man in whose company one always feels warm and secure. Indeed, we may regard the Hasid's quest for communion with his rebbeh as being basically a quest for psychic security and protection.

Satmarer (like all Hasidim) seek communion with the Rov both publicly and privately. Opportunity for being with the Rov publicly arises on festive occasions, during prayer and the "tables." The desire to attend services at the main bet-midrash where the Rov prays, visibly increases with the seriousness of the occasion and the anticipation that the Rov will assume leadership. Thus Rosh Hashanah, Yom Kipur, Hoshanah Rabah, Simhat Torah, and the first day of Shabuot are prime occasions, and rare is the Satmarer Hasid living in New York City who will not attempt to be with his rebbeh on the days of heavenly judgment, participate in the joyous hakafot on Simhat Torah, or listen to the Rov's reading of the Ten Commandments. These are also the times when those living elsewhere come occasionally to Williamsburg.[31] Secondary occasions are the remainder of the once-a-year holidays and a number of special Sabbaths on which there is certainty that the Rov will lead. On a regular Sabbath only the veterans who make up the hard core of the community attend regularly. The rest prefer the comfort and more regular hours of the smaller shteebel and only occasionally venture into the main bet-midrash.

Merely attending a worship session in which the Rov participates carries the reward of having one's prayers go to Heaven in the company of those of the Rov, thus giving one the comfortable feeling of being close to the holy man. He who is willing to invest additional effort to push his way close to the Rov (a few privileged individuals have reserved seats not far from the Rov) can reap the additional benefits of actually beholding the Rov's face while the latter prays and of hearing every word the Rov utters. At the maximum-reward occasions, attendance alone is physically difficult, for the long hours in the packed hot bet-midrash render these occasions into virtual fast days (Satmarer do not eat before worship).

The table, or public meal, we recall, is one of the most typical Hasidic patterns. Lacking any element of legal compulsion, it is far more informal than the worship session. Since only the Rov and a few privileged guests are served at these meals, the average Hasid attends for the purpose of beholding his ideal man serve the Lord even in such a prosaic activity as eating, occasionally grabbing or receiving a bite from what the Rov ordinarily leaves in each dish. Even more rewarding are opportunities to exchange with Rov a wish of lehayim, to listen to the Rov's Torah exposition, or, on some occasions, to partake in dancing and singing that the Rov joins. All this may be interrupted by the Hasid at any time to engage in light conversation a few feet away. In all, table participation requires relatively little effort and is thus highly rewarding.

Private Hasid-Rov meetings are of three general kinds. First, each Hasid visits with the Rov at regular intervals, two or three times a year, one of which is during the Days of Awe. No appointments can be made[32]; each individual must go to the Rov's home during reception hours and wait his turn in one of the anterooms. When the Hasid enters, he remains standing in a position of reverence in front of the Rov and hands the latter a *kvittel*, a piece of paper on which all names of the members of his nuclear family (of procreation) are written, as well as any other name of a relative he may wish to add. Some also write needs and requests near a name, (e.g., a grown son or daughter needing a proper match, a sick person wishing to be cured). He also places on the table his pidyon, or redemption money, which may be any amount one wishes.[33] After the Rov reads the kvittel, the Hasid may also ask the Rov for advice on a problem he may have encountered. The Rov normally offers advice, often in short phrases which his Hasidim have learned to understand. For example:

> hasid: I received two suggestions for a match for my son, one is the daughter of Reb Dovid from Budapest, and the other, the daughter of Reb Chayim from Debreczen, may he rest in peace, whom, I believe, the Rebbeh knew.

> rov: Yes, I remember Reb Chayim. He was a true scholar and pious, too.[34]

The Rov did not have to state explicitly his choice, for he has indicated it by mentioning the desirable characteristics of Reb Chayim and by ignoring Reb Dovid, a fact that left no doubt in the Hasid's mind as to the direction he ought to follow. Finally, the Rov bestows his blessing on the Hasid, "May the Creator help you succeed!" which is a sign for the Hasid to leave. This he does reverently, backing out from the room and allowing the next Hasid to enter.

A Hasid visits the Rov each time an important event happens in his family, as when a child is born or a son becomes bar mizvah or a child marries. The procedure on these occasions is essentially the same as that during the annual visits, except that the requests and the wishes are likely to concentrate on the hero of the occasion, who, if he happens to be present, may receive from the Rov the priestly blessing (Numbers 6:24-26).

The third type of visit is occasioned by special problems or emergencies. Shall one move to a new apartment? Shall he take a new job? enter a new business? So and so is ill, and so forth. These visits differ from the first two types in that they are brief, to the point, and do not usually involve a kvittel and a pidyon. In cases of illness, the Hasid may attempt to see the Rov in the bet-midrash and briefly mention the sick person, giving the patient's name as well as that of his/her mother and saying what seems to be the matter with him, occasionally also asking some specific advice, such as whether or not to rush into an operation.

All these private meetings suggest an intense dependence on the Rov for guidance. The Hasid appears to be unwilling (or, perhaps, unable) to decide important matters for himself and to face the hazards of living without first seeking protection from the man whom he believes to be capable of providing it.

Since the culture with its focus on religion has, as already noted, remained virtually intact, little change has occurred in behavior discussed in this chapter. Two minor developments, though, deserve our attention. First, the community holiday on the day of the Reb Yoel's liberation has become an occasion for conflict. The old Rebbetzen arranges her own "all are invited" banquet for the occasion, apart from the one given by the established leadership. Different comparative attendance figures are cited by each side as proof of relative strength. Some establishment spokesmen, apparently irritated by the phenomenon of a onetime community-identifying day having turned sour, opined that in view of the fact that Reb Yoel is no more among the living, it may be time to abolish the celebration of his liberation from the Nazis. While it is impossible to predict the outcome, the situation does not, by itself, seem to portend any serious future explosions.

The second, at this time more subtle, trend involves capacity (or lack of) for important decision making. On the surface, the pattern of private visits with the Rebbeh continue unaltered (with the obvious exception of open opponents). Yet, interviews with establishment supporters, as well as fairly extensive information on a variety of patterns of deviance, indicate considerable emotional weakening of Rebbeh-Hasid ties and a corresponding rise in Satmarer's ability to decide. Unlike the first phenomenon, this one does have potential for significant future change. It touches on a central nerve of the very nature of Hasidic community systems. Lacking information on other contemporary Hasidic communities, it is idle to even speculate on whether we have at hand a peculiar Satmar situation or a wider trend connected with global trends of ever-expanding communication. Only time (and, perhaps, additional information) will provide the answer.

Notes

1 See Chapter 1, n. 12.

2 As is the case with social structure—and with all religious behavior, for that matter—sex, age, and marital status are important variables here. The reader will no doubt notice throughout this chapter the frequent insertion of such qualifying adjectives as "male," "over thirteen," and "married."

3 The common reference to Orthodox Jews' attendance at the synagogue "three times a day" is a misstatement that derives from the fact that there are three services: morning, afternoon, and evening ones (patterned after the sacrificial services in the Jerusalem Temple). It is theoretically possible to have services at three different times, but with the exception of academies, where the teachers and students are always present, this is hardly feasible. As a rule, Orthodox Jews schedule the afternoon and evening services together, beginning the former close to sunset, when it is officially still afternoon, and following it soon thereafter with the latter. Synagogue attendance is thus twice, not three times, a day.

4 This is an abbreviated pronunciation of *bet-hamidrash*—literally, "house of study"—which denotes one of the two types of Jewish houses of worship. The other is a *bet-hakeneset*, or "house of assembly" (for which "synagogue" is an accurate translation). The bet-hamidrash, being the more informal of the two, is naturally preferred by Hasidim everywhere.

5 On holidays the smaller places do have an approximate schedule, because their clientele includes time-conscious worshipers whose preference for the shteebel may actually depend on their relative punctuality.

6 Loose interpretation enters, especially when the Rov is involved. In the presence of the one person regarded as the ultimate authority, it would be presumptuous for a Hasid to worry about legality. The Rov's "morning" minyan is usually in mid-afternoon, and a number of people wait each day to pray together with him. This does not count holidays when the Rov's is the main minyan, in which the bulk of the congregation participates.

7 "Meaning" is to be taken not only in the literal, but, even more important, in the symbolic sense. Here again we find an opportunity for individuation, since the meaning one reads into a particular phrase naturally depends on one's knowledge as well as one's interpretation.

8 This is the plural—not the grammatically correct one but the one used in Satmar for "taalis."

9 More about this custom and its meaning in Chapter 7.

10 The discussion in this section is closely related, and may actually be considered as a preface, to the discussion of the educational institution in Chapter 8.

11 Note the similarity, in this respect, between prayer and study.

12 See Table 2. Those marked "intermediate" in significance do not constitute a distinct category, but are either intermediate days of major holidays or minor holidays that nevertheless require fairly extensive behavior changes. It should also be repeated that here, as in many other behavior areas, we are describing behavior not restricted to Satmar but common to Orthodox Jews (except, of course, those marked "community" on the chart). The mode of observance, however, occasionally contains peculiar elements.

13 Even though they consider themselves as the true representatives of contemporary Orthodoxy, Satmarer nevertheless concede the existence of other Orthodox Jews, though of a lower level.

14 In Hebrew and Yiddish, *Shabat*, the term from which the "Sabbath" derives and which literally means "rest" or "rest day," is actually the name for Saturday.

15 The connection between the Sabbath and the manna stems from the biblical account of the latter (Exodus 16), which includes references to the Sabbath—that the manna did not fall on the seventh day and, instead, a double portion was collected on Friday. There the Bible also mentions the necessity to cook and bake for Shabat on Friday, and states that no one ought to leave his residence on the seventh day. The latter admonition became the basis for numerous Sabbath laws.

16 Most married men wear a *shtraamel* (a velvet hat with a broad rim of brown fur strips) and a long black satin or silk coat called a *kaaften*. Another Sabbath man's set—consisting of black loafers, white knee socks, and short breeches which, abroad, used to be worn by sheyneh yidden exclusively—came into wide use among newly married Satmarer in the United States. Similarly, many unmarried adolescents wear a kaaften, once an exclusive custom of the upper stratum. In Chapter 5, n. 8, above, I referred to this downward diffusion of patterns of dress, interpreting it as a reflection of the evolving positive value of equality. But many sheyneh yidden—especially kelay-kodesh—are recognizable on weekdays when they wear a kaaften and in some cases even loafers and black knee socks. The Rov is the only person whom I have seen wearing white socks on weekdays. The shtraamel is thus the only garment worn exclusively on holidays.

17 The twenty-fifth hour is added partially because of some doubt about the exact time a day begins and partially because some addition from weekday time to the Sabbath, at both the beginning and the end of the holy day, is required as an expression of welcome to that day.

18 Although a somewhat festive atmosphere is maintained for the remainder of the evening, including a meal named the "Queen's Farewell," for all practical purposes the Sabbath ends with the recitation of the habdalah. On the long winter Sabbath evenings most storekeepers even open their shops for a few hours.

19 I have omitted here an important holiday behavior pattern: participation in the Rov's "table" (*cf.* Chapter 1, "The Rift Between East and West—In Eastern Europe.") It will be mentioned with all specifically Hasidic aspects of Satmar later in the chapter.

20 As I have noted in the case of prayer, where the Satmarer follow a standardized procedure, I consider it unnecessary to repeat the easily available details. This applies to the seder as well.

21 Officially the kittel should, as on Yom Kipur, remind its wearer of his finiteness and thus caution him against taking himself too seriously. I do not know to what extent the official objective is achieved, but I have the impression that the kittel has acquired the latent function of validating the complex roles that the father takes on at the seder by giving him a distinguished appearance that sets him apart from the rest of the participants.

22 For example, the Passover season had been for centuries a time of bloody anti-Jewish rioting (in Russia it lasted into the twentieth century), largely incited by fire-and-brimstone Easter sermons against the "Christ killers." The massacres often occurred at the very point of the seder; the resulting anxiety no doubt contributed to the evening's mystery. Yet few Satmarer, if any, are likely to be aware of the temporal associations.

23 In the late 1960's, as the children began growing up and marrying, the number of weddings grew to an average of four or five a day. As a result, they lost their festive character, and one has the impression that they even became somewhat burdensome, as most persons felt obligated to attend at least one wedding every day.

24 More about this rite in Chapter 7.

25 Literally a "doorpost," so called because it is affixed there. It actually consists of a piece of parchment on which a scribe wrote the two biblical passages (Deuteronomy 6:5-9; 11:13-21) that contain the command for its attachment.

26 It is a source of pride and prestige for one to be able to claim that he has never touched his beard or side curls. Relating the Rov's escape

from the Nazis, an informant underlined the fact that the Rov had managed to keep his beard and curls intact even during his captivity. The informant pointed to this as testimony of the continuous heavenly vigilance over the zadik.

27 The widespread Jewish custom of naming children after deceased grandparents or other relatives tends to fortify the above pattern, which is found among many Jewish groups.

28 Because belonging to the group is voluntary, loyalty is, in most cases, an automatic concomitant of affiliation.

29 The Pentateuchal laws regulating menstruation have not only been retaineded but have actually undergone elaboration, as have the laws concerning mikveh construction. I mentioned above the campaign throughout the United States to build mikvehs that are absolutely kosher, and needless to say the Satmarer women's mikveh has been built without leaving out a single restriction. More details about this behavior in Chapter 7.

30 An informant once dropped a remark to the writer that reveals the attitude of at least some Satmarer toward both mikveh-going and the Rov. The man mentioned that he needed to talk some matter over with the Rov, and the writer asked him why he did not go to the Rov. A seemingly spontaneous reply came: "I do not want the Rov to see me on a day when I was not in the mikveh. I have the uncomfortable feeling that he sees on my face that I am not pure."

31 On these prime occasions many Hasidim from other countries visit Williamsburg. From Western Europe, where larger numbers live (Antwerp, London), chartered flights are usually available during the Awe season.

32 As noted in Chapter 4, n.4 the visiting pattern has recently changed to an appointment system.

33 The Rov, as noted earlier, distributes the pidyon money for any cause he deems worthwhile, but not for the maintenance of his household.

34 This is a true story related to me by the Hasid involved. The match with the girl indicated by the Rov's choice was consequently concluded and the writer knew the couple as parents of some half-dozen children. The names and places of origin have, of course, been altered.

PART THREE

FAMILY AND
EDUCATION

A USEFUL way of classifying Satmar institutions is by degree of autonomy, which may be viewed in two ways. One way would involve the examination of respective norms. Satmar behavior is guided by two types of standards: one is shared with the larger culture, the other is derived from Satmarer's interpretation of Jewish religious law. In fact, Satmarer themselves clearly distinguish between the two types, assigning the first to the domain of *mentshlichkeit*, or humanity, while subsuming the second variety under *yiddishkeit*, or Jewishness.* An institution is thus autonomous to the degree to which it is oriented toward standards of yiddishkeit rather than those of mentshlichkeit. A second dimension of autonomy is the extent to which the social organization involved is confined to the community's boundaries.

Part Two dealt with the most autonomous of Satmar institutions—religion. The two next most autonomous areas—the institutions of family and education—involve some standards shared with the outside, and their social networks extend beyond the community. Yet both are basically yiddishkeit-oriented, and are bulwarks of support for the core elements of the culture Satmar wishes to preserve.

*To be sure, the two areas of Yiddishkeit and mentshlichkeit overlap. For example, Satmarer frequently claim that the former encompasses the latter. This theoretical claim should, however, not obscure the fact that in practice a clear difference between the two is recognized. On many occasions I heard this kind of remark: "Such behavior is not only not *yiddish* [Jewish], but not even *mentshlich* [human]," or "Moshe does not lead a yiddish life, but he is at least a *mentsh*," i.e., a decent human being.

VII

The Family

Values and Norms

SATMAR places a high value on family. Appropriate family background, although not sufficient by itself, is nonetheless essential for the attainment of high or even average status in the community. While it is not entirely free of notions about biological inheritance, the importance assigned to lineage consists mainly of legal, social, and mystical components. Legally, products of forbidden unions are either totally ineligible or highly undesirable as marriage partners, and the stigma is, moreover, transmitted to offspring. The quality of one's family is thus an index of one's eligibility to marry into "the Lord's congregation." Satmarer also recognize the importance of socialization, believing that an individual's behavior is greatly determined by upbringing and by experiences in the home during one's formative years.[1] Finally, the mystical element is the belief that parents' and especially the father's, overt and covert behavior during intercourse resulting in conception influence the quality of the child's soul.[2] The offspring of a pious man is thus believed to be a likely possessor of a high-quality soul, and vice versa.

The great emphasis on family also orients the individual toward perpetuating the family tree, regarded as one of the main purposes of life. The childless are considered unfortunate, whereas those who fail to marry altogether are deprived of status.

Also important is the attitude toward sexual behavior, which underlies numerous aspects of family life. Satmarer regard the sexual act as basically desirable for several reasons. First, pro creation is both a biblical command (Genesis 1:28) and a main goal in life. Second, sexual satisfaction is in itself valued as a deterrent to sinful thoughts.[3] Finally, a number of mystical notions suggest the sexual union to be symbolic of spiritual unions involving the divine. The latter are particularly useful for justifying the sexual life of highly revered individuals of all times.

Nonetheless, as the strongest of passions, sex is also regarded as man's most vulnerable point, the avenue through which he can be most easily tempted into sin or degeneration. One must therefore exercise caution, avoiding activities that arouse one's drive and opportunities for transgression. Even with a legitimate spouse, an individual must observe restrictions—such as the post-menstrual and post-partum taboos—and abstain from vulgarity, thereby preserving the basic dignity and mizvah-character of the act. Because of its crucial importance, proper sexual behavior is synonymous with holiness.[4]

Monogamy became an important norm among Ashkenazim despite the fact that the Bible does permit polygyny. Even though traces of the original leniency are still to be found in special cases, monogamy is taken very seriously. But the tradition does not go to the extreme advocated by Catholicism. Divorce, while discouraged, is nevertheless officially permitted, as is remarriage of both parties.

The standards guiding mate selection may be divided into two broad categories, religious norms and practical considerations. Most important in the first category are the specific rules barring eligibility on the basis of incest,[5] illegitimacy resulting from adulterous relations, incestuous ones, or from previous marriage.[6] The primacy of these rules is reflected in the severity of their enforcement. Not only is a would-be violator refused marriage, but his mere suggestion of marriage is likely to result in ostracism. Of almost equal importance is minimum religiosity by Satmar standards. Although marriage cannot be refused in case one of the partners lacks this quality, such a marriage nevertheless results in effective rejection by the community. Next in importance is family background. Marrying into an unacceptable family may result in considerable loss of status, though not in ostracism. Finally, a number of traditions, such as those involving first names or double intermarriage,[7] impose further restrictions which are, however, often disregarded without incurring sanctions.

"Practical considerations" include such desiderata as approximate age equivalence, good health, normal intelligence, feminine beauty and adroitness, and earning capacity or occupation of the male. Satmarer define these as preferences of a practical nature rather than as cultural values (not even of the mentshlichkeit variety). Hence individuals consider them as their private concerns, which they may disregard at will,[8] expecting strangers not to interfere unless consulted.

Expectations concerning division of labor between husband and wife are undergoing radical change. At their root is the emerging view that, unless confined to the house by pre-school children, women share with their husbands the responsibility of providing for the family. Concomitantly, the husband is expected to lend a hand in housework, as well as to allow the wife a larger share in the process of family decision-making. Performance of most of the religious ceremonies in the house and supervision of boys' religious education remain the only responsibilities assigned to the husband exclusively. In secular domains, lip service is still paid to the old ideal that the husband be the leader and the wife the follower, while in reality new norms of cooperation, mutual trust, and flexibility on the part of both marital partners are clearly on the rise.

Children are expected to obey fully and respect their parents and, until marriage, to relinquish to the latter all important decisions. On their part, parents ought to socialize their young, to provide for them until marriage, to take an active role in selecting a suitable mate for them, and to help them become established after marriage.

Finally, kinfolk are expected to help each other in case of need. This norm has also been undergoing change of late, as Satmarer have come to rely increasingly on resources outside the family and even the community for taking care of welfare needs that had traditionally been alleviated within the confines of family and kinship.

Structural Features

Despite the presence of a strong familistic sentiment that distinguishes Satmar from the surrounding American scene, structurally the Satmar family appears to be, with few minor exceptions, much like the American middle-class family. Social scientists refer to this type as the conjugal family (or the Eskimo type, in anthropological literature).[9]

The main characteristic of this family type is that the nuclear unit (husband, wife, and unmarried children) is not entangled in extended kinship ties, consequently enjoying a great deal of freedom and flexibility. Relationships with kinfolk outside the nuclear unit are voluntary, selective, and have little if any official sanction.

Structural, terminological, and behavioral indicators point in the direction of a conjugal system. To begin with, no distinct kinship unit beyond the nuclear family exists in Satmar. Instead, each individual recognizes his relatives on father's and mother's, as well as on a spouse's, side whom one feels obligated to invite to family celebrations and with whom he/she generally has stronger ties than with strangers. Likewise, in case of need one is expected to turn to relatives before going to strangers. There are no rules as to how close or distant a relative is to be considered kinfolk (or kindred); this allows one a degree of freedom in selecting a set of desirable relatives. While mutual attraction is no doubt a factor in the selection process, the main factors seem to be religiosity and community membership.

The most intense associations maintained outside the nuclear unit are along vertical lines. While one has no specific obligations toward collateral relatives (brothers, sisters, brothers- and sisters-in-law, nephews, nieces), one does have obligations toward parents and children. This appears to be related to the emphasis on perpetuating one's family tree, which focuses attention both upward from where one originates and downward where the chain is to continue.

As in all conjugal systems, every line of descent is of equal importance. The Yiddish terms used to designate kin relationships tell the story rather effectively; just as in modern

English, the terms fail to differentiate cousins, uncles and aunts, grandparents, grandchildren, or in-laws of any direction.[10] Incidentally, one pair of terms has no English equivalent at all. Mechuttan (*mechitten* in Satmar Yiddish) for male and mechutteynesteh (*mechitteynesteh* in Satmar) for female refer, respectively, to the father and mother of one's son-in-law or daughter-in-law. In fact, the terms have come to include all recognized relatives of in-laws. What these probably reflect is the importance placed on family background in selecting a mate. Hence, once a marriage is contracted, both sides acknowledge their mutual acceptance by referring to each other as *mehuttonim or mechittonim* (plural for mehuttan/ mechitten).

Even more revealing are the regulations on incest (see Figure 3). Being of ancient origin, the rules suggest that the basic elements of a conjugal family system date back to antiquity. Satmar incest rules are the same as those of all Orthodox Jews and consist of two categories: primary and secondary restrictions. Primary restrictions are those mentioned in the Bible (Leviticus 18:6-18), whereas secondary incest restrictions refer to the proscriptions imposed by the Talmud (Tractate of *Yebamot, passim*).

Analysis of the rules reveals that they faithfully reflect the basic features of the family structure outlined above. First, the restrictions apply equally to the male and female lines in all directions. Second, the greater emphasis on the vertical dimension stands out clearly, since cousins and even nieces, again in all directions, remain eligible, while vertical relatives are forbidden to a point beyond imaginable applicability. Finally, almost as many relatives of ego's wife as of ego are included in the ban, which, furthermore, remains in force not only in case of divorce but also (with the exception of a wife's sister) even after the wife's death. All this is congruent with the already noted importance of the family of a spouse.

Forms of both the sororate—the custom of marrying a wife's sister in case of the wife's death—and the levirate—marrying the deceased husband's brother—have always existed among Jews. With the elimination of polygyny, the levirate became in many cases impossible, for the duty to marry a deceased brother's wife was the responsibility of the oldest surviving brother, who was likely to be married at the time. It thus became customary

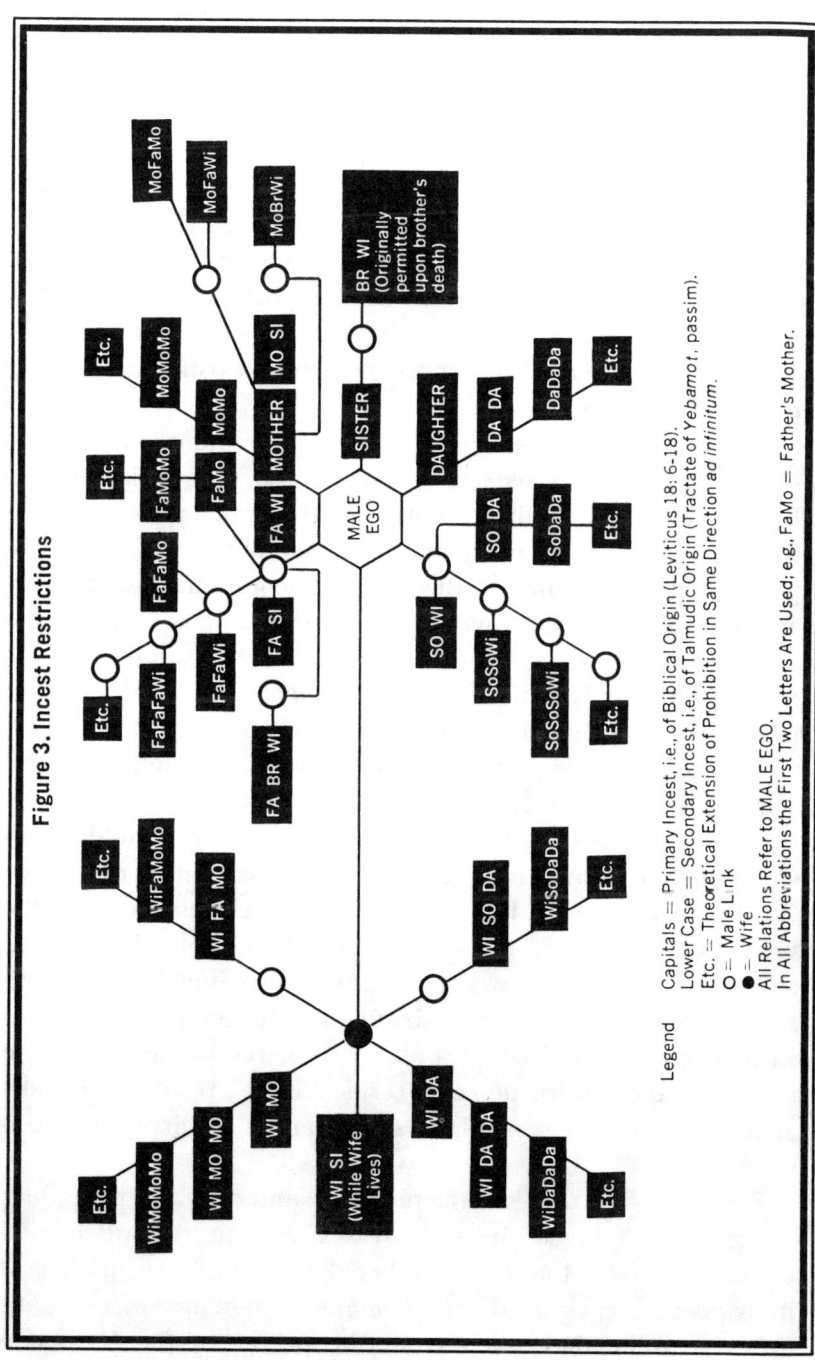

Figure 3. Incest Restrictions

Legend   Capitals = Primary Incest, i.e., of Biblical Origin (Leviticus 18: 6-18).
Lower Case = Secondary Incest, i.e., of Talmudic Origin (Tractate of *Yebamot*, passim).
Etc. = Theoretical Extension of Prohibition in Same Direction *ad infinitum*.
○ = Male Link
● = Wife
All Relations Refer to MALE EGO.
In All Abbreviations the First Two Letters Are Used; e.g., FaMo = Father's Mother.

among Ashkenazim to resort to the ceremony prescribed in the Bible for those refusing to marry the widow[11]—and this is what the Satmarer do today.

When a wife dies and is survived by an unmarried sister, the husband is expected to consider her a preferred candidate. Unlike in the case of the levirate, however, no rule exists to that effect, so that such marriages depend on the consent of both partners. Before World War II such marriages were common. At present only two cases have been reported (probably a few more exist.) The small number may be due to the abnormal circumstances under which most presently existing secondary marriages were contracted.

Community endogamy[12] is not a requirement, for all that one is supposed to seek is religiosity and appropriate family background. The available data reveal no penalty—formal or informal—for marrying an outsider who otherwise meets the prescribed requirements. Beyond this, community endogamy appears to be a tendency. In case of exogamous matches the couple is likely to end up in the husband's community, for membership in Hasidic fellowships involves the husband to a much greater extent than it does the wife.

Another—and for the moment final—index pointing in the same direction concerns patterns of residence. As would be expected in a conjugal system, not only are households overwhelmingly confined to members of nuclear units—only ten of 762 households were found to include other relatives—but the residential pattern of the independent households is random, showing no tendency toward geographic proximity to any given set of relatives of either husband or wife. Sample interviews with newlyweds and couples about to marry yielded the same results. The quest for neolocal residence (i.e., residence equally apart from both sets of relatives) appears to be virtually universal.

Exceptions to the general picture painted in the preceding paragraphs do exist. In some cases descent of one line is emphasized over that of the other. For example, a number of individuals, recognized as *kohanim* (singular: *kohen*), are believed to be descended from the priests of the Jerusalem Temple. Others, known as *leviyim* (singular: *levi*), trace their descent from the Levites of old. In both cases, transmission is through the male line. Except for certain religious purposes of a ceremonial nature, neither plays an especially important role.

On the other hand, for the purpose of determining Jewish identity, the female line counts more heavily. The offspring of a Jewish mother and a non-Jewish father is automatically a Jew, whereas in the reverse case the child is not considered Jewish unless duly proselytized. The practical significance of this rule for Satmar is virtually nil, for mixed unions do not exist in this community and are not likely to be tolerated in the future without radical cultural change.

The fact that religious law favors, in the first case, patrilineal, and, in the second instance, matrilineal descent may be taken as further evidence of the absence, even in theory, of basic preference for one or the other.

Somewhat different structural patterns at the upper stratum appear to be undergoing change at the present time.

Genealogical information on the Rov's family reveals a tendency to marry relatives. Of the twenty-four marriages shown in Table 3, nine—the six Teitelbaums, two of the Halberstams, and at least one of the others—were with cousins, seven of whom were first cousins. The main motive here seems to have been a search for equivalent status, which can be seen from the fact that not a single match involved a commoner and from the additional fact that those with higher prestige were not necessarily the ones who married relatives.[13] This quest, while general throughout the entire Satmar population, seems to have generated among the rebbeyic dynasties a heightened tendency to marry within the family, for the simple reason that available choice was quite narrow.

In addition to the high incidence of cousin marriage, perhaps partially a concomitant of it, kinship boundaries in the past were considerably larger than among commoners. Individuals tracing descent from the founder of a dynasty maintained kindred relationships even after five or six generations. Those who emerged as leaders served as rallying points for the numerous scions who sought to retain their family identity. In our case, first it was the Rov's brother who was the center of gravity for the Teitelbaums; then the Rov assumed the position.

Table 3
Marriage Pattern Among the Leaders
of the Teitelbaum Dynasty*

Children of Teitelbaum Dynasty Leaders	Family Background of Spouses			
	Teitelbaum Family	Halberstam Family	Other Rabbinic Background	Totals
Rov's grandfather's children:				
Sons		1	3	4
Daughters	1	1	1	3
Rov's father's children:				
Sons (Rov and his brother)		1	1	2
Rov's second marriage		1		1
Daughters		1	2	3
Rov's brother's children:				
Sons	2			2
Sons second marriages	1	1		2
Daughters		3	2	5
Rov's daughters	2			2
Totals	6	9	9	24

*These figures include all the children of the listed leaders.

Despite these differences, which often gave the impression of an extended kinship unit, the Rov's family shared with the rest of the community the basic structural characteristics of family. Descent has been bilateral, and a closer look at the aggregate of relatives suggests that it has not really constituted a well-defined extended kinship structure. The boundaries were undefined, and identification with the unit depended on individual choice and carried no specific obligations or privileges. It seems, therefore, that it was simply a case of intensification of the general cultural theme of family consciousness, except that here additional motives were in operation. Scions had been able to reap economic advantages from their family background, as they felt entitled to financial support both from the leaders and the followers. Too, identity with a rebbeyic family naturally carried greater prestige. All these factors contributed to the enlargement of the kindred perimeter.

Within the confines of today's Satmar community there is hardly any trace of the above pattern. The Rov has no living descendants. Of twenty-five household heads of rabbinic background who are members of Satmar, only two are married to relatives. Those relatives of the Rov who are trying to continue the quest for marrying "holy seed" are not formally part of Satmar but heads of small satellite congregations. It is therefore difficult to predict whether or not a nucleus of high-prestige families will eventually establish a somewhat different family structure than has the remainder of the community.

Family Behavior

The ideal marriage age for both boys and girls is considered to be eighteen, though eligibility begins at about sixteen. The early twenties are regarded as the upper normative limit. Single status beyond that age begins to be regarded as a reflection of difficulty in marrying, and, as time passes, it turns into a stigma which may eventually isolate an individual from age mates and prevent one's normal incorporation into the community.

Courtship as it is understood in Western culture does not exist in Satmar. Despite the failure of the professional matchmaker to reappear on American soil, matchmaking—now everybody's business—has remained the only approved way of initiating a serious male-female relationship.[14]

The sequence of events leading to engagement is more or less as follows. A married adult of either sex is "struck with an idea" of a potential match which seems appropriate in terms of relative statuses and aspirations of the two families. The suggestion is carried to one set of parents, and then—in the absence of a definite "no"—to the other set. The matchmaker normally withdraws at this point, to reappear only in case the matter comes to a successful close, upon which a fee for the suggestion will be demanded—and received.

If either set of parents objects, the matter normally ends. If both are serious, however, they will initiate exploratory steps. The girl's father will seek to have a closer look at the boy, whose mother will do the same with respect to the girl (all adults consider themselves experts in evaluating youngsters of their own sex). If both pass the initial inspection, the suggestion will be passed along to the youngsters who may, as a first step, attempt to glance at one another inconspicuously in order to assure themselves that they have no *prima facie* objections.

The next step is to bring the candidates together, usually in the girl's home. There they are given an opportunity to talk in the presence of elders—but in most cases also in semi-privacy, i.e., out of earshot of others. If the meeting is a success, the two family heads now must resolve whatever practical problems—possibly including details of financial support for the couple[15]—they may face before setting a date for the official engagement.

Traditionally, the engagement is formalized at a party given by the girl's parents to which only relatives, the closest friends, and several prominent individuals are invited. At the affair the fiancee attempts to deliver a scholarly Torah speech, which is customarily interrupted by singing.[16] A dignitary then delivers a Torah talk into which he weaves the theme of matrimony. The main formal event is the reading of the official engagement document known as "Conditions" (the entire affair is referred to as "Conditions Writing"), in which the details agreed upon by the parents are spelled out. The document is signed by both parents or their representatives, the engaged, and witnesses. A plate is then broken[17] to the accompaniment of exclamations of *mazeltov!*, or "Good luck!" Since, as at all formal Satmar gatherings, the women are seated in a separate room, the boy is led to the women's division where he wishes his fiancee mazeltov! At this point the engaged are not yet allowed even to shake hands, as all physical contact must be delayed until after the wedding. Refreshments are then served, over which the participants wish each other lehayim! or, "To life!" and, again, mazeltov!

In recent years, most people have omitted the engagement party, formalizing the engagement by a handshake between the boy and the girl's father and then leaving the writing and read-ing of Conditions for the bridegroom's reception that precedes the wedding ceremony. This changing custom reflects the fact that the function of the engagement party has been declining for centuries. The Conditions document, despite its legal form, has never had any true binding power (except over the financial obligations of the parents), since the engagement itself may be broken by either side with no serious legal repercussions. True, informal tradition militates against the breaking of engagements, but the same applies to all engagements, regardless of the way in which they were formalized. The recent abolition of dowries divested of significance even the financial clauses of the document; the blanks provided for these details are nowadays filled in with the meaningless phrase "according to the private agreement of the parties." Consequently, the Satmarer consider the engagement party superfluous.

The period between engagement and marriage is usually a short one, a few months in most cases. During this interval, the engaged meet frequently, but only for practical purposes, such as shopping and other preparations. Whenever possible, the encounters are chaperoned in order to avoid the temptation of physical contact.

A major consideration in setting the wedding date is that it be during the "pure" period of the bride, i.e., at least twelve days after menstruation, thus enabling the marriage to be consummated without delay.

During the last few days before the wedding, the prospective bride and groom are not permitted to meet. They spend these days in last-minute preparations in the company of relatives and friends. During the last week, the fiancee counts her "seven clean days," i.e., she inspects herself every day in order to be sure that her menstrual bleeding has disappeared. This is a prerequisite for the immersion in the mikveh on the wedding day, which is her final act of purification.[18]

On the Sabbath before the wedding, a gay ceremony takes place in the synagogue, where the bridegroom prays. The boy is called to the Torah scroll where a section of the weekly portion is read to him. After the reading, someone begins to sing, which serves as a cue to the women to throw into the men's section—aiming at the fiance—candy and nuts which they have prepared for this purpose. The symbolic emphasis is on the nuts, which, as a fruit, implies the wish that the new couple be fruitful. The sweets are picked up by the young boys present, often helped by their fathers. The ceremony, variously referred to as *bavaarfen* or "throwing at," or *aufreef* or "calling up," unlike among other contemporary American Orthodox, is not made much of by Satmarer. Some serve liquor and cake at the conclusion of the services, which becomes one more occasion for congratulations and well-wishing.

Both bride and groom spend the wedding day at home. The day is considered a private Yom Kipur for the two, as both fast and recite prayers of atonement. Some weep and pray that the unknown relationship they are about to enter may prove a happy one. On this day they enter a privileged period that is to last for seven days, during which they are exempted from work. All their needs are taken care of by relatives and close friends who constantly surround them.

The wedding normally takes place in the evening, as American circumstances have rendered day weddings impractical. The actual ceremony is preceded by preliminary simultaneous receptions for the bride and bridegroom, arranged in separate sections of the hall.[19] The bridegroom, dressed for the first time in his shtraamel-and-kaaften—the Sabbath attire of married adults—is seated at the head of a table, where he is flanked by his oldest male kinfolk as well as by guests of distinction. His reception resembles the engagement party described above, especially in cases where the latter has been omitted, thus necessitating that the reading of the Conditions take place now. A semi-professional entertainer, a *badhan*, who chants rhymes that he composes for each occasion, usually begins his entertainment at this preliminary reception. This is also the occasion for someone to hand the bridegroom a present from his bride—a prayer shawl and kittel, the latter to be worn at the main ceremony.

Meanwhile, at her reception, the bride has been sitting on a throne-like chair, also surrounded by close relatives and friends. Musicians are usually hired to play, while women and girls dance with one another.

Neither the bride nor the groom partakes of the refreshments and gaiety that surround them. They continue in the serious Yom Kipur mood, fasting, meditating, and occasionally weeping, until the ceremony. The wearing of the kittel by the groom and the white gown by the bride is also seen as part of the Atonement Day syndrome which includes the wearing of white.

All halls catering to Jewish Orthodox weddings have the roof over the corner reserved for the ceremony built so that it can be opened, for traditionally the canopy under which the ceremony is to be performed is to be opened "under the stars"—that the couple may multiply like stars. In New York City it is often inconvenient to perform weddings outside, and the open-roof corner serves to preserve the canopy-under-the-stars tradition.

When the canopy is prepared, the bridegroom puts on the kittel; some also spray ashes on their heads as a reminder of the destruction of Jerusalem, which ought to be remembered at the height of one's personal joy. He is then led by the *interferers*[20] to the canopy where a welcome is chanted for him. A few moments later the bride—her face thickly veiled—is brought by the wives of the interferers, who, before placing her alongside the groom, lead her in a circle around him several times while she too is welcomed in chant.

The ceremony itself lasts just a few minutes, for Satmarer do not permit such modern additions as speeches. The ceremony is confined to the traditional essentials, which are, in brief: recital of the betrothal blessings, placing of the ring by the boy on the girl's finger, reading of the *ketubah*—the important marital contract which must be in the couple's possession as long as they live together—breaking of a glass to interrupt the joy with a reminder of Jerusalem's destruction, and the recitation of the standard "Seven Blessings."

When it is over, the bride lifts her veil. The newlyweds now shed their serious airs and walk joyously down the aisle, surrounded by guests eager to congratulate them. They retire to a room in which they remain locked for a few minutes.[21] They are now permitted to eat, as the Yom Kipur mood gives way to one of restrained joy and gaiety.

At this interval the bride is removed to another room, where her head is shaved and covered by a wig or other headdress, not to be uncovered henceforth except in times of solitude. She is now a married woman, not only officially but readily recognizable as such.

The dinner proper does not differ greatly from its counterpart in the larger American society. The differences consist of segregated seating for men and women, more restrained entertainment, an extremely low level of alcohol consumption, speeches which are largely devoted to discussion of Torah, and the conclusion of the meal with the standard Jewish grace, followed by another recitation of the "Seven Blessings" by attending dignitaries and/or relatives.

After the dinner comes a specifically Jewish traditional entertainment known as a "mizvah dance."[22] The bride and groom are seated in the center of a circle. The badhan begins to chant a rhyming call for each male guest of some importance to come and dance with the bride. The man called comes forward, picks up one end of a handkerchief, the other end of which is held by the bride,[23] dances for a few seconds, and then continues to dance in a circle of men. The climax comes when the bridegroom is called upon to dance with his bride (without a handkerchief),[24] but he too is taken away from her by the men, in whose company he continues to dance. When this dance ends, the wedding is over.

Although the marriage is expected to be consummated during the first night, it is, according to scant information, usually delayed a day or two. Both bride and groom have received instruction from their respective parent of the same sex regarding sexual experience, in spite of the fact that parents assume their youngsters to have acquired the necessary information from reading and hush-hush conversation with peers. The parental instruction is thus meant to give the novices the benefit of the doubt and assume naivete on their part, as well as to add a practical touch.

Virginity of the bride is a definite expectation. Its absence is legal ground for divorce. All available evidence indicates that disappointments are rare.

After their first experience the newlyweds are required to avoid any physical contact for eleven days,[25] after which the woman's visit to the mikveh is again necessary for purification.

The wedding of a girl (as distinct from that of a divorcee or widow) is followed by "seven feast days," during which a holiday atmosphere is maintained around the new couple. Neither of the two is left unattended during waking hours. In the course of this week, parents or relatives of either side may arrange for a "Seven Blessings feast," i.e., a dinner reception to which they invite, in addition to all immediate relatives, at least one guest who did not attend any of the previous occasions. At the conclusion of the dinner they recite the "Seven Blessings." Due to the ban on continued sexual activity, as well as the custom of spending the seven feast days amidst relatives and friends, an American-style honeymoon is out of the question for a Satmar couple.

The young people now enter a new stage in their life cycle, in which life is radically different from what it was before. Marriage carries with it the acceptance of responsibility for earning a livelihood and managing a household. It also allows incorporation into the adult community as a full-fledged member. Outward signs announce the new status. The woman is especially recognized as married because of the substitute she wears for her hair. And even the man, whose new status is not as conspicuous, has ample opportunity to communicate it publicly. During Sabbaths and holidays he wears a shtraamel and a kaaften,[26] and on weekdays during morning prayer, in addition to the phylacteries he began wearing at thirteen, he now wears a prayer shawl. The addition of the talit marks the married man not only in the synagogue but also when he walks to and from the bet-midrash each morning, for the size of the bag he carries under his arm has become considerably larger. These signs, the new community status and the new way of life embarked on upon the first marriage, are retained for life, even in case one remains single after divorce or death.[27]

Marriage also marks the beginning of sexual satisfaction. We have noted that, on the one hand, the norms encourage sexual activity and, on the other, they define it as, in a way, unclean. Both these aspects seem to be reflected in behavior. My evidence suggests that the act itself causes no severe guilt feelings. Rather, it is enjoyed as a legitimate and healthy activity. The negative aspect finds expression in the insistence on strict privacy in all matters related to sex and in the emphasis on moderation. The post-menstrual taboo constitutes the greatest specific limitation. For at least twelve days[28] after the initial discharge, all physical contact is strictly forbidden. While it is, of course, impossible to ascertain extent of adherence, numerous behavioral indicators suggest a high degree of observance.[29] Even during the pure period, one is encouraged, informally, not to indulge excessively. For example, a man is taught desirability of submerging in a mikveh on the morning after intercourse, before prayer or Torah study. Originally instituted to discourage scholars from "being constantly at their wives like roosters,"[30] this practice also has the inevitable effect of associating intercourse with impurity from which one must cleanse oneself before engaging in religious activity. The literature also emphasizes that excessive sexual activity is detrimental to health.[31] These encouragements, while lacking specificity and significant sanction, probably do have some moderating effect. All things considered, it seems probable that, though they do not regard sex as basically sinful and bad, Satmarer nevertheless engage in it not too frequently.[32]

While Satmarer do not live in homes that can be called indigenous in a strict sense, since they rely on the apartment houses or two- or three-family homes that Brooklyn has to offer, they nevertheless occupy dwellings that meet their cultural requirements. Most important, they seek large homes that include at least three or four rooms potentially convertible into bedrooms. These have become necessary because of the various restrictions connected with sexual behavior. The strict privacy required for marital relations results in the early exclusion of children from the master bedroom. Then, separation of boys and girls from the very beginning necessitates at least three sleeping rooms for a family that has one child of each sex. Like all Orthodox Jewish homes, Satmar dwellings are marked by a *mezuzah*, a rolled piece of parchment containing two biblical passages (Deuteronomy 6:4-9 and 11:13-21) which is attached to the right doorpost at the entrance of each room. Within the home, master bedrooms are equipped with twin beds to accommodate the required separation during taboo periods. The beds are usually placed at opposite ends of the room in order to avoid any temptation that physical proximity may cause. Interior decoration, while generally similar to that of other middle-class homes, also includes a few indigenous elements. Practically all Satmar homes have many nicely-bound religious books, displayed in quite expensive bookcases. Silver articles, spice boxes, and others—are also found in most homes, as part of the displayed furnishings.

Couples strive to have children as soon as possible, not only to comply with the mizvah to procreate but also to reap the mundane joys that children are seen to offer.[33]

The post-partum taboo on intercourse is a rather short one, roughly matching current medical advice,[34] except that as in all cases when sex is forbidden, the proscription extends to all physical contact. The short interruption makes possible frequent pregnancies, and age differences of a year or so between siblings are rather common.

The current tendency in Satmar is toward large families. Again, the reasons are both religious and selfish consideration of a mundane character. Although religiously forbidden, women concerned about their health or wishing to escape burdens of excessively large families do practice forms of birth control, not in outright violation of the norm, but by finding legally sanctioned ways to bypass it.[35] Therefore, religiosity by itself would not necessarily result in large families. However, practical considerations enter the picture. Informants frequently expressed opinions to the effect that limiting oneself to, say, two or three children carries the risk that death of a child may leave one without the number considered necessary for one's happiness.

Sons are preferred, but after one or more sons birth of a girl is welcome and, in either case, once born, a daughter is loved and cared for as much as is a son. The difference is in religious ceremonial. A daughter is named in the synagogue soon after birth and then officially ignored until engagement. Even her assumption at age twelve of religious duties, such as fasting on Yom Kipur, goes unnoticed, whereas a boy goes through two major ceremonies before marriage. The first is circumcision when he is eight days old, usually performed at home by a lay specialist who is also a high-status individual. The ceremony is religiously important, for with it the boy enters "into the Covenant of Abraham,"[36] i.e., he becomes a Jew. It is an occasion for inviting guests, who are treated to a short meal follow-

ing the circumcision. The other major ceremony occurs when a
boy reaches the age of thirteen and becomes a *bar-mizvah*—one
officially obligated to keep the mizvot. In the synagogue the bar-
mizvah is recognized by being called to witness the reading of a
biblical passage on the Sabbath nearest to his birthday. Unlike
most American Jews, who turn it into an elaborate affair, Satmarer hardly notice the synagogue occasion. But on the very
day a boy enters the age of mizvot, his parents arrange a major
festive meal at which the bar-mizvah delivers a Torah talk. Satmarer have adopted the American custom of giving gifts,
mostly religious books, at the occasion. As already noted, at this
age a boy begins to be counted as an adult and hence as one of
a minyan, the ten-men quorum required for public religious services. Nothing comparable marks a girl's arrival at her age of
mizvah.[37]

Various interaction patterns within the nuclear unit make it
clear that the husband is still the head of the family in many
respects. He dominates its religious aspects, performing, as a
rule, all necessary ceremonies (except candle-lighting at the onset of holy days) and guarding the religious character of the
household.[38] He is also the representative of his unit to the
community, in which status of the entire unit is determined by
the position of its male head. However, he is the sole bread-
winner only when his wife is confined to the home by the presence of pre-school children. Otherwise the wife usually works
and makes a considerable contribution toward the family
income. This is clearly demonstrated in Table 4, in which we
see the percentage of working wives rise sharply as the
youngest child reaches school age. According to most
informants, this has led to a rise in the wife's share in making
family decisions of a practical nature, such as allocation of
available income. As we have noticed, this trend toward greater
equality of power between marital partners has been gaining
legitimacy within the normative system, thus ceasing to be
considered an anomaly.

Socialization of children, though generally considered a
mutual enterprise of both parents, is nevertheless characterized
by some division of labor between the two. The mother carries

Table 4
Wife Working and Age of Youngest Child
(N = 657)

| Wife Working | Age of Youngest Child | | | |
| | 5 or Below | | 6 or Above | |
	N	%	N	%
Yes	80	18.4	116	52
No	354	81.6	107	48
Totals	434	100	223	100

most of the burden during the first two years of a child's life, whereas the father gradually assumes an ever larger role in the process thereafter.[39] He becomes the main disciplinarian as the child reaches an age when use of physical punishment begins to enter the picture, while the mother normally resorts to the threat of "telling father." The man assumes the main responsibility for guiding his sons' Jewish education, whereas daughters' upbringing has traditionally been assigned to the mother. Of late, however, the introduction of a girls' school in the community has taken away some of the role of the mother in this area, whereas the father continues to monopolize his domain.

Because complete child-rearing data could not be obtained—with the exception of extensive information on sex and independence training—I can have only modest confidence about the following paragraphs.

Lactation, once universal in the culture, is still highly valued, though mothers who have insufficient milk supplement it with a bottle rather than hiring a wet nurse, which was the custom abroad. Addition of solid food at an earlier age than was customary in Hungary has also been accepted on medical advice. Satmarer attempt to extend lactation, at least in part, for as long as possible.[40] (I have no information regarding feeding schedules or weaning techniques.)

Satmarer seem to have abandoned swaddling without any difficulty as soon as American pediatricians advised them that a child develops better when given an opportunity to move about freely.

It is a different story with sex training, a behavior area that, unlike that of feeding or swaddling, does relate to the basic value system of Satmar. They are, therefore, not amenable to outside advice on how to proceed. Available evidence indicates little indulgence in masturbation, though transgression does not seem to meet with severe sanctions beyond strong disapproval or slight slapping of an offender's hands. Similar behavior was observed with regard to heterosexual play, except that in this case control is accomplished by strict separation of the sexes, both within and outside the home, a separation that begins almost at birth.

Boys are gradually introduced to the subject of sex in school, where, accompanied by a degree of embarrassment, they encounter it in the Bible, the Talmud, and the law codes. Girls, on the other hand, are formally kept ignorant until immediately before marriage.[41] As we have noted, however, both boys and girls discuss the subject with peers. Rare indeed is the youngster who learns the facts of life from a parent.

I found traces of autoerotic behavior among boys between puberty and marriage, but it is impossible to even guess its extent. Its existence, however, does not seem to constitute a problem. Its sinful character is constantly reiterated in the morality literature to which boys are exposed, as well as by their teachers. Hence the transgressor knows that he commits a violation which must be kept in strict secrecy and for which he must atone.

As for heterosexual contact, compliance with the ideal norm of abstinence before marriage seems almost total. All barriers to violation noted in connection with the post-menstrual taboo —cultural emphasis, severity of sanctions, fear of betrayal by the would-be partner—operate here, as well as others. The unmarried lack the privacy of a bedroom (automobiles are not made available to unmarried youngsters for any length of unaccounted time, especially after dark). Neither is a partner with whom one has already had intimate contact; early separation of the sexes is not conducive to development of social skills necessary for approaching a stranger of the other sex. Finally, though not instructed on specifics, a girl is usually warned by her mother against permitting a boy to touch her. This admonition, together with information acquired informally regarding sanctions risked by loss of virginity, are sufficient to frighten a young girl from even coming close to a boy.

Although a measure of aggressiveness, reflected in their intense militancy, has marked Satmarer all along, in the United States they seem to tolerate more aggressive behavior on the part of their young than they did abroad. One finds rather intense sibling rivalry, expressed in tattling, frequent quarrels, and mild physical aggression. Similarly, quarrels and mild fighting with peers may be seen wherever Satmar boys congregate and are not under the direct supervision of a significant adult, such as a teacher. Boys also show open disrespect toward adults —parents and teachers excepted—talking back, pushing, and stepping on the feet of anyone in their way, without even bothering to apologize. Youngsters begin to join rather early in aggressive behavior against such hated out-groups as Zionists and their allies, using derisive language, demonstrating, and occasionally even violating property.[42] What is remarkable in all this is that, at the same time that minor aggressive acts abound, they are kept within limits, and serious aggression of the kind that would run afoul of criminal law is practically absent in Satmar.

Independence training cannot profitably be dealt with as a single behavior category but must be viewed as consisting of at least two subcategories toward which Satmarer display quite distinct attitudes. First is the matter of taking care of personal needs, such as dressing and feeding. I have no specific information on extent of parental indulgence or on the age at which a child is expected to master a particular task. In general, parents display considerable impatience and appear eager that their youngsters should reach independence in the performance of these necessities as soon as possible.[43]

The picture changes radically when we look at the second subcategory—training in important decision-making. Such decisions are deferred to parents and occasionally to other significant elders until marriage. For example, an adolescent boy does not have the right to choose a school from among those approved in the community. He may suggest his choice to his father, who then has the ultimate word. The same is true in the case of a girl who leaves school at sixteen and must decide whether or not to go to work before getting married and, if so, what kind of work to seek. No adolescent has the right to spend considerable time on anything without accounting to his parents. Even in mate selection, parents, rather than the candidates, have more influence, though youngsters are permitted to veto choices they definitely dislike. In case of rebelliousness, parents resort to physical punishment until age fourteen or even fifteen. Lack of training in the making of important decisions appears to be a significant feature of the culture, one to which we shall return.

Affection toward children, except in infancy, is minimized, especially on the part of the father.[44] This is part of a wider tendency to avoid public expression of affection; even spouses meticulously avoid display of even verbal affection in the presence of others, including their own children.

The ideal of total obedience to parents is rarely approximated. On the other hand, open disrespect is practically nonexistent. This is true for all age levels, including married children. There is, however, no evidence of maintaining in behavior the related ideal of respecting older brothers or sisters. On the contrary, intense sibling rivalry appears to pervade the entire structure, cutting across age and sex lines in spite of attempted separation of males and females.

Boys and girls are not only separated whenever possible but are also treated differently in several respects, in line with differences in adult roles. Beginning at an early age, girls are encouraged to use their free time for helping with household chores and for learning to knit or sew, whereas boys are driven to study Torah whenever possible. This corresponds to the expectation that adult women will manage a household and, when possible, supplement family income by working outside the home, thus rendering industriousness a chief virtue. Whereas adult men are expected to be the religious heads of their homes, for which role they need familiarity with Torah. Interestingly, until about the age of sixteen no attention is given in the home or at school to preparation of boys for adult occupational roles, the prevailing attitudes being that a normal individual will eke out a living as his father managed to do, without extensive preparation. This reflects the fact that prestige in this community is more a correlate of scholarship and piety than of occupation, which is but a secondary, indirect factor. Also, as we shall notice in chapter 9, Satmarer are confined to a rather narrow range of occupations which do not include those needing extensive preparation-practice of law or medicine, for example.[45]

Adolescence as a stress-filled transitional period is, at least on the surface, nonexistent. At the same time, the community faces no open problems associated with adolescence in American culture. In Satmar this period is curtailed at both ends: a degree of childlike treatment extends to about fourteen, and sixteen is considered the beginning of eligibility for marriage. The rapid transition is possible because childhood, as known in contemporary Western society, barely exists among Satmarer, who do not recognize any qualitative difference between childhood and adulthood, viewing the former as an imperfect form of the latter.

A year or two before marriage, both boys and girls are encouraged to begin working. The purpose in threefold: to prepare for postmarital roles, to earn money which will be needed in establishing new families, and to prove one's ability to earn money, which is as asset in finding a desirable match, especially for the boy who must be prepared for the time when he alone will provide for his family.[46]

Launching children into marriage is exciting and fulfilling for parents. The increased financial burden connected with more and better clothes, weddings, feasts, and other necessities, is alleviated by the fact that money has usually been saved for this purpose. And the standard of expenditure for the occasion is left to the individual parent, his financial capacity being a factor in his planning.[47] Above all, the joyous experience of having reached the pinnacle of *naaches*[48] compensates for any financial burden.

The prospect of having all one's children married, though considered a major fulfillment[49] and the beginning of fewer worries, also has its negative side. Aside from parents' realization that they are aging, it also means the loss of their children's companionship on which they have learned to depend.

In contemporary Satmar the situation contains two mitigants: the large number of children extends the process over a decade or more, allowing for gradual adaptation; and the geographical concentration of the community places married children within easy accessibility of parents, so that communication and companionship continue to be possible.

It is impossible to gather adequate data on life in old age in Satmar, since the Germans exterminated most of the older people, leaving rather few cases to be observed. Only eighty-three of 1,525 adults (some 5.4 per cent) were reported to be sixty or over, and only fourteen (.9 per cent) were seventy or above. Of these, most prefer to live by themselves, as do their married children. A few live with their children but feel that were it not for their financial contribution (derived from social security, city welfare, or savings) their situation would be intolerable. From these meager data one may infer an emerging trend toward weakened ties with parents after marriage.

Divorce is rather rare. Of 1,565 once-married adults, only sixteen—twelve men and four women[50]—had been divorced once during their lives, and this despite the troublesome period between 1944 and 1950 during which social disorganization of every sort was much more prevalent than in normal times. The few cases justify no conclusion concerning causes. The law codes are of no great help either, for such legal grounds for divorce as failure of the woman to bear children during the first ten years after marriage are rarely applied. On the other hand, complaints about a partner's deficient religiosity seem to figure more prominently. One change is worth noting: a divorcee, once a stigmatized person, seems to have lost her stigma and has no apparent difficulty remarrying. Of the four women who were divorced, three were remarried.[51] Informants expressed the view that when one considers marrying a divorced person—man or woman—one ought to investigate "whose fault caused the divorce." Such an inquiry, of course, rarely yields clear-cut results.

In all but a few cases, then, death ends the family life cycle. Most of those who become single, whether by death or divorce, remarry. Only eighteen men and fourteen women who had been married were single at the time of the research, as against

218 men and forty-eight women who remarried after dissolution of their prior marriages.[52]

Behavior at the time of death, burial, and mourning is largely the same in Satmar as it is among all Orthodox Jews. With the exception of a few minor changes in custom, it follows rather closely the description in the standard code.[53] A few of the patterns are worth mentioning because they reflect a variety of basic cultural attitudes.

Regard for human life as being sacred is maintained until the very end. With the exception of an attending physician, no one is allowed to touch or move the dying for fear that such action may hasten death—which is considered tantamount to murder.

The dead body, though considered ritually impure, is treated with utmost reverence, especially in the case of one whose life was marked by a high degree of scholarship and piety. Status is also considered in the choice of a burial plot, which is done with an eye to proximity to family, friends, and status equals. Between death and burial and the body is continuously guarded and in front of it silence is maintained and candles are burned. Handling and washing are done exclusively by approved individuals, mostly by members of the Holy Association, who are in charge of all matters concerning burial. Mutilation of the body is strictly forbidden; Satmarer resist medical requests for autopsies. Showing one's last respect by walking behind the casket is considered an important mizvah. The custom is maintained today even though the distance to the cemetery forces the hiring of an undertaker for transportation. Before driving to the burial, the mourners let the hearse ride slowly through a few Williamsburg streets, and those who wish to pay respect (in fact, anyone who happens to be in the street) may walk behind the hearse for a while.

Simplicity characterizes all behavior connected with death and mourning. The body is dressed in a white shroud made of new but plain cotton; in addition, males are also wrapped in their own old prayer shawls. The casket is make of plain undecorated wood. Neither flowers nor music is permitted, and those attending the funeral—family and all others—wear their simplest weekday attire. No exception is made in cases of deceased individuals of high prestige. Rather than using luxurious equipment, respect to those of high-status is expressed through eulogies; by confining the handling of the casket to highest-status individuals; by submerging the body in a mikveh instead of just washing it; by making the casket, in the case of a scholar, of wood taken from and benches and chairs on which he studied, taught, and preached; and through mass attendance at the funeral, for the death of such revered men is considered everyone's loss.

Several cultural themes underlie this emphasis on simplicity and equality. It originated, the Talmud relates, as a reaction to the vogue of extravagant expenditures on burial outfits that resulted in widespread abandoning of corpses by survivors who could not afford the expenditures but felt embarrassed not being able to provide respectable outfits.[54] Later, as Jews settled amidst foreign cultures, modesty assumed the added function of providing one more symbol of dissociation from the surrounding cultural patterns that often called for display of affluence at such occasions. Above all, however, absence of luxury at burial and mourning came to express deeper cultural attitudes with wider ramifications: death demonstrates man's basically humble nature, regardless of the status one occupies while alive, and ought to serve as a reminder for the living against indulgence in self-aggrandizement. The message would be lost if luxurious display were allowed to create an artificial air of festivity.

Another basic attitude—that death is inevitable, that, like life, it is the work of God and should be accepted by survivors without excessive grief—finds expression in numerous patterns. Solemn silent meditation and soft-voiced short remarks, rather than tears, are considered appropriate, though the latter are not banned and are common at the time death actually occurs and during interment. Death's finite and irrevocable nature is underlined by covering the body from the moment of death, not to be uncovered thenceforth except during purification and dressing, which are performed out of sight of the mourners (open-casket funerals are thus unthinkable). Also, except in cases where the body is carried to the Holy Land, which is considered the ideal burial ground, burial is attempted as soon after death as is technically possible, which seems to have the function of preventing extended grief. Finally, the recited prayers explicitly emphasize the acceptance of God's verdict as just. In fact, the prayer most associated with mourning, the *Kadish*, contains no reference to death but expresses praise for the Lord's holiness and greatness, mentioning that He has created this world according to His will and closing with a prayer for peace. The Kadish was not originally designed for mourners and is even today recited upon many other occasions; but its adaptation to mourning shows the suitability of its contents to the underlying theme, that no matter what happens one ought to praise the Lord, for it is His world in which humans are but temporary dwellers who must accept the inevitable limitations of their finite existence.

Mourning behavior, as prescribed in the code and followed in Satmar, reflects the basic family structure. Only primary relatives—parents, children, siblings, spouses—are required to follow formal mourning procedures of any kind, and among these it is the child, and especially the son, who must observe the longest-lasting and most extensive procedures. He must recite the Kadish each day in the synagogue for a period of eleven months and then do so on each anniversary of the death—the yoortzaat. The latter, with the possible exception of the first year, becomes less a day of mourning and more one of solemn commemoration of parents whose line one continues.[55] The theme of continuation is also evident in the custom of naming one's children after deceased parents or grandparents (when these are exhausted, also after other relatives), thus forming a living reminder of one's origin. Clearly, no prescribed structure exists beyond primary kinship, and no appreciable distinction is made between the sexes or lines of descent since secondary and more distant relatives are all exempt from formal mourning whereas primary ones all have initial obligations. The added obligations of children further show the greater accent of vertical relationships, whereas the greater emphasis on the son[56] relates to the religious framework that surrounds these symbolic expressions, a framework that, as we have seen repeatedly, emphasizes the male as a participant.

One final area of family behavior to be noted is that of inheritance. Here is further corroboration of the real family structure, namely, basic equality of children regardless of sex or

birth order. The unwary may be misled by the official letter of
Torah-based law, which denies the right of inheritance to
daughters when there are sons, prescribes a double share to the
first-born son, and, in the absence of children, reverts the property to the father or brothers of the deceased rather than to his
wife, at the same time that it designates the man as the exclusive heir of his wife. Al these remain official laws which, in the
absence of a will, may be insisted upon by the parties.

The fact is that most Satmar men do leave wills, dividing their
estates equally among all children and their wives.[57] Even in the
absence of a clear testament, rabbinical judges will usually make
a strong plea for the accepted standard of fairness to prevail, a
plea which few can afford to ignore stubbornly. Again, the pattern bears a sharp resemblance to the situation in the larger
Western culture—a similarity which comes to the surface again
and again in family structure and behavior, despite important
differences in matters of sex and courtship or training in
important decision-making. This amalgam of similarity to, and
difference from, the larger culture underlines one of the most
important general characteristics of Satmar culture: adaptability
to changing conditions without the loss of core values.

In the last thirty years, family structure and behavior have
remained virtually unaltered. Contrary to expectation based on
experience with most ethnic immigrant populations in this
country, American-born Satmarer not merely continue the pattern indicated by their parents, but seem to have intensified it.
For example, the matchmaking pattern is now so well established that it is absolutely inadmissible for a boy to take out a
girl for a date, even in the way non-Hasidic yeshivah-type young
men take out girls to a restaurant for a meal or a drink. Note
that these Yeshivah-variety dates are arranged by third parties
and before the actual date each side thoroughly investigates the
other to determine acceptability of the individual, as well as
his/her family. Since reputation is of crucial importance,
attempt at physical contact is virtually impossible, not only
because it carries the risk of strong rebuff, but primarily due to
the fact that an individual prone to violate such a basic proscriptive norm is likely to have his reputation ruined to a point of

eliminating the offender from the reputable dating circuit. Yet, Satmarer strictly forbid any encounter other than boy and girl meeting under controlled conditions in the house of the girl. One informant, criticizing another Hasidic group, pointed to the fact in that community dating is practiced, something which, according to the informant, is forbidden among all Hasidic groups except that one.

Another indication of intensification I found in the visibly heightened consciousness concerning *shiduhin* (sing. *shiduh*), the mate-selection process. Almost from birth of a child parents are anxious about any occurrence that might damage the child's reputation and thus constitute an obstacle in the way of finding a proper match. (Incidentally, a similar intensification of awareness in this area seems to have occurred among all contemporary Orthodox groups, except the most modern type.) A child has some learning difficulty? The fact must be carefully camouflaged, lest it might hurt later when it comes to a shiduh. A youngster is retarded or has some other mental difficulty? The fact must remain a secret (some are shipped out of the country), because public knowledge of it is sure to hurt in shiduhin, not only of the individual, but of all siblings. Reports indicate that some marry off retarded and other mentally defective children, to partners with similar difficulty and—according to one report—sometimes to normal individuals (the pattern of limited pre-marital encounter facilitates deception) usually followed by severe consequent conflict between the two families. Etc., etc.

A few modifications of the behavior patterns described in the chapter are noteworthy. Nowadays, instead of entering the world of work/business a year or two before marriage, virtually all men not only continue their studies until marriage, but spend at least a year or two thereafter studying Torah in the *Kollel* (see update to Chapter VIII), the quasi graduate division of the school system. This also requires another modification, namely support of the young couple by parents during that period and agreement prior to engagement about the exact nature of it, how much each set of parents will contribute. As we would expect, reemergence in importance of financial arrangements is paralleled by reappearance and wider practice of engagement parties, even though details of arrangements are still concealed by usage of "in accordance with the parties' agreement."

Married women continue to be gainfully occupied after marriage whenever possible. However, in addition to the general occupational changes in the community as a whole (noted in the Chapter IX update), I noticed an emerging new phenomenon among women. Many married women are now employed, not because they need the money, but out of a desire to leave the house and spend at least part of the day doing something which offers more satisfaction and creative fulfillment than housework. In a curious twist, some women are reported to be motivated to have children by the opportunity provided by the community's *Yeled Sha'ashuim*, an interesting facility which accommodates mothers and their newly born to take a few weeks rest, for a nominal charge, in an all-needs-provided environment. Thus, insulation not withstanding, a mild beginning of feminism, with potentially serious future consequences, seems to have arrived in Satmar.

Notes

1 Comments on misbehaving individuals are likely to include reference to family background. If the culprit stems from a "good" family, a common reaction is: "I wonder where he saw such behavior, certainly not at his father's!" Whereas if the parents are of low esteem, there is a ready explanation: "The apple does not fall far from the tree!"

2 *Cf.* Chapter 1, "The Rift Between East and West."

3 The Talmudic literature frequently refers to the desirability of having "bread in one's basket," i.e., a ready outlet for one's desires.

4 Modesty in sexual matters is considered an earmark of a religious Jew and, to a lesser degree, of Jews in general. An informant who had lived among Gentiles during World War II told me his impression that, in the best of Gentile company, conversation inevitably turns to women and sex.

5 Details of incest rules follow in the next section, dealing with family structure.

6 For example, a *kohen*, who traces his lineage to the priests of antiquity, may not marry a divorcee. Or a man may not remarry his own divorced wife if she has been married to another since he divorced her.

7 A girl and her mother-in-law or a boy and his father-in-law should preferably not have the same first names. Two pairs of siblings should not, if possible, intermarry.

8 This does not mean that sanctions like ridicule are not effective. For example, I found only a few cases in which the wife was older than the husband, the difference being no more than two or three years; even these were not generally admitted. Also, parents and close relatives feel free to interfere without being asked. This does not detract from the fact that none of these standards are true social norms, and no wrong doing is imputed to one who disregards any of the practical desiderata.

9 For a concise summary of conjugal family characteristics see William J. Goode, "Industrialization and Family Change," in B. F. Hoselitz and W. E. Moore, eds., *Industrialization and Society* (UNESCO-Mouton, 1966), pp. 237-255, esp. pp. 239-41. See also G. P. Murdock, *Social Structure* (New York: Free Press, 1965), *passim*, for discussion of the Eskimo-type structure.

10 The term *geshvesterkind* ("cousin") does not discriminate between parallel and cross cousins, father's and mother's side, or male and female.

Likewise *fehter* ("uncle") and *meehmeh* ("aunt") apply to both father's and mother's siblings as well as their spouses. Vertically, secondary relations are marked by distinct terms, though lines of descent remain indistinguishable. Thus, on either side "grandfather" is *zeydeh* and "grandmother" *baabeh*. In the case of "grandchild," *eynekel* fails to differentiate not only between a son's and daughter's child but even between grandson and granddaughter. Affinal relatives have distinct designations: "father-in-law" is *shvehr*; "mother-in-law," *shvigger;* "son-in-law," *eydem*; "daughter-in-law," *shneer*; "brother-in-law," *shvohgger*, and "sister-in-law," *shvehgerin*. As a matter of fact, many Satmarer have begun to adapt "cousin," "uncle," and "aunt" into their Yiddish, no doubt because these are fully equivalent to the Yiddish terms. No similar adoptions are noticeable when the designations differ.

11 See Deuteronomy 25:5-10. In addition to the difficulty caused by monogamy, Ashkenazim have often given an additional reason for abolishing the levirate: the surviving brother is supposed to marry the widow with the pure intention of complying with the biblical command, but in reality few men are capable of such purity when it comes to sexual behavior.

12 "Community" is used here to designate the Hasidic fellowship, not geographical location, which is relatively unimportant among Hasidim. See Chapter 1, "The Rift Between East and West," and also I. Rubin, "Chassidic Community Behavior," *Anthropological Quarterly*, 37:3 (July 1964), 138-148.

13 For example, the Rov was married twice (the second time as the main Teitelbaum leader), both times to a nonrelative.

14 Occasionally a boy will spot a girl he likes, and will then attempt to find an adult willing to play the role of matchmaker. He does not want to go home with the story that he likes a particular girl and thus expose himself to the censure that surrounds "falling in love."

15 Abroad, it had been a nearly universal custom among the Satmarer to give a dowry to a daughter. The custom began to disappear after World War II when many almost middle-aged men returned to find that their wives had been murdered (more women than men were murdered because they refused to abandon their small children). These widowers began to marry girls who were almost a generation younger than they, causing an intense shortage of marriageable girls for the young men. A young man was so happy to find a suitable girl that he did not even think about a dowry. In the United States, the custom has completely disappeared.

16 The custom of interrupting the fiance's Torah talk was widespread in Hungary, where everyone attempted such a talk. Those who lacked scholarship had to be instructed by others, but even with instruction they were not always capable of delivering the talk flawlessly. In order

to avoid embarrassment, it became customary to interrupt all such talks, including those delivered by scholars.

17 The breaking of the plate has a dual symbolism. It is supposed to underline the irretrievable nature of the act, since a broken plate cannot be mended. It also serves as a reminder of Jerusalem's destruction, which ought to be kept in mind even at the height of joy.

18 In case an accidental discharge upsets the plans, the wedding is rarely, if ever, delayed. Instead, a child is sent to sleep with the newlyweds until the bride has a chance to complete her seven clean days, which she starts counting anew. Before the first experience, temptation is considered to be so great that the couple cannot be trusted to control it. The child's presence is believed to prevent cohabitation without publicizing the mishap, as would be the case if the young people were to return temporarily to their parents' homes.

19 Satmarer have adopted the American custom of arranging weddings in a catering hall rather than in the bride's home, as had been customary abroad. Since hallowed tradition is not involved, they have had no difficulty in adopting this convenient practice, for which they can now afford to pay. Usually the expenses are expected to be met by the bride's family. Occasionally some of the cash gifts (another newly adopted custom) are used to help pay for the wedding, though in most cases the gifts are left entirely with the new couple.

20 A married couple from each of the two families—parents or other close relatives—is given the honor of leading the bride and groom to the canopy. The males lead the groom and the females the bride.

21 This is known as *yihud*, "being by themselves," which is forbidden to any man and woman (except close kin) not married to each other. After the canopy ceremony, yihud is formally required to complete the procedures necessary for the bridegroom to "acquire" the bride as his legal wife.

22 The dance is so called because the Talmud considers it a mizvah to dance with a bride.

23 It would be unthinkable for a man to touch an adult female stranger, especially if she is married.

24 This is the only time in a man's life when he is permitted to dance with his wife in public.

25 I have reason to believe that the delay of consummation mentioned above, though attributed by most informants to initial bashfulness and inexperience, may also be motivated (perhaps not entirely consciously) by the requirement to abstain soon thereafter. The initial taboo period understandably requires unusual self-control, especially since heretofore both man and wife had been totally deprived of contact with the oppo-

site sex. Thus, the delay of a day or two may have the function of prolonging permissible contact, which in turn may facilitate compliance with the norm of abstinence thereafter.

26 Often there are older men who do not wear a straamel or a kaaften, for many of the present adherents of Satmar are not of Hasidic background and, upon joining the Hasidim, do not change their mode of dress. Among the younger generation, however, the Hasidic dress is universal. This is one respect in which the Satmarer have become more conservative in the United States. They insist that the increased dangers of assimilation in this country demand increased countermeasures, of which distinctive dress is considered highly important.

27 An exception to this rule is the return to parents' households of those widowed or divorced at an early age and—in the case of women—even later in life. The return is usually temporary, since most remarry as soon as possible.

28 Occasionally the taboo period is even longer, for seven days must pass after complete cessation of discharge. For an accurate summary of all essential legal details involved, see Rabbi S. B. Hoenig, *Jewish Family Life: The Duty of the Woman*, 8th rev. ed. (Cleveland: Spero Foundation, 1961).

29 The taboo on the topic of sex left me without recourse to direct large-scale questioning, a la Kinsey. Therefore in all matters concerning sex I had to rely on bits of conversation with selected informants, plus indirect indicators. As for adherence to the above taboo, I became aware of parents' "tying it to the soul" of their youngsters about to marry—that the rules must be observed and that children born of relations during the impure period are highly undesirable marriage partners. Also, the complaint of one spouse that the other has attempted violation is ground for immediate divorce; therefore making such an attempt is extremely risky. The man also risks loss of face in his wife's eyes and loss of any claim to serious religiosity. Above all, adherence to the taboo is a source of pride to the Satmarer, who claim they have taken the initiative in restoring it in the United States. I feel that this claim would not have been made had there been large-scale violations.

30 Babylonian Talmud, Berakot, 22:1. Although this custom has gradually declined, all the latter-day codes mention it, and Satmarer emphasize its observation, which is seemingly widespread.

31 Originally Maimonides in his code, Deot (Deyos), chapter 4, cautioned against excess on grounds of health. Since Maimonides was a respected physician, he has been widely quoted on the subject. His sixteenth-century admirer and interpreter, Karo, who composed the more popular code, *Shulhan Aruk*, quotes him verbatim in *Orah Hayim*, 240:14. A supporting psychological theme can be traced to the *Babylonian Talmud* (*Nidah* 31:2), where the postmenstrual taboo is explained in terms of its

psychic benefits: the return of the woman to her husband, after the break, renders her as welcome as a bride.

32 A strong theme in the culture accentuates Friday night as the preferred time for intercourse. Originally suggested for scholars (*Babylonian Talmud, Ketubot 62:2*), this theme became diffused among lower strata as well. An entire lore grew up around it: that it is part of the enjoyment of the Sabbath; that rest from work and relaxation create the appropriate mood; that it is congruent with the symbolism of the Sabbath, which includes reference to another union—of the Jew with his Maker; and that, by engaging in procreation, man becomes a partner to the Lord whose act of creation the Sabbath commemorates (Genesis 2:1-3; Exodus 20:8-11, 31:16-17). The Friday evening liturgy includes numerous allusions to the various symbolisms. The ideal thus prescribed is to restrict intercourse to the night following the woman's purification of her menstrual impurity and to Sabbaths and holidays that occur during the ensuing pure period. How many persons actually adhere to this austere schedule is difficult to say. What is certain is that many keep it in mind as an enviable ideal

33 Whether the desire to escape the monthly twelve-day taboo on sexual activity enters the motivational complex here, is of course, difficult to establish. The fact is that intercourse is permitted during the entire pregnancy period; moreover, it is believed to have a healthy influence on the mother and the fetus.

34 Originally the taboo period lasted seven days following the birth of a boy and fourteen days in the case of a girl (*Leviticus 12:1-5*). Later, rabbinic authorities amended the period to extend until seven clean days had passed following the cessation of all bleeding. Today's norm is in accordance with the rabbinic amendment.

35 Several informants remarked about the seeming lack of religious objection to the use of pills or even diaphragms, as long as it is the woman who applies the measure, because women are not obligated to procreate. A physician who practices in the community told me that women increasingly demanded information about the Pill, which was at the time beginning to appear on the market at a reasonable price.

36 See Genesis 17:7-14.

37 In addition to the two occasions mentioned, a boy who is the firstborn child goes through another public ceremony at the age of one month. The ceremony is known as the Redemption of the Son. In it the father hands a kohen five dollars with which he "redeems" his son in accordance with biblical command (Exodus 13:13, 34:20). We shall note later in this chapter that the ceremony does not have any social significance, i.e., the firstborn son is not socially distinguishable from another son.

38 This aspect of the husband's role is closely tied to the tendency already noted toward a measure of Torah literacy among practically all Sat-

marer. Without a minimum of such literacy, a husband finds if difficult to validate this aspect of his role in the eyes of his wife and children.

39 The trend toward equality seems to have invaded this area, though to an extent unknown to the writer. For example, many fathers admitted, apparently without embarrassment, helping their wives with such chores as diapering and feeding.

40 Some informants expressed the belief that lactation prevents impregnation and thus is a legitimate technique of temporary birth control.

41 Even at the onset of puberty, all a mother will tell her daughter is that at this age females begin to have a periodic discharge; she then instructs her on the accompanying problem of keeping clean.

42 In the above-mentioned case of swastika painting (ch. 5, n. 16), the Rov expressed disapproval of the act. Nevertheless, it enjoyed wide popularity in Satmar.

43 This is in line with the general cultural emphasis on growing out of childhood early. In the United States, conditions that keep the father, or both parents, absent from home most of the day have intensified the emphasis on early self-sufficiency. The writer once observed a father chastising his two year old for soiling his clothes with candy: "You bad boy! A big boy like you does not do this anymore!"

44 Cf. Ruth Landis and Mark Zborowski, "Hypothesis Concerning the Eastern European Jewish Family," in Psychiatry, 13:4 (November 1950), 447-464, for interesting speculations on interactional patterns reported to have characterized Jewish families in Eastern and Central Europe, which includes the region of the Satamar's origin. This study has not concentrated on many of the reported patterns (hostility of mother toward daughter, for example), though a later note will indicate what seems to the writer to be a definite error.

45 An exception is the small number of occasions open to the Torah scholar—occasions for which those so inclined are, of course, given an opportunity to prepare. Even this possibility is kept in the background and rarely mentioned as motivation for study.

46 In connection with the third motive, boys often choose a type of work on the basis of its prestige rather than pay. Earnings carry greater weight after marriage, when switching of occupations is rather frequent and occupational prestige recedes in significance.

47 If one is not capable of footing the necessary bills, especially for a daughter, two respected individuals will collect money in the community for the hallowed purpose of "bringing in the bride," i.e., marrying off a girl—such assistance being one of the important mizvot. The collectors normally do not identify the needy person, in order to preserve his dignity.

48 No English equivalent exists for this term, which stands for the continuous progress of one's offspring in the desirable direction (occasionally it is also applied to pupils) and which is highlighted by each significant milestone the child reaches.

49 Having an aging bachelor or spinster in the family is viewed as a tragedy.

50 There may have been a few more women who lived with their parents and escaped my attention. Investigation, however, failed to yield further information. In any case, it is highly doubtful that there were more than a few such cases.

51 Even in the case of the single woman, the stigma seems to be not the divorce but the fact that, prior to her last marriage, she was married twice and both husbands died. Such a woman is referred to in the literature as a "killer" (not that she is suspected of having killed her husbands, but that she is considered to have unlucky fate), and marrying again is considered dangerous. I was surprised that she had acquired a third husband.

52 The large number of secondary marriages is due to the German exterminations, which account for 195 of the men's 218 cases and for forty of the women's forty-eight.

53 Joseph Karo, *Shulhan Aruk, Yoreh Deah,* Sections 337 ff.

54 *Babylonian Talmud, Moed Katan, 27:2.*

55 Belief has it that the soul, on each return of the day it left the body, is considered for promotion to a higher and more desirable position in Heaven. The son, by reciting the Kadish and studying the Torah on that day, helps the process along, for he testifies to the merit of the parent who brought him up in the proper way. Hasidim have developed the custom of serving liquor and cake to the congregants in the synagogue. This is known as "giving tikun," meaning "improvement," and refers to the wish that the soul may receive improved treatment henceforth. Those who partake of it utter the wish that "the soul be granted ascension."

56 In the absence of a son, another close relative-a daughter if she is married, expects her husband to keep the ritual regularly. Otherwise she asks one of the male relatives to perform those synagogue duties that may not be performed by women. As for naming children, both daughters and sons consider it an equal privilege to have children, named after their parents. In fact, an informal rule gives a wife the privilege of naming the firstborn after a relative of hers; the husband has to wait until the second child is born. Exceptions are many, but the rule again shows equal regard for all descent lines on the part of both males and females.

57 The only exception here is the norm prescribing a double share for a firstborn son. Beyond this, and a few purely ritual formalities, that son has no privileged status. For some reason, Ruth Landis and Mark Zborowski in "Hypothesis Concerning the Eastern European Jewish Family," Psychiatry, 13:4 (November 1950), 447-464, assume a system of primogeniture among Eastern and Central European Jews. To the best of my knowledge, this has not been the case. When an important inheritable position, such as that of a Hasidic rebbeh, was at stake, in many communities the following was split among several heirs. And even where the pattern was to select a single heir (Lubawitsh or Belz, for example), the oldest son was preferred only if he happened to be regarded the most capable one and/or if this was the expressed wish of the father (who, however, often favored a younger son or even a son-in-law). Also, daughters usually received an equal share of the estate. Although no one may override the Torah's commandments, there is a legally sanctioned way out. The Torah mentions inheritance, not gift giving. A person is always free to "give" his property to anyone he wishes. Thus, in the text of traditional Jewish wills, the term "inheritance" is replaces with "gift".

VIII

Education

BECAUSE the preservation of religion is thought to depend on the appropriate education of the young, formal education in Satmar comes close to being an adjunct to religion. Yet it requires separate treatment, first, because long ago boys' education was taken out of the home and synagogue and handled in a formal school by individuals whose occupational specialty was teaching, and, second, because of the structure of education in the United States. State laws requiring youngsters to be enrolled in a licensed school until the age of sixteen have forced the small, private-enterprise type of school (which flourished abroad alongside community schools) out of business. In order to set up a secular department to meet the state's minimum requirements, Satmar's schools had to be centralized. For the first time in Satmar's history, all boys are exposed to some secular instruction.

Even more basic have been the changes with regard to girls, for in Hungary Satmar had no formal structure for educating them. Jewish book learning is considered not only unnecessary but actually undesirable for women; the few skills and laws a woman needs to be able to fulfill her role in the home were taught informally by the mother. As for secular education, girls, unlike boys, were in most cases permitted to attend elementary public schools. Things are different in America. A girl too must stay in school until she is sixteen. Satmarer were forced to start a girls' school of their own, in which, moreover, the entire personnel had to be recruited from without.

All these changes have resulted in a large, centralized school system serving some three thousand students. The system thus exceeds the community's boundaries in several ways. It caters not only to internal needs but to external requirements. The personnel include many outsiders. And, being a kind of organization without precedent in Satmar, it inevitably developed behavior patterns that are, to a degree, peculiar to its own character.

Basis of the System

The underlying norm that serves as a foundation of and rationale for the educational system is the high value placed upon bringing up children who will continue to live by the religious standards of their parents. It is a value with individual, familial, and community dimensions. Individually, each person is under strict religious obligation to transfer the Torah heritage to his offspring. The fulfillment of this mizvah is taken to be among the main purposes of life on earth and even in the world to come, for the soul is believed to benefit from having left behind worthy children, whereas dying without this accomplishment is considered tragic. Family consciousness, as we have seen, extends in both vertical directions, including concern that someone will continue the family's tradition. Finally, continued existence of Satmar is seen to depend on the success of the school.

Within this broad framework are more specific norms, chief of which is the desideratum of learning Torah and teaching it to one's sons so that they too may be able to study and obey it. Supporting Torah study are several related norms which elevate the dignity of the teacher of Torah and even of the books that contain any form of Torah. These serve as the foundation for school discipline which is thus administered in the name of the revered subject matter.

Complementing such goals as Torah study are numerous prescriptions that are expected of the school, such as to tolerate no breach of any religious law, no profanities of any kind, no degree of open disrespect, or, in short, no behavior that threatens the community's self-imposed standards.

In the secular department of the boys' school and in the girls' school as a whole, there appears to be as yet no rationale other than the desire to comply somehow with the law and thus maintain the frequent claim to good citizenship and loyalty. Some expectations are beginning to emerge, however. For example, now that the English department exists anyway, plus the fact that adults experience a need for knowing and using English, many parents have begun to demand that the school do a better job teaching boys the English language. Abroad, girls were permitted to attend public schools and many parents were proud of their daughters' high grades, if for no other reason than as an indicator of the girls' "brightness." This same motivation continues to be apparent in the United States. As for the girls' Jewish studies department, a great deal of confusion about its purpose still existed a decade after its coming into being. Conservative elements which felt guilty about its presence have, at best, hoped that it will do no harm. More liberal parents, however, have begun to feel that it may also perform a positive service, namely, teach girls those essentials of Judaism they had in the past learned informally from their mothers, most of whom now lack the required time and skill for this task.

Satmarer have not regarded their schools as having any significant relationship to one's occupational role in adulthood, except in a very limited sense. The boys' Jewish department, which is the heart and soul of the school system, absorbing most of the energy and money invested in the system, has practically no relationship to occupation, because the overwhelming majority of Satmarer do not plan to have their children utilize Torah knowledge for occupational purposes. This, incidentally, brings to light an interesting side aspect: the absence of any striving for intensive scholarship in the entire enterprise of Torah study in Satmar, despite the great value placed on this activity and the high prestige bestowed on the scholar.

In the case of girls, some connection with adult occupations does exist. Many parents and several school administrators expressed the hope that some of the girls will develop an interest in joining the teaching staff and gradually replace out-group teachers who make up practically the entire faculty.[1] Interestingly, however, the possibility that the girls will eventually use their secular knowledge to seek office jobs, instead of needle factory work that most women workers now perform, has not only failed to delight parents and community leaders but has actually become a source of worry. Office work is seen by many as an opportunity to escape the community's control—a subject to which we shall return.[2]

In summary, Satmarer want their school to serve primarily as a bastion against undesirable acculturation, as a training ground for Torah knowledge in the case of boys, and, in the case of girls, as a place to gather knowledge they will need as adult women. Only in a minor way do Satmarer want their school as a place to receive knowledge that may one day be put to practical use in earning money.

Social Structure

As in the case of religion, the social relationships surrounding the educational process have both formal and informal aspects. But here the formal structure, because it carries the actual burden of the operation, is much more important than it is in the religious sphere.

Figure 4 shows the main features of the formal organization.[3] The Rov is the head of the system, and all but one of the principals are directly responsible to him. they consult him in all important matters of policy. The exception is the individual in charge of the boy's secular division and the girls' school as a whole, who is an outsider and is responsible to Principal 2 instead of to the Rov.

Informally, the zealot-liberal rivalry mentioned in chapter 5 focuses sharply on this nerve center of the community, concentrating especially on the operation of Bais Ruchel, the girls' school which the right wing has not entirely accepted. Both sides are represented in the administration as well as on the faculty, but the struggle involves many individuals not formally connected with the school.

Principals 2 and 4 play a key role in the system, much beyond that indicated on the chart. Both also serve as stabilizers in the informal struggle which might otherwise threaten the operation of the system. Principal 2 is a recognized scholar and has right-wing leanings, though he is not actually a zealot. The Rov trusts

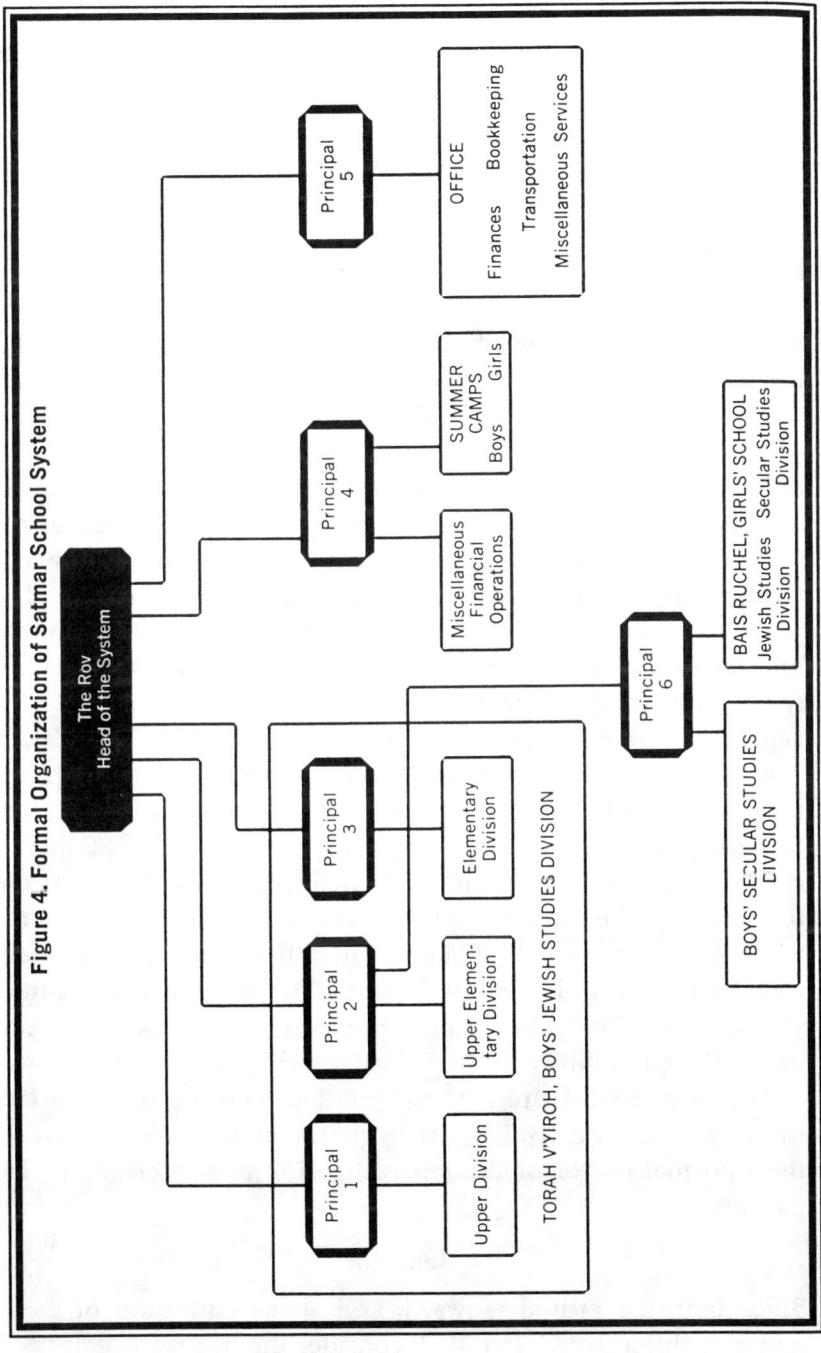

Figure 4. Formal Organization of Satmar School System

The Rov
Head of the System

Principal 1 — Upper Division

Principal 2 — Upper Elementary Division

Principal 3 — Elementary Division

TORAH V'YIROH, BOYS' JEWISH STUDIES DIVISION

Principal 4 — Miscellaneous Financial Operations / SUMMER CAMPS Boys Girls

Principal 5 — OFFICE Finances Bookkeeping Transportation Miscellaneous Services

Principal 6 — BAIS RUCHEL, GIRLS' SCHOOL Jewish Studies Division Secular Studies Division / BOYS' SECULAR STUDIES DIVISION him and therefore placed the controversial Bais Ruchel under his supervision, thus pacifying the zealots. He also keeps an eye on the system as a whole, and those formally in charge do not dare question his intrusions in view of the apparent confidence the Rov has in him.

Principal 4 is a principal-at-large, without a specific organization to operate except the summer camps. But he has many responsibilities in matters of finance and several other technical areas. An extremely capable individual with an extraordinary memory, he initiated the activities, including the camps, for which he is now responsible. His success rendered him virtually indispensable and thus quite powerful. He too enjoys the Rov's full trust and moreover is highly respected by practically everyone in the community. The esteem he enjoys relates to another of his gifts, namely, high social intelligence. He rarely utilizes all his power and thus avoids antagonizing people. As a middle-of-the-roader he often mediates between extremists, who usually yield to his undisputed practical sense. Like Principal 2 he also penetrates many areas of the school that are not formally under his jurisdiction, but he is usually welcomed because of the high regard he enjoys. Together, Principals 2 and 4 serve as a cementing force for the organization.

Many parents have not yet become accustomed to accepting the formal authority of the school administration. The reluctance is understandable in view of the fact that most Satmarer communicate with each other informally, and it is often difficult to submit to the authority of individuals with whom one interacts informally as well. Thus when fathers request that their sons be transferred to other teachers, the administration often yields, especially if the father happens to be a respected member of the community.

The formal structure is thus modified by three informal factors: the conservative-liberal struggle for influence and control, the informal power of Principals 2 and 4, and interference by parents.

Behavior

Since both the attitude toward, and actual education of, boys and girls differ greatly, we shall consider the two separately.

The Education of Boys

As soon as a boy begins to talk, his father begins to teach him the rudiments of religious practice, especially prayer. In the two or so years that follow, the little fellow learns to recite many short prayers and blessings, as well as to participate in some parts of the services in the synagogue where his father takes him periodically. In other words, in the years roughly between one and three, a child acquires "readiness" for his school experience that is to begin soon.

The third birthday is an important point in the boy's life. Until now he has worn his full hair and has hardly been distinguishable from a girl. But on this day he receives a Satmar-style haircut, i.e., a close head-shave, except for the side curls that remain dangling on his cheeks as an outward sign of his identity as a male and as a Jew.

As part of impressing on him his male identity, the boy is taken to the school where he is made comfortable by the teacher who introduces him casually to the new environment and routine.[4]

Few boys actually begin school at three, but most do so within the coming year. Guided by the child's apparent maturity, rather than by a fixed age, a father who thinks his son is ready will ask the school to accept him on a trial basis, which the school gladly does. If the child is judged not ready by the teacher on the first try, the experiment will be repeated as many times as needed, and, as noted, by the age of four, most boys are in for good. They do not enter the secular department until age six or seven, so beginning school means spending most of the day in the serious business of learning Torah, which continues to be a boy's central activity until he is sixteen or seventeen.

The first subject taught is reading Hebrew. The technique continues to be the one used successfully for ages. The child learns, successively, to identify the basic consonant letters by their names *(Aleph, Bais, and so forth)*, to add the vowel symbols, and finally to read the whole words. All this is done mechanically, in a persistent manner, until the boy masters the skill. The prayer book is used as a text for this initial subject. As soon as a satisfactory level of ability has been reached, reading is dropped as a subject of instruction but continues to be practiced during prayer sessions which become part of the school routine.

The central subject now becomes *Humash* (*Chimmish in Satmar*) "the Pentateuch. An old tradition prescribes that a child's Bible instruction shall begin with the first few verses of Leviticus. As soon as these are mastered, instruction turns to the portion read each week in the synagogue. A child learns as much of that portion as he can grasp, but the following week he begins the next portion, regardless of how much of the previous one he studied. The Hebrew text is translated into Yiddish, which continues to be the daily language in Satmar. This is the learning technique for all subsequent subject matter. In the beginning, emphasis is on precision of translation rather than on meaning and explanation. The latter appear gradually according to the student's maturity.

Later the biblical text is taught together with the commentary of the eleventh-century Rabbi Shelomoh Yizhoki, known as *Rashi*. This commentary has become revered through the ages and is printed in most editions of the Pentateuch alongside the biblical text.

Next the child is introduced to the *Babylonian Talmud*, the voluminous compendium of basic rabbinic literature. This gradually becomes the center of the curriculum for the remainder of the school years, as the amount studied constantly expands and numerous commentaries are added. Talmud remains the central subject even when parts of Karo's code are introduced in the more advanced stages and despite the retention of the weekly portion of Humash-and-Rashi as a subject to be reviewed and expanded each year.

These works constitute the core curriculum. In addition, several "softer" subjects are occasionally added,[5] not systematically but at the discretion of each teacher, who is left with a great deal of leeway as long as he covers the core subjects effectively. Curiously, writing belongs in this category of secondary, haphazardly taught subjects. Neglect of writing instruction is partly a result of the fact that the basic technique of instruction and examination at all levels of the religious division is oral, not written. Then too, in combating undesirable outside influences, Satmarer tend to de-emphasize subjects emphasized in the larger culture. For the same reason they exclude grammar, either Hebrew or Yiddish, from the curriculum of both boys' and girls' schools, and modern Hebrew is actually a forbidden language, not only in school but outside as well. To be sure, teaching of language skills has been declining among Central and Eastern European Ashkenazim for the last few centuries. But with the establishment of modern Hebrew schools with a Zionist orientation which concentrate specifically on language, omission of the latter has become an element of the official Satmar ideology.

Each teacher must maintain strict discipline in his classes, by physical force if necessary. The teachers of classes I visited kept a belt or rod within clear sight of the students, serving as a constant reminder. While occasional use of the rod is expected and approved, its excessive use is taken as a sign of a teacher's basic weakness and is greatly resented by both administrators and parents.

In addition to classes, fathers normally urge their sons to spend their free time in the evenings with Torah study, mostly polishing up on subjects studied at school. Fathers help in the process, as most are sufficiently literate to do so. The purpose is not only for the child to do better in school but to acquire the habit of spending free time on Torah, not on idling, which is considered a sin.

Probably as an outgrowth of the Pentateuchal division into weekly portions, the week is the basic time unit for study, even when Talmud becomes the central subject. A student's capacity is expressed in terms of weekly coverage, e.g., "David learns already four pages of Talmud a week." Examinations are held toward the end of each week by the teacher, by the principals (who use these as a check on teachers' effectiveness), and by fathers at home—normally Friday evening after the meal—as a constant check on the children's progress and indirectly on the effectiveness of the school.

Satmarer have nonetheless adjusted their yearly calendar toward the American pattern. Abroad the school year was divided into two terms: the "winter," which started after Sukot and lasted until close to Passover, and the "summer," which began after Passover and ended before Rosh Hashanah. Here the normal school year parallels the American. For the summer months Satmarer have camps in the Catskills at which they accommodate most of the students—but these really are summer schools, as most of the day is spent in Torah study, with teachers recruited from the regular teaching staff of Torah V'Yiroh, the boys' Jewish studies division. At the same time, some camplike atmosphere is maintained, classes are held outdoors, and some camplike activities, such as swimming and occasional hikes, take up time spent on Torah during the regular school year. Furthermore, unlike regular school, not every Satmar parent sends his children to the Torah V'Yiroh camp. This relates to another change in Satmar behavior, namely, the widespread trend to send women and children for summer vacation to bungalow colonies in the Catskills. Thus many a colony finds itself with enough children to hire a teacher of their own, a situation many prefer to sending their youngsters to camp.

The religious division has no long-range goals beyond the instillation of Torah literacy and piety in the male population. Hence there are no formal props such as classes with grade numbers (first grade, second, and so on) or graduation at any point. Each teacher is known to teach at a certain level (e.g., one teaches two pages of Talmud per week), and students are assigned to a given teacher according to the level at which they are judged to be on the basis of past performance or examination by a principal. Although the school naturally prefers to transfer entire classes from one level to the next, a great deal of shifting of individual students takes place. Similarly, transfer of a class from the elementary department to the yeshivah (upper division) is accomplished without fanfare, merely upon the judgment of the teacher that the class seems to be ready for it. The yeshivah continues to emphasize the same basic subject matter, except that the coverage increases, more commentaries are added, and the technique changes in the direction of allowing students greater independence and initiative in the use of time. When a boy leaves the yeshivah, he does so not because of having finished a certain grade or having graduated, but because he has reached with his father a decision that it is time to seek an occupation in preparation for marriage. Those who bring their education to a formal climax are the few who have the drive to continue their study to a point at which they are ready to be examined by the yeshivah head for the purpose of being ordained as a rabbi. Such ordination is granted upon the student's demonstration that he is acquainted with the codes of Karo and is thus able to answer authoritatively any question of Torah law that may be brought to him by a layman. But, as we noted in our discussion of the underlying norms, the community does not particularly encourage professionalization and in fact few opportunities exist for utilizing the rabbinic certificate for occupational purposes. Thus the few who persist in study are more likely to have been encouraged by a father with a lofty self-image. The majority go through twelve or so years of study and then leave it without having at any point symbolized their arrival at a certain level of achievement, and without connecting the labors of these years with any practical end. This is certainly one of the noteworthy features of Satmar education, and contrasts sharply with the increasing emphasis of American education on its practical use, with a proliferation of "graduations," "diplomas," and so forth, thought to be essential.

In the secular, or "English," department the picture changes radically. Virtually everything is different here. Students enter secular classes quite reluctantly at the age of six or seven when they are forced by law to attend. With the exception of a few English words they have picked up in the street, they bring practically no readiness skills with them. The reluctant attitude, apparent practically from the first day, may be traced to the fact that, far from being the innocent curious youngsters who often delight a first-grade teacher, these first-grade boys have been attending school for several years. They have already been socialized in the culture of a system that includes a negative attitude toward the secular department. The classes meet in the afternoon, by which time the boys have been at school for several hours and are thus a bit tired. The material is strange, not only in language but also in content, for the aesthetic and ethical values of the larger American culture often bewilder the Satmar child.

In a second-grade class I observed, the teacher read a story about a boy named Peter who found a new friend in a stray dog he took home as his pet. Not only is Peter from a world that is mysteriously strange to a Satmar boy, but a dog is an "unclean" animal (touching it requires handwashing) avoided by Satmarer. The idea of having one as a pet is revolting. The fact that the teachers are mostly strangers to the community creates still another barrier between them and the students. To overcome all these handicaps, teachers would have to be superior individuals, whereas they rarely are even average. Underlying all shortcomings of the secular department is the lack of community involvement, which in turn stems from absence of expectations as to what the department ought to produce beyond compliance with state law. What concerns community leaders most is the possibility that the exposure of youngsters to strange people and materials may be an avenue for undesirable acculturation, a gap in the isolating wall they try to build around the young until they grow up and are ready to deal with the environment from the more favorable vantage point of adulthood and full-fledged incorporation in the community.

This attitude influences the behavior of all actors in and around the secular department of Torah V'Yiroh. The negativism of entering students persists through the entire ten years of attendance and is reflected in numerous behavior patterns in and around classes. The few minutes between dismissal of religious classes and the beginning of secular classes are among the most difficult for the principal, who must struggle with the multitudes who are trying to run home on phony pretexts ("Mommy wants me home," "Daddy told me to go to the doctor," and so forth, and so on). Despite his restraining efforts, large numbers manage to escape, often through sheer physical overpowering of the policing personnel.

The classes proper are disorderly and noisy. The same boys who on mornings sit with utmost respect in front of their Talmud and Bible teachers and study seriously, now crack nuts, eat sandwiches, and often turn their backs to the teachers, forming little conversational groups. Teachers who attempt in vain to maintain some semblance of a classroom, eventually become apathetic and acquire a sense of helplessness and purposelessness.

Most of the time classes are in session, the principal is in his office, handling cases of extreme breach of discipline or of attempted escape, attempts that continue throughout the teaching period. While he goes through the motions of disciplining and threatening to tell parents, both the culprits and he know that nothing serious can be done. Most parents show annoyance when called by the principal about misbehavior during secular classes. In the very process of admonishing a youngster to behave, many a father looses a smile that betrays his basic satisfaction with the son's disenchantment with the strange world. This smile, imperceptible as it may be, is not lost upon the boy, who has learned to distinguish between father's genuine and simulated indignation.

The principal is well aware of the attitude of the parents and community leaders. He knows that if any serious complaint is to come from any source it will concern a gap in the acculturation-resisting structure, not effectiveness of instruction. For example, one of the tasks imposed on the principal is a continuous combing of textbooks for potentially subversive content (e.g., love stories or pictures), a task to which he devotes a great deal of his available time.

Under the circumstances, it is surprising that boys do acquire rudiments of the "three R's" in the course of their secular schooling. The fact that none of them wishes to continue beyond the point of requirement not only fails to worry anyone but actually delights the school's significant leadership as well as the community as a whole. It is testimony to the successful operation and control of the basic structure.

Girls' education

Historical background is especially important in understanding behavior in and around the girls' school. In Hungary, circumstances had conspired to give a peculiar twist to the cultural norm against undesirable acculturation, resulting, oddly enough, in greater permissiveness toward secular education.

Roughly, the historical sequence seems to have been as follows. An age-old tradition forbade teaching to girls Talmudic and, to a lesser degree, original biblical texts.[6] But this had been a dormant and oft-violated norm[7] until the twentieth century, when many Orthodox leaders who felt a need for more extensive and systematic Jewish education of females founded the Beth Jacob girls' schools which spread rapidly to most parts of the continent. Satmarer, however, fought Beth Jacob on two counts. First, it was affiliated with Agudath Israel, an organization that mildly sympathized with the movement to resettle the Holy Land. Second, it was an innovation, and, in the Hungarian Orthodox tradition, the Satmarer invoked the Hatam Sofer's dictum that "the Torah forbids the new." The opposition removed the old ban on teaching females from its dormant status and placed it among the explicit norms that Satmar has committed itself to enforce. Meanwhile, state laws made secular school attendance mandatory till a given age. The state laws, while widely resisted in the case of boys whose Torah education they threatened, came gradually to be heeded in the case of girls who had not much to do with their time. As a result, Satmar women, while remaining mostly on the ignorant side when it came to Torah, became far more imbued than men with the surrounding secular culture, speaking mostly Hungarian (as, in fact, they still do in Williamsburg) and enjoying such alien cultural products as fictional literature and movies. When the women's acculturation did not cause them to rebel against their own culture, the community relaxed its vigilance and increased its tolerance toward this otherwise novel phenomenon.

In the United States, Satmarer found themselves in a predicament. Here they also found compulsory education laws, in fact more extensive ones than in Hungary, extending the mandatory age to sixteen. The problem arose, to what schools should girls be sent? The coeducational structure of public schools, plus their general reputation as breeders of poor sexual morality, placed them beyond the pale. The Beth Jacob schools, by then fairly well established in this country, might have been the solution were it not for Satmarer's past opposition which would now make for an awkward situation. Reluctantly, Satmar established Bais Ruchel, a school system somewhat similar to the one they once opposed, but with the compensatory ideal of being able to adhere strictly to norms to which they are committed. All these circumstances must be considered when we look at community politics connected with Bais Ruchel and at the educational process that takes place within its walls.

The original reluctance to establish a girl's school left a residue of guilt and uneasiness about Bais Ruchel's existence, especially among the conservative elements that strongly opposed its creation but were forced to capitulate when they heard that the Rov was in favor of it. Their anxiety finds expression in continuous vigil which concentrates on the religious department and its alien personnel, for it was religious instruction the conservatives opposed to begin with. The object of the vigil is to assure strict observance of the ban against teaching substantive Torah to the girls and generally to watch that the alien teachers should have no undesirable influence over the students. On the other hand, the secular department has been left alone, more or less. The net result has been a rather well-functioning English department and a tension-ridden, ineffective religious division, a situation we would normally not expect in a community that otherwise centers on religion and suspects outside cultural currents.

In many respects, the educational patterns at Bais Ruchel are closer to those of American schools than the ones found in Torah V'Yiroh. Girls begin in school around the age of five and spend a year in kindergarten, where the emphasis is on the creation of readiness skills for both the religious and the secular school experience. The girls' school day is also normal by American standards, ending at around 3:30 or 4:00 P.M. (boys are kept till six, because religious instruction lasts more than half a day). Finally, the secular classes resemble their American counterparts, with a few exceptions. The nature of the division between secular and religious classes is clearer when one understands the workings within the religious department.

Adherence to the rule against Torah teaching results in serious problems beginning with second or third grade. By then the girls read Hebrew fluently and are familiar with most of the prayers and blessings. The question arises, what to teach next? Several attempts by a few liberal-minded administrators to compromise and allow teaching of peripheral subjects, such as the Ethics of the Fathers or Psalms, have been nullified by zealots who ran to the Rov and protested the new heresies, as a result of which the controversial subjects were withdrawn from the curriculum. In their place came a number of substitutes: Bible stories, moral teachings, simplified law-and-custom codes,[8] few in number and anemic in character, thus far too inadequate for satisfactory teaching over a period of seven or eight years. The students become bored, restless, and disrespectful. Their attitude finds overt expression in classroom misbehavior,[9] absenteeism,[10] and complaints at home that are often fed back to the administration, irritating the teachers and keeping the situation under continual stress.

In contrast, the secular department functions rather well. This may be attributed not only to the appreciably lower degree of anxiety and vigilance on the part of the community, which leaves the staff with more freedom to develop an effective program, but also to the malfunctioning of the religious classes, which creates a vacuum easily occupied by the secular part. Bored with the meaningless, childish content of the Jewish class and annoyed by the constant suspicion and fuss raised about anything that looks like an innovation, the girls find relief and an outlet in the secular class where they are taught interesting material that suits their respective age levels and where both their teachers and they are not continually suspected of subversion. The classes I observed functioned remarkably well. Signs of their success are also visible outside the classroom in such things as interest and pride shown in the work done in and for the English classes,[11] as well as in satisfaction expressed by both students and parents.

The English department has its limitations, of course, as well as its tensions. Textbooks are censored in advance and purged of all suspect stories and pictures. Nonacademic subjects such as music, physical education and dancing (even with other girls) are totally absent. Probably the most important limitation is its orientation toward complete termination of the educational process at sixteen, which precludes encouragement of any activity that might stimulate desire for continued learning. Library book borrowing, for example, is forbidden, because one ought not to acquire the habit of reading books with uncensored content. Attempts have been made to start the cooling-out process several years in advance by de-emphasizing academic subjects in the upper grades, offering in their stead sewing classes where the skills taught have practical application after graduation, both at home and in the shop.

Despite the limitations, effectiveness of the department seems beyond dispute. For example, girls talk mostly English among themselves, violations of the ban on library visits do occur, and they seem sufficiently extensive to have aroused the attention of conservatives and to have warranted public admonitions by the Rov. Occasionally girls, with the help of liberal elements, actually resist conservative pressure in organized fashion. For example, an eighth-grade class demanded to have a formal graduation with all the props of marching, a commemorative yearbook, and so forth—all unprecedented, foreign, and hence fiercely fought by the zealots. Yet the girls had their way and instituted the procedure for future graduating classes. Similarly, the substitution of sewing instruction for regular subjects has met resistance, and terrific pressure was brought on the school to permit at least typing instruction in order that girls need not depend on the needle industry for work. These are the more remarkable in view of the fact that they took place despite the Rov's general opposition and despite the fact that both mothers and daughters share the awe and admiration for the Rov characteristic of all Satmarer.[12]

In all, the girls reap from their ten-year school experience a fairly good knowledge of academic subject matter taught in the first ten years of American public schools and a fair appreciation of language, literature, and some social studies. On the Jewish side they acquire, in addition to a knowledge of Hebrew reading and the use of prayers, some familiarity with Jewish law and custom, as well as with the story content of various biblical books.

It is more difficult to appraise the degree to which the community achieves its most important objective, that of guarding the girls against undesirable outside influence, an objective they seem to achieve so effectively in the case of boys. On the one hand, no case of actual rebellion against parents or community has come to my attention. On the other hand, the above-noted cases which violate community norms suggest a higher degree

of outside cultural influence than the community considers
desirable.

This is an area in which serious and far-reaching changes
have occurred in the organizational sphere, even though the
basic thrust of the system, educationally speaking, remains basically unaltered.

First and foremost is the already-mentioned decentralization
of the huge system which now comprises over 10,000 students.
Each of the four geographic concentrations—Williamsburg and
Borough Park in Brooklyn, Monsey and Kiryas Yoel some thirty
miles north of New York City"has a separate network from pre-
kindergarten to and including the equivalent of junior high
school. For girls it includes complete high school. Only boys of
high school age are directed to a central school located in
Kiryas Yoel, a school that has about 400 students. Thus, over
95% of all Satmar students attend local schools. Due to the central position education occupies in Satmar life, local schools
translate into local power. Each of the four units is responsible
for its own financing, which includes setting-and-collecting
tuition, arranging for fundraising affairs (banquets, parties,
etc.), and getting larger contributions from well-to-do individuals. This puts a high premium on fund-raising know-how and on
financial support. Consequently, effective organizers, generous
contributors, and the local communities in general, possess a
great deal of power.

In addition to the fourfold division, each sub-system is internally decentralized. While each network has a director who
coordinates the budgetary as well the organizational and office
components, his role is managerial, not educational in nature.
There is no central head principal to coordinate the educational process. Instead, there are many principals, each heading
a manageable subsection (one or a few grades, depending on
size). The Rebbeh is the titular head of the entire Satmar system. However, sheer size coupled with the multiplicity of the
Rebbeh's role, make it impossible for Reb Moshe to effectively
supervise on a daily or even weekly basis. His role is limited to
periodic visits in which he orally examines a given class of boys,
to consultation, and to settling occasional disputes with which

local administrators are unable to cope. In other words, as chief executive of the entire Satmar community, he is also the titular head of its educational network. (It reminds one of the role of the President of the United States which includes being the Commander in Chief of the Armed Forces, except that in the Satmar community the equivalent of Defense Secretary is missing.)

Local power means local variation in response to local needs. For example, Borough Park Satmarer are more affluent than those residing in Williamsburg. Greater affluence is associated with more involvement in business which means more exposure to outsiders, thus greater awareness of other cultural patterns in general, and greater recognition of the importance of certain skills, especially those needed for success in American society. The difference between the two communities is especially mirrored in the two girls' schools. The Borough Park Bais Ruchel has an excellent secular studies' division, headed by a most capable woman who is neither a product nor a member of Satmar. The classes I visited were well-taught, stimulating, and rich in content. (I could not believe my eyes when I saw Bais Ruchel 14 and 15 year old girls play simulated Wall Street investment , checking their short-term and long-term success against quotes in the daily newspaper.) Among other things, this remarkable educator edited and published an outstanding anthology in which she included first-rate selections of English-language literature, from which a few minor passages offensive to Satmarer (especially love scenes) were edited out, but with little damage to literary value. In addition, she constructed an effective science curriculum (dubbed "environmental" study; "science" is an unwelcome term in Satmar), including a magnificent set of slides. In addition to curriculum, this principal fought for numerous innovations she considered important (e.g. trips to Washington, D.C. and other outings, the addition of a twelfth grade), winning concessions from conservative elements who automatically resist change. In sum, we are witnessing an outstanding illustration of how local power resulted in local policy in response to local conditions. In contrast, the Williamsburg Bais Ruchel is much more conservative (a trip to the nation's capital is unthinkable) and the secular instruction cannot be compared with that of the dynamic Borough Park system.

While organizational changes abound, in the curricular sphere we have a rather mixed bag. Most of the changes found are in girls' secular studies departments (throughout the system, just more so in Borough Park), though even here we observe a trend that began a generation ago. I emphasized the fact that general studies for girls were generally of high quality, especially when compared with Jewish or religious study. Even the push for change is not entirely new. What we are seeing today is intensification and elaboration. A generation ago, the girls (with the active help of their mothers) fought for and gained an eleventh grade, a graduation ceremony, and an American-style yearbook. Their daughters today (again assisted by their mothers) push for things such as trips to the world outside and for a twelfth grade, which in Borough Park they attained during the 1988-89 school year. Today's mothers led the drive to get typing lessons, in order to be able to work in offices, instead of following their mothers to the needle shops, while conservative educators and watchdogs pushed sewing machine instruction, fearing exposure involved in office work. The daughters today receive instruction in the use of computers/word processors and office work is not merely accepted, but community leaders and educators brag that Satmar girls are so well trained that they are preferred choice in many business establishments.

In contrast, little has changed in the girls' Jewish studies departments, even though Satmarer, realizing that something is amiss here, have been publishing numerous textbook materials for classroom use, materials they claim to be in demand by many non-Satmar schools. I have examined quite a few of these publications and, with very few exceptions, found them wanting, a bit on the childish side. I have also observed classrooms and they remain, in my opinion, as poor as they ever were. Teachers lecture most of the time and when they ask a question, it is likely to be one for which a "right" answer can be found in some handout. I have not observed a single instance of a teacher asking a provocative question, one that would stimulate thinking rather than searching for an available answer. (In one case, I observed a group of sharp students challenging the teacher along an uncharted path, totally confusing the poor woman who was unprepared for such an occasion.) No doubt contributing to the situation is the fact that, with one minor exception involving a remote outpost, no one seems to dare breaking the rules established by the old Rebbeh and based on Talmudic dicta which are mentioned in the standard Jewish codes as precedents to be followed where possible. These rules/precedents prohibit teaching girls authentic Hebrew texts such as the Pentateuch or the Siddur (prayer-book). The substitute publications are all in Yiddish and, in most cases, contain an amalgam of materials culled from writings which span thousands of years, without any attempt to indicate what is what. Thus the gap between the religious and secular divisions seems to have widened over the past three decades, raising some eyebrows of even a few insiders who comprehend the problem but feel helpless in the face of Satmar reality.

Before turning to the boys' division, one more development deserves our attention. A generation ago, all Bais Ruchel teachers, in both religious and secular divisions, were outsiders, for the simple reason that qualified insiders were not available. Today, all teachers in the Jewish division and quite a few of those in the general studies department are insiders, former Bais Ruchel students who were trained for their jobs within the walls of the system. It is a development which has many consequences. It makes Satmar less dependent on outside talent when it comes to operating their school system. It also created more opportunities for employment of women within the community (a subject to which we shall return in due time). These changes also bring more control, as both reduced reliance on outsiders and increased internal employment assist in the attempt to close gaps in the wall of cultural insulation the community has erected. It should be noted, however, that complete insulation remains a dream especially cherished by arch conservatives, but one not likely ever to be attained. In addition to other opportunities, especially in the economic sphere, for meeting strangers, Satmarer still encounter outsiders as administrators and as general studies instructors, in both the girls' and boys' schools. We shall have ample opportunity to further discuss the twin dualities of insulation-exposure and control-change which are central to this study.

Turning to the boys division, the curricular changes are even fewer than in Bais Ruchel. Here there is an abundance of textual material as there always was. Furthermore, the materials used have been essentially the same for centuries, some of them for millennia. Similarly, the basic educational objectives of instilling Torah knowledge for its own sake, as well as for the purpose of knowing how to conduct oneself as a Jew, with occupational prospects touching but a small minority, all remain unaltered. Here and there one hears of a minor change in emphasis; e.g., one educator noted that Satmar has been somewhat influenced by the Lithuanian non-Hasidic systems and has shifted away from its erstwhile accent on quantity to an emphasis on depth of understanding. Even though phenomena like this do point to the fact that Satmar is, after all, permeable, they are clearly of little importance at this point.

One change, though, deserves our attention, namely, the addition of a kollel, a sort of graduate division for married men (cf. addendum to the last chapter). After resisting for some two decades, the old Rebboh consented to create such an educational arm, (which, incidentally, exists in virtually every yeshivah in this country as well as in Israel). Immediately after marriage, every man is expected to continue his Torah study at the kollel for at least a year or two. However, the main objective of the kollel is to train religious specialists of various sorts (religious teachers, dayanim, scribes, congregational rabbis, etc.). Talented young men who show inclination in that direction are thus encouraged to stay in the kollel beyond the initial one-to-two-year period and study until ordination/accreditation which qualifies them to practice a given specialty. Thus, in spite of the absence of such institution in Hungary, Satmar has adopted this basically Lithuanian pattern and established it as a standard division of its educational network.

Things have changed even less in the boys' secular division. Despite the fact that today's teachers seem to be somewhat better qualified than their predecessors of a generation ago, all the old factors—afternoon fatigue, limited time, persistent use of Yiddish in the home, lack of real interest on the part of students—combine to make it a poor excuse for secular education. This, in spite of increased awareness that a good knowledge of English is important for all who live in this country. A partial explanation for this paradox lies in the fact that as they reach adulthood, most Satmar men seem to be able to speak the language adequately and some of them manage to attain a fairly high level of proficiency which, in turn, enables them to enter and succeed in a variety of business and technical endeavors, including the various areas associated with computer technology. It is an interesting phenomenon, which, in my opinion, merits our attention not merely for its own sake, but for its wider implications for some of our well-established educational axioms regarding the importance of attained formal degrees for successful entry into certain occupations.

A final note: education being one of the nerve centers of the Satmar system, it tends to register important developments in the community at large. The conflict between the Old Believers and the present leadership has lately shifted its focus to the school system where it intensified and assumed critical dimensions. The rebels have recently begun creating their own school network, an act that has aroused the ire of the present leadership which reacted with severe measures against supporters of the fledgling countersystem. The situation is especially critical in Kiryas Yoel, a town of which the established leaders (primarily the present Rebbeh and his son Reb Aaron whom Reb Moshe installed as the Rov of Kiryas Yoel) consider themselves to be the legitimate owners, at least in the sense of controlling the town's religious establishments. Thus, supporters and participants of the new Bnai Yoel schools have been de-facto excommunicated and are officially denied physical access to most of the synagogues and, above all, the sacred grave of the Old Rebbeh. The latter is uniquely critical, because there are enough synagogues in town outside the establishment. Similarly, rebels have jumped the gun and quickly built their own ritual baths which are essential to Satmar religious life. The grave, however, cannot be duplicated. Attempts at access on the part of dissenters have, allegedly, been met with physical attacks, allegations denied by the establishment. Another critical battleground developed in the schools proper. Since the new system is incapable, as yet, to accommodate all age groups of both genders, school administrators, principals, and teachers have been ordered to expel all students who have siblings attending the new schools. An interesting "dialogue" resulted. Supporters of Bnai Yoel argue that precisely because the establishment uses the schools as a political weapon (some years ago, several students were thrown out of school because their parents openly defied the Rebbeh and his son) the new schools are necessary. The Rebbeh and his followers, on the other hand, argue that the early incidents were few and belong to the past and that the new schools system detracts funds necessary to run the one operated by the establishment. Therefore, Bnai Yoel supporters have no right to expect the established schools to meet their needs. On a considerably smaller scale, a similar conflict developed in Williamsburg where opponents have created a new school for girls named Ikvey Hatzon. This ongoing conflict is one I regard as a crucial process. Creating a measure of structural independence now, has potentially wide-reaching consequences for the future of Satmar when wider fission may be attempted.

Notes

1 The above hope has proved to be largely without foundation. I shall speculate later in the chapter about the causes of this disappointment.

2 As a matter of fact, at the time of my research the conservative elements were attempting to replace the teaching of office skills with sewing instruction in the upper (eighth through tenth) grades.

3 What is not included in the chart is the Education Committee, which consists, in addition to the five in-group principals, of several lay members. The committee has no significant role, however, as the principals communicate directly with the Rov in all important matters.

4 Some go as far as protecting the youngster from seeing anything "unclean" during this day. These fathers carry their boys, enveloped in a prayer shawl, to and from school. Most of them also take him to the Rov for a blessing. During the visit, the Rov asks the boy a routine question: Would he permit his side curls to cut off? The boy, prepared for the question replies with a definite "No!"—to the delight of the Rov and the father, who take the answer as a good sign that the youngster will continue to resist efforts to divest him of his Jewish identity marks.

5 *Cf.* Chapter 6, "Study of Torah."

6 *Babylonian Talmud, Sotah 20: Shulhan Aruk* (Code of Karo), *Yoreh-Deah*, Section 246:6

7 Women were allowed to study by themselves. Many who were motivated found ways to combine limited instruction with self-study and became quite learned. Such women even enjoyed a degree of prestige, though having a learned daughter was not among the cherished aims of parents.

8 All these materials are taught in Yiddish, for Hebrew as a spoken language is strictly forbidden in and out of school as part of the Zionist heresy. The Rov published a lengthy thesis on the subject (C. Y. L. Deutsch, Ed., *Taharas Yom Tov*, Vol. 8 [New York 1957], 120-150), in which he reiterates the ban against teaching the Torah to girls, emphasizing especially the undesirability of teaching Hebrew as a language to both boys and girls.

9 In one ninth-grade class which I observed, the teacher read aloud her notes on laws about blessings—laws I was sure the girls had known for years—while the students took notes. This went on for about an hour, during which the students fidgeted restlessly but refrained from open misbehavior and disrespect. A student whom I knew rather well inti-

mated that the girls, knowing in advance about the visit, had decided to control their usual riotous behavior. Certainly such behavior would have been quite understandable in view of the hour-long lecture and its boring content.

10 While not as acute as in the boy's English classes, absenteeism among girls is visible in the Jewish classes. One administrator told me that when parents request that a girl be excused from school for some reason, they invariably specify absence from the Jewish, not the secular, half of the day.

11 In several instances I saw girls working on social studies projects with which they showed extreme resourcefulness, in both gathering and arranging the necessary materials. The finished products were proudly displayed to friends and acquaintances. This brings to light another aspect of their success—available social reward for work done—which is largely absent in the case of the Jewish studies.

12 In the 1960's not only instruction in office skills but consequent employment in offices became legitimized, even among the conservative elements.

PART FOUR

ECONOMICS, POLITICS, AND WELFARE

Moving along the independence-dependence continuum, we now come close to the dependence end of the line. Part Four includes those institutional areas in which Satmarer depend heavily on the surrounding society, yet are not completely absorbed by the latter. Norms of their own channel their behavior in distinct directions, encouraging them to embrace some, but not all, behavior patterns of most Americans.

IX

Economic Behavior

FOR many centuries, European (like other) Jews did not live an autonomous economic life but were part of economic systems surrounding them. Satmarer in the United States continue in the same direction and, like their European forebears, have become enmeshed in the economic life of their country. But, again like their ancestors, their norms have prevented full absorption, resulting in economic behavior that has a somewhat distinct character, in spite of basic dependence on the united States' economic/technological reality.

Normative Guidance

Satmar religious norms—obviously most important in a religion-centered culture—play a significant role in guiding consumption and are of but slight import in shaping work and production patterns. To the complicated set of rules and regulations for kosher food that all Orthodox Jews accept, Satmarer bring an extra measure of zeal.

Mainly, kosher food rules involve a number of limitations on the eating of meat and meat products. First, not all animals and birds are "pure," i.e, permitted to be eaten according to Torah law. The latter category consists of cattle, sheep, deer (rarely used), chicken, domesticated geese and ducks, turkeys, and, also rarely used, pigeons. Of cattle and sheep, only certain parts may be eaten. All animals and fowl must be slaughtered by a certified expert called a shohet, who must use a perfectly smooth-edged knife to cut the wind and food pipes of the animal in a prescribed way. Further, in cattle and sheep the lungs must be checked for certain disease symptoms which, if found, may render the animal nonkosher. Finally, the meat that conforms to requirements must be soaked and salted, again in prescribed fashion, before it may be cooked. If even one specification is missing, the meat and anything produced from it is nonkosher. Also, any mixture of meat and dairy products is not kosher.

With regard to seafood, biblical regulation (Leviticus 11:9-12) bans eating of all but those having fins and scales. Unlike in the case of animals, however, there are no further regulations regarding killing and preparation except for the belief that eating fish and meat together may cause skin disease.

Wine and, to a lesser degree, bread must be handled exclusively by religious Jews. The regulation is intended for the prevention of close social contact with individuals with whom intermarriage is undesirable or forbidden. For somewhat different reasons, similar restrictions govern the processing of milk.

Partially related to the year-round regulations are those which apply to special occasions. Most of these are prescriptive in nature, i.e., they prescribe the eating of certain foods on certain occasions.[1] In the case of Passover, however, the proscriptive element, the ban on *hamez* (grain and grain-products that are leavened) and foods that contain hamez, is far more important than the positive prescription for eating *mazah* (unleavened bread). In fact, the laws and regulations concerning hamez match in complexity the above-mentioned rules governing kosher meat and meat products, with quite extensive behavioral consequences.

Also significant are the prescriptive rules on specific modes of dress for various occasions. As we have noted, these affect all members of the family, male and female, adults and children.[2]

While in many respects anti-modern, Satmar culture does not restrict the use of modern technological products. Some items, however, are thought to constitute an acculturating threat. Thus television (and by the standards of some extremists, radio too) is forbidden because it provides audio-visual access to such undesirables as half-nude women and violence. The same reasoning underlies a community ban on theater- and movie-going as well as on reading of secular philosophy, fiction, and scientific writing in religiously sensitive areas (e.g., evolution).

In addition, normative guidelines of a basically secular character play an important role in Satmar consumptive behavior. Lack of strict rules naturally leaves room for ambiguity, conflict, and change. We find this to be the case in moderate versus conspicuous consumption. Indigenous Satmar culture favors moderation, but it does so very ineffectively. Their middle-class urban origin have accustomed Satmarer to comfortable living. Upon their arrival in the United Sates they raised their aspirations to the level of middle-class existence common in this country. An additional factor moves them in the same direction: in the United States, unlike Hungary, Satmarer find themselves surrounded with open and frequent challengers, even from Jewish Orthodox elements, triggering a need to defend and justify the Satmar way of life, both to themselves and to outsiders. As it turns out, the ability to live comfortably has become part of this defense. Informants often emphasized that, in the last analysis, Satmarer live as well, even materially, as do others; hence, the restrictions they accept do not really lead to deprivation. The combination of middle-class habit and defensive posture tends to weaken any urge toward moderation.

Religious rules of a negative character also apply in matters of work and production. Here, proscriptions involve time rather than substance. They forbid work activity on Sabbaths and major holidays[3] but have little to say about the type of work one ought to avoid.[4] This leaves the bulk of the substantive area of work at the mercy of motivations that tend to bring into play the dynamics of conflict and change.

Take, for example, the problem of whether to seek a livelihood within the community or outside of it. On the one hand, numerous factors converge to encourage intra-community occupational activity. Norms of eating and dressing, coupled with the Satmarer's intense distrust of others in matters governed by religion, create opportunities in production and distribution of desired articles. Finally, satisfaction of religious and related educational needs call for the services of numerous specialists such as teachers, ritual slaughterers, scribes, and ordained rabbis. In addition to available opportunity, proscriptions against working on Sabbaths and holidays makes it convenient to confine one's activity to an environment of which the limitations are an organic part.

Yet, in the absence of rules requiring or even making it preferable to work within Satmar, countervailing motives of a secular nature have emerged. Outside business and work is often more profitable. It is also more convenient from a human-relations point of view, for it reduces opportunities for intra-community friction which inevitably results from involvement in the secondary relationships of employer-employee and merchant-customer.

In consequence, when confronting decisions on occupational choice, Satmarer find virtually no guidance from indigenous norms. Abroad,they preferred commerce to manual work, and the clergy—especially the rabbinate—enjoyed high esteem. But these preferences had no religious sanctions, and upon arrival in this country the value system painlessly changed toward more positive valuation of work, even of the semi-skilled variety. A new hierarchy of occupational prestige has been emerging in Satmar, in which the preference of business—especially the small store type—over work has virtually disappeared. Even the rabbinate lost its attractiveness to most members. Instead, certain "clean" and relatively lucrative occupations (e.g., diamond cutting) have begun to be coveted.

Finally, attitudes toward women working have been undergoing radical change. In Hungary it was acceptable for a wife to help her husband in business or run a business by herself. At the same time it was inconceivable for a woman to work for wages in a factory, and employment in an office or business establishment was extremely rare. Again, due to a lack of religious sanction, the norms in the United States easily adapted to local conditions. Motivated by the desire for respectable middle-class consumption, it became not only accepted but generally expected that a woman without small children at home should have a job.

Trends of Behavior

In order to abide by the kosher food rules, all households maintain two sets of cutlery and dishes, one for meat and the other for dairy products. Two more sets are reserved for the week of Passover when the ban on hamez extends to all dishes that were used for hamez-containing products. In this respect Satmarer do not differ from other Orthodox Jews. But when it comes to purchasing products such as meat, mazah, or bakery and dairy products, Satmarer do not trust anybody except their own members or members of satellite groups. They are also extremely careful in searching ingredient lists of processed foods for questionable items and are thus relieved when a trustworthy individual begins to manufacture a product that had heretofore been available only from the outside.

When purchasing religious articles—such as phylacteries—production of which is guided by strict rules, Satmarer again seek out trustworthy artisans or merchants. In the case of clothing or ornamental religious artifacts, however, in which appearance is what counts, Satmarer have no problem trusting the producer and will shop wherever prices are most reasonable.

The trend toward acceptance of conspicuous consumption is especially reflected in the behavior of younger people. When a young man becomes engaged to marry he considers it virtually obligatory to seek out a nice-sized diamond stone for the engagement ring. In turn, the engaged girl frequently brags to friends about the expensive stone she received. Furnishing a new couple's home follows the same trend of high spending on furniture, rugs, curtains, and lighting fixtures, and so it continues down the line in clothing (especially women's), catered affairs, gift giving, and lately even automobiles. True, in the last few years a slight reaction has set in against what some consider to be ruinous behavior. But this reaction is far from a widespread revolt. In fact, many of the critics confine their moderation to a single area, namely, catered celebrations, while riding along the high-spending road in most other matters. Lack of any restraining norms on technological products reinforces this general trend, for it renders Satmar just as vulnerable as the general population to the appeal of a new gadget.

The behavioral effect of the values that surround work and employment activity is clear in several areas. Besides the trend toward sending wives to work, the job-picture among husbands has also changed. The occupational distribution of male household heads is given in Table 5. Item 6 is especially instructive, as it indicates that some 30 per cent of male household heads have drifted into occupations that, according to reliable information, virtually did not exist among Satmarer abroad. Spot checks further suggest that members of this category have not lost status as a result of their occupation.

We may also note that among those listed under "professionals" (category 1) we find only specialists in fields that are of

Table 5
Occupational Distribution of Male Household Heads

Occupation or Source of Income*		*N*	%
1. Professional, technical, and kindred workers:			
Teachers and principals in Satmar and similar schools' Jewish studies division	54		
Minor clergymen	50		
Others	5		
Total professional, technical, and kindred workers		109	14.2
2. Managers, officials, and proprietors:			
Manufacturers	70		
Wholesale and retail trade	113		
Real estate owners and/or managers	20		
Others	8		
Total managers, officials, and proprietors		211	27.4
3. Clerical and kindred workers		8	1.0
4. Sales workers		20	2.6
5. Craftsmen, foremen, and kindred workers:			
Diamond workers and contractors	33		
Others	46		
Total craftsmen, foremen, and kindred workers		79	10.3
6. Service workers, operative and kindred workers		234	30.6
7. Miscellaneous combinations of productive occupations		20	2.6
8. Semi-productive† and nonproductive sources of income		76	9.9
9. Combinations of productive occupation and nonproductive or semi-productive income source		12	1.6
Totals		769	100

* The classification of categories 1-6 is adapted from the one used by the U.S. census.

† The "semi-productive" included in this category refers to so-called collectors (N=39), individuals who collect money for various nonprofit organizations and receive a share of their collections. Alleged abuses are responsible for the fact that collectors" are in rather low esteem in the community, not much above those who live on charity. Hence their inclusion here.

interest and value to the community; physicians, attorneys, and, in fact, all general-type professionals are conspicuously absent. The reason for this must be sought in educational rather than occupational norms. There are no prohibitions against the practice of medicine or engineering, but there are proscriptions (as we have seen in Chapter VIII) against higher education, without which one cannot attain either the knowledge or the license necessary for practicing any of the common professions. In milder form, the same process operates with regard to most types of white-collar work.[5]

In addition to the limitations imposed by their culture, Satmarer share with most Diaspora Jews certain restrictions which have developed as a result of the peculiar circumstances in which Jews, especially in Europe, have lived for centuries. The historical details do not concern us here, beyond the observation that even today few Jews are involved in basic industries and in farming, either at the entrepreneurial or the labor end. Satmarer are no exception.

Finally, data on the working environment clearly reflect the underlying normative ambiguity. Table 6 shows that about half the population works with outsiders despite the advantages of intra-community occupation and despite opportunities created within the community by consumptive restrictions. Again, there

Table 6
Sociocultural Characteristics of the Occupational Environment

Sociocultural Characteristics	Customers, Business Associates, and Employees or Self-employed		Employers and Fellow Workers of Employees		Totals	
	N	%	N	%	N	%
Includes only members of Satmar and/or other Orthodox Jews	103	29.9	172	69.3	275	46.4
Includes non-Orthodox Jews and/or Gentiles	242	70.1	76	30.7	318	53.6
Totals	345	100	248	100	593	100

appears to be no status associated with the sociocultural nature of one's occupational surroundings.

Satmarer now experience no serious economic deprivation,[6] yet the situation contains some built-in difficulties. Foodstuffs are expensive, and so are many of the required and desirable religious articles. Passover alone, for example, entails several hundred dollars in extra expenses on mazah and other foods, new dishes, and new garments that are customarily purchased at this time, as well as on the required thorough housecleaning that lasts several weeks. The exclusion of the professions and white-collar work from the occupational horizon is a serious limitation. We should also keep in mind the changes in economic behavior that we just discussed. Both the economic limitations and the occurring changes may one day have some serious consequences for Satmar, as we shall suggest at a later point.

Two significant changes in the economic sphere came to my attention. (Although I do not have new census data, the following developments which I have observed were confirmed by several informants in positions to know, including the manager of an internal job-placement service.)

One concerns the nature of occupations. Today's Satmarer— both men and women—do not work in needle shops. Instead, they have been drifting into occupations related to the Jewelry trade, photography and photo equipment, electronics, as well as into business connected with, but not confined to, these three popular areas. We already mentioned (update to Chapter VII) that women have been flocking to office work, especially the operation of computer systems. While on the subject of computers, it is interesting to note the emergence of top notch specialists in the area who seem to have undergone a great deal of training. The phenomenon is not entirely surprising. While the ban on higher education is as strong as ever, it does not include higher technical training,a distinction one would expect in the light of the fact that the prohibition is based on the perception that it constitutes an acculturative threat. Thus, what Satmarer (and other Hasidic, as well as yeshivah-type Orthodox Jews) object to is the study of such matters as philosophy or evolution and the overall exposure to the college environment, both to professors and students. These are considered potentially harmful. Technical training is an altogether different matter. Computer training of the highest order can be obtained today in Orthodox training centers where nothing else is taught and where all the instructors are strictly Orthodox Jews. While an outsider may view this exception as a crack in the insulating wall (an employee of a giant corporation in New Jersey who read my book phoned me several years ago, asking: "How come a Satmarer joined our company as a computer specialist?"), Satmarer and Jews in general, unlike resistors to assimilation such as the Old Order Amish, have never felt threatened by technological innovation. This is evident from the fact that this development has, to my knowledge, not encountered any resistance, even on the part of the ever suspicious ultra-conservative elements.

The second development meriting notice is the apparent shift toward employment within the community. This has been spurred by the huge growth of the community, especially the educational system which offers a large number of jobs, as well as by the emergence of Kiryas Yoel which opened a new market for goods and services within an exclusive setting. One of the important by-products of this trend is that the Satmar community leadership has acquired significant economic power, a fact which, as we shall see, has radically altered the nature of community control, especially (but not exclusively) in Kiryas Yoel.

The two developments seem to work in opposite directions, thus possibly balancing each other. The occupational transformation, especially the leap into electronics, tends to create wider contacts with the outside world. As such it is beginning to act as an agent for weakening control and, correspondingly, increasing the tendency toward both change and deviance. Contrarily, the drift toward internal work and business activity reduces outside contact and thereby strengthens internal control. The leadership now has vastly greater economic control than it used to have. Whether it uses these wisely to serve its interests is, to a degree, a matter of opinion. We shall return the subject when we come to the vital subject of social control.

Notes

1 *Cf.* Chapter 6, "Festivals and Festivities," and especially Table 2.

2 See details in Chapter 6, "Symbolization of Identity."

3 *Cf.* Chapter 6, especially Table 2.

4 The only minor exception is the ban on dealing in foodstuffs that observing Jews are forbidden to eat; this ban applies even when the merchandise is intended for a non-Jewish clientele.

5 On account of their superior secular education and their general higher acculturation, women are beginning to break through on this front. Beginning in the 1960's they have drifted into another advantage over men: in their outward appearance they do not differ so radically from the general population as do their male counterparts. A wig, long sleeves, and a high neckline do not appear bizarre, while a beard, dangling side curls, and a long coat are definite obstacles when it comes to holding, for instance, the job of bank teller.

6 Since the census data in this study were obtained from informants, income figures are at best only good guesses at approximate incomes. For what they are worth, these 1961 figures for 737 of 860 families show the following percentage distribution of annual income, as compared with census figures for urban white families:

Income	Percentage of Satmar Families	Percentage of Urban White Families in U.S.[*]
Below $5,000	5.8	31.9
$5,000-$6,900	45.6	24.9
$7,000-$9,900	30.7	24.1
$10,000-$14,900	13.7	13.2
$15,000-$24,900	3.9	4.3
$25,000 and above	0.3	1.7

[*]U.S. Census Bureau Figures (1960).

Assuming that our figures are not completely distorted, they indicate that Satmar is characterized by neither great wealth nor extreme poverty. The percentage figures at both ends are lower than those for the U.S. urban white population as a whole, while the middle-income percentages are considerably higher.

X

Politics

BY politics we mean thought and action oriented toward solving problems of the entire collectivity.[1] This includes minimization of interpersonal conflict, funding-and-administration of community services, defense of the group, relationship with various categories of outsiders, and allocation-and-distribution of power in connection with all such matters.

As in the case of the economy, Satmar has no autonomous political structure. All we find is, again, some prescriptions, proscriptions, and attitudes that modify behavior to a significant degree.

Normative Guidelines

Refraining from criminal behavior is not only dictated by the Torah but has become, in the case of Satmar, an important component of the community's self-image. This is especially true in the United States, where the contrast to the high rate of criminality in New York City serves to justify Satmarer's claim to cultural superiority and their resistance to assimilation.

When interpersonal conflict does arise, an age-hallowed regulation renders it a sacred duty to settle the dispute through the mechanism of a *din-Torah,* a Torah-based judgment, rendered by an ordained individual or a panel of several rabbis who constitute a *bet-din* (a court of judgment). Only upon refusal of one of the litigants to accept a din-Torah may the other bring the matter before a civil court, and this only after obtaining permission from a rabbi or bet-din.

As for attitudes toward and relations with the body politic, they have become rather complex as a result of centuries of

Jewish minority existence. On the positive side, the Talmudic sages have laid down the well-known principle of *dina demalkuta dina!*, (the law of the government is law!), thus making it mandatory even for the rabbinical bet-din to operate within the law of the land. This principle is based, first, on the basic acceptance of the necessity of government: "You should pray for the well-being of the government, for if not for the fear of its presence, people would devour each other alive."[2] Beyond this is the practical recognition that a powerless minority depends on the good will and protection of those in power.[3]

This positive set of attitudes is balanced by counter-notions originating in unpleasant experiences which reinforce the cultural distance that Jews have felt to exist between themselves and their non-Jewish overlords. The Talmudic sages who insisted on respect for the law and the government also warned against becoming too intimate with ruling officials, who tend to cater to Jews only when it serves their purposes.[4] The admonition to settle conflicts at a bet-din rather than in a non-Jewish court is symptomatic of this attitude, for it indicates only a partial acceptance of the majority's rule. In fact, resistance on the part of a minority to assimilation and even acculturation requires that a given distance be maintained and that the host culture be perceived, at least to a degree, as negative.

In Satmar these opposing sentiments continue to exist side by side but have undergone a rather interesting adjustment in the United States. On the one hand, the United States government is referred to as a *malkut shel hesed* (a government of grace), a complimentary term employed for a ruling system seen as just and kind toward all its people, including its Jewish inhabitants. The sentiment is expressed when, for example, the freedom here is favorably contrasted to the lack of such freedom in Hungary or Rumania, even in the pre-Nazi period. Even the State of Israel is frequently mentioned as a negative contrast. Observing a policeman's rerouting of traffic in order to accommodate the outpour of worshipers from the Satmar synagogue on a holiday, a Hasid remarked: "What a contrast with the police in the 'Jewish' land! There, instead of protecting religious Jews, they beat them up for interfering with traffic!"

On the other hand, "America" is also perceived as a strange land; a land in which lawlessness and sexual immorality run rampant; a land in which one cannot walk the streets safely; a land whose public officials are both inept and corrupt; and therefore a land in which one must expend an enormous amount of effort if one is to avoid being attracted to and absorbed by this strange culture with its easy pleasures. This negative perspective, unlike the positive one, focuses especially on concrete groups within the larger society. Puerto Ricans and Blacks who commit aggressive acts against Satmarer and others, delinquent youths in general, corrupt policemen and other public officials, unwed mothers, Jews who become assimilated or attracted to Zionism—all these are singled out by Satmarer in support of their uncomplimentary appraisal of American society. When I pointed out the contradiction to an informant, he merely shrugged his shoulders and retreated behind the defense line already familiar to us: "Well, I see your point, but both views are true. If we have difficulties reconciling the two, it is merely our inability to understand how all things fit together!"

While such duality is common among immigrant groups, Satmarer are unique in two respects: they do not see any ethnic, religious, or other group as the embodiment of positive values in this country, and at the same time they harbor no illusory self-image of representing the "real America," for they not only see themselves as culturally alien and a minority in this country, but they are ideologically committed to retain both their separate culture and their minority status.

In fact, commitment to remain a minority until Messianic redemption is the basis for what is no doubt the most significant single political norm in Satmar, namely, anti-Zionism. The theological foundations for this corollary of the belief in an ultimate redemption by a God-sent Messiah have already been noted (Chapter III), as were the historical circumstances that have cast Satmar in the role of standard bearer of ant-Zionism within the Jewish Orthodox camp (Chapters I and II). This is an extremely important commitment, one that has become an inalienable component of the community's image.

Political Behavior

As part of the community's self-image, the avoidance of major intra-group conflict is rather deeply internalized and faithfully translated into actual behavior. Fully aware that their image would be severely shattered were they to collide with police and be dragged into court for property violation, assault, or murder, Satmarer have learned to completely shun such "non-Jewish" behavior. The absence of criminality is unequivocally confirmed by the police captain of the precinct, who told me that the only way Hasidim are involved in a crime is as victims.[5]

Disputes in financial matters are rather common, however, especially in connection with joint business ventures. Again, all litigation is brought to a din-Torah. Submission to it is theoretically voluntary, but refusal either to heed a summons[6] or to abide by the court's decision may result in a mild form of excommunication—something which few dare to risk. In fact, in the United States this form of litigation has become more formalized. Abroad most rabbis engaged for a din-Torah were also employees of the community and thus had a secure income. Consequently, while litigants normally paid a fee, the judges could afford considerable flexibility in the matter of fee assessment and collection. This meant that cases involving small amounts or poor litigants could be brought before the rabbis with little concern about fees. Here the rabbis involved lack such stable employment and are thus more dependent on din-Torah income. The Rabbinical Congress has become the organizational vehicle for channeling litigation and for securing standard fees, a process that has generated considerable resentment. Informants complain of excessive fees which make it difficult to process small claims, resulting in encouragement of dishonesty.

Loyalty to and acceptance of the larger political system is expressed not only in reliance on police and fire protection, road building and maintenance, and other such services that the community cannot possibly provide for its members, but also in participation in the political process. Satmarer enjoy their franchise and use it. In the tradition of the mainstream of immigrants, their vote has been, according to both community and outside informants, solidly Democratic. Since Satmar has numerous satellites that follow its lead, it is a political force of which politicians take note. Thus, periodically, especially before elections, New York City mayors and mayoral candidates make it their business to pay a formal visit to the Rov; even the state governor has thought it advisable to follow suit.

In contrast, the negative attitude toward particular groups has not generated any overt action, organized or individual, against any of the despised cultural types. Negative sentiments thus go no further than verbal expression.[7]

It is an altogether different story when it comes to Zionism and the State of Israel. Satmar plays a leading role in organizing demonstrations against Israel (in the late fifties they once organized a demonstration in front of the White House). Usually such demonstrations focus on a specific issue, such as the heavyhanded practices of the Israeli medical establishment in indiscriminate performance of autopsies, or on the part of police in violating religious sentiments in Jerusalem, Bnai Brak, and other non-Zionist Orthodox enclaves. In other cases the goal is more diffuse, an attempt merely to convey to outsiders that Zionists do not speak in the name of all Jews. Satmarer prefer to and often do stage demonstrations under a wider banner, not only because they know that "Satmar" is an unpopular symbol but because of their conviction that they struggle in the name of authentic Orthodox Jewry. Indeed, on issues such as autopsies they do have many allies not only among their satellites but within the Orthodox camp in general.

In addition to demonstrations, Satmar lends financial support to various groups in Israel that maintain cultural and educational establishments of their own and who refuse to accept government aid for fear of losing their independence. They also maintain ties with the older and the more militant Neturey Karta in Jerusalem (see Chapter II). The upshot is that while Satmarer do not come into direct conflict with any of the non-Jewish groups whose behavior they abhor, they do collide frequently with most American Jews who tend to sympathize with and support the Jewish state.

The anti-Zionist stance creates two sets of problems. One has to do with controlling the behavior of extremists in this country and in Israel. For reasons already discussed (Chapter 5), the Rov, with all his prestige, found it difficult to prevent the zealous defenders of his teaching from engaging in violence. This becomes more than embarrassing, for violence and illegal acts go against the grain of Satmar culture. Thus, when a Satmarer Hasid commits a violent act that is publicized, the responsible leaders feel that the act is a *hilul hashem*, a sacrilege for which the community receives an undeserved black eye.

The second problem area reaches into the inner depths of the Satmarer's self-image as authentic Jews. Through ages of precarious relationships with the non-Jewish world, a collaborator who helped to work against Jews in any way was one of the most despised of characters. This has been true even in the case of the informer whose motivation was money and who therefore limited his activity to financial matters. Abhorrence was, naturally, much greater vis-à-vis Jews who, for ideological reasons, chose to collaborate with anti-Jewish elements against the Jewish collectivity of some part of it (e.g., members of the infamous Yevsektzia, the Jewish Section of the Soviet government which was instrumental in pursuing Jews who were suspected of anti-Soviet activity or persuasion). Now anti-Zionism occasionally casts Satmar in a role that comes uncomfortably close to that despised role. Unwittingly, Satmarer find themselves talking the language of seasoned anti-Semites who, in the post-Nazi era, often find it more convenient to hide their anti-Jewish sentiments behind anti-Zionist rhetoric. Satmarer are aware of the problem and shudder from its implication. The dilemma finds expression in the Rov's major thesis on the subject of Zionism. After arguing theologically that the presence of a Jewish polity is an obstacle to Messianic redemption, he struggles with the implication that if the Messiah is to come, the Jewish state would have to disappear: "However, we are in need of Heavenly mercy that this state disappear, but only via a superior force emanating from His Blessed Name and not at the hands of the Nations, for if, Heaven forbid, it be through the Nations, it will, understandably, constitute a grave danger to Jews."[8]

As in the case of aggression, Satmarer feel that they are being misunderstood and undeservedly blamed for something they do not intend. Yet they do not know how to cope with this public relations problem; they do not know how to convince outsiders that their anti-Zionism is not intended as a stab in the back of Jews who do not share their views. More broadly, they have difficulty communicating the essential meaning of their anti-Zionism to perplexed outsiders who see it as highly paradoxical that a group whose chief effort is channeled into maintenance of total cultural independence should embrace a political philosophy that opposes any form of political independence.

Despite these serious problems, no relaxation of this political line is in sight. The 1967 war has, if anything, intensified Satmar's anti-Zionism and apparently increased the ranks of the militant faction. The alteration of this foundation stone would have profound consequences for the sociocultural mosaic of contemporary Satmar.

While the normative guidelines to political behavior have remained the same, actual behavior has undergone (and is still undergoing) a variety of rather significant developments. The very fact of the repeatedly mentioned internal conflict is probably the most important one in this context, particularly because it goes against the important norm of avoiding internal strife. New is also the already reported resort to sanctions for the purpose of control, as well as the attendant claims and counterclaims (see Update to Chapter VIII). Without unnecessarily probing to establish the actual details, it seems beyond doubt that the level of internal strife is unprecedented in the history of Satmar.

External relations are also undergoing modification. It has already been noted that the communities sympathetic to the Satmar line begin to feel uncomfortable with the "satellite" label. An informant knowledgeable in the affairs of the Rabbinical Congress, the chief instrument for maintaining relations with allied units and with friendly individuals of rabbinic status (Chapter V), related a few seemingly minor changes in that organization, which, however, have the potential of assuming greater significance in the future. Like his uncle, Reb Moshe is the president of the Congress. However, he undergoes periodic elections for the position, elections conducted through a secret ballot, an innovation which the informant claims to have been instituted at the insistence of the Rebbeh himself. Until now nobody has challenged his leadership, thus assuring his repeated unanimous election. How long this situation will continue is anybody's guess. When asked whether anybody has ever refused to go along with one of the Rebbeh's policy positions, the informant replied: Meanwhile, nobody said no to him, but neither do the members feel that they have a holy obligation to go along with all his demands. He did not elaborate on how he reached this conclusion. Since the informant is loyal to the Rebbeh, his statement, clearly, was not meant to belittle the leader. Rather, he seemed to have made his assessment on the basis of extensive interaction with the organization's members. (Incidentally, similar assessments of different situations were volunteered to the researcher by many knowledgeable insiders whose loyalty to the establishment appeared beyond question. A few years following the above interview, another informant related to me a case in which the Rabbinical Congress actually refused to go along with a proposal of the Rebbeh's, thus affirming the accuracy of the first informant's assessment.) It all adds up to the inevitable conclusion, once again, that the basis of the Rebbeh's authority has shifted from its erstwhile charismatic foundation to a more practical administrative one. The new ethos was summarized by a loyal insider in the establishment's employ: "Somebody has to be the boss!"

At the same time that Satmar's grip on its former satellites apparently weakened, the community has become more involved in relationships with organizations which throw a wider net, encompassing all Orthodox organizations and individuals in the New York City area. They cooperate with and often play a leading role in undertakings concerned with health and welfare of Orthodox Jews. In a few cases we are dealing with Satmar-run organizations which extend assistance to any Orthodox Jew. Examples of the latter is their well-known *bikkur holim*, literally: "sick visitation." This volunteer organization not merely visits sick individuals in hospitals as well as in homes, but also, in fact mainly, organizes assistance, including monetary help, where needed. Another organization, perhaps unique, is the already mentioned facility for new mothers and their newborn. All of these gave Satmar additional political clout, for even where they are merely cooperating, sheer numbers command a high level of regard for the community within New York City's Orthodox Jewry.

Finally, looking at Satmar's relationship with the general political establishment on the local, state, and federal levels, the unwavering loyalty to the Democratic party of a generation ago has, as in most ethnic groups, yielded to a more selective stance in which a given candidate's assessed commitment to furtherance of the community's goals, rather than party affiliation, is the chief determinant of Satmar's support. The new position was clearly stated to me by one of the community's political activists in charge of maintaining contact with various significant outsiders. It was also echoed by a community-relations officer active in one of the areas inhabited by Satmarer. Emphasizing the importance of all Hasidic groups to those running for elective office, regardless of party affiliation, the officer put it this way: "Where else could one count today on this type of secure voting block? All a candidate needs to do is make a credible commitment to support within reason a given group's interests, and the leader will issue an order to his followers to vote for that person, an order that will in most cases be obeyed one hundred percent."

Whereas careful selectivity is the rule on the district level, when it comes to the presidency of the United States Satmarer have thrown their support to Republican candidates. According to informants, the changeover began with Nixon in 1968 and has since continued uninterruptedly. The apparent reason for the switch is the perception (common among the majority of Orthodox Jewish established organizations) that since the Sixties the Democratic Party has become the domain of the New Left, which, in turn, is seen as the force behind the moral decline manifested in such aberrations as urban riots directed to a large degree against Jewish store owners, the sexual revolution, the feminist movement, etc. At the same time, Republicans are seen as the guardians of the old values of family and decency. This perception has, incidentally, begotten a strange bedfellowship between many Orthodox Jews and a variety of elements on the right of the political spectrum, an alliance admitted by many of its backers to be fraught with danger, but considered necessary in today's political climate.

Notes

1 In our case this would exclude the religious and educational spheres; these may not, however, be excluded by definition because occasionally they are part of the polity. Of course, there is a political aspect of every institution, which, as a matter of fact, we have discussed in each case.

2 Tractate of *Abot*, Chapter 3, Mishnah 2.

3 During the Middle Ages, Jews were often under the direct protection of the ruling prince, who benefited from the Jews' presence and frequently protected them from attacks by zealous monks and wild mobs. An excellent view of this complex situation is provided in fiction form by Joanne Greenberg in *The King's Persons* (New York: Holt, Rinehart and Winston, 1963).

4 Tractate of *Abot*, Chapter 2, Mishnah 3.

5 Abroad, many Satmarer made a living from illegal activities like smuggling and dealing in forbidden articles, such as foreign currency and saccharin. Here, however, the Rov told his followers that, in view of the fact that Jews are not barred from normal activities, they have no right to engage in any illegal dealings. In one case, a Hasid flew out of the country with contraband in his baggage. While the Hasid was in the air, a friend of his came to the Rov and asked him to pray for the smuggler's safe arrival. The Rov angrily refused: "Did he consult me before he went? Who says that one may do these things here?"

6 There is no contradiction between the just-mentioned voluntary character of submission to a din-Torah and the summons. First, one does not have to submit to the judgement of the rabbis who issued the summons, having the right to request a judge more to his liking. Then, of course, one can ignore the summons if one is willing to suffer the consequences.

7 I suspect, though I have no data to support my suspicion, that in the late 1960's these feelings found some expression in "backlash" voting patterns.

8 Teitelbaum, Reb Yoel (The Satmarer Rov). *Vayoel Mosheh* (New York: "Jerusalem" Publishing, 1959), Introduction, p. 9.

XI

Welfare

IN that area of behavior which centers on the need to take care of individuals who, for reasons of age, illness, or unemployment, are incapable of providing for themselves, we find strong cultural traditions which are increasingly giving way to reliance on resources outside the community.

Several cultural values encourage extensive mutual aid. The most basic of these is the value of *zedakah,* often translated as charity but which is actually broader than that, including all kinds of help and implying obligation rather than voluntary benevolence. The value of zedakah is buttressed by the values of family and community solidarity. The lofty Satmar self-image adds another dimension. The distribution of large sums of money is one way of demonstrating Satmarer's character, and an important one at that, for it allows them to rebut the frequent accusation that they are pious merely in ceremonial matters but cruel in human relationships.

Thus collection and distribution of money are a permanent year-round feature of Satmar. Few, if any, individuals fail to collect at least once a year for some purpose. Collectors are of several kinds. Some collect each week, receiving a standard contribution of a nickel. Most collect only once or twice a year, accepting not less than a quarter contribution but receiving mostly a dollar from each adult they approach. Then too, the Rov's wife collects several times a year for organizations she sponsors, demanding and receiving several dollars each time. On certain occasions the Rov sends a few men to collect for a special purpose. These identify themselves as the Rov's messengers and thus receive larger contributions. Finally, some out-of-community individuals come to the Satmar synagogues to collect, and the Satmarer pride themselves in giving to them—it is added proof of their charitable character.

Collection is done mostly in the synagogues, where Satmarer can be found mornings and evenings. Although it is a daily activity, near the High Holidays the pace of collections increases considerably, and on Purim it reaches staggering proportions, starting in the morning in the synagogue and continuing all day in the homes. Many youngsters travel all over Jewish New York to collect, risking rejection and frequent humiliation, but feeling that it is worthwhile for the sake of accomplishing a good deed.

The purposes of the collections are numerous and varied: individuals in permanent need on account of illness, old age, or just unemployability;[1] emergency cases; organizations engaged in charitable work; schools both in America and in Israel;[2] certain sheyneh yidden—especially eineklach—who feel a right to demand various forms of support, and so on.

Many Satmarer set aside regularly a tenth of their income for contributions. Others give sporadically. Rare, however, is the individual who can avoid giving away at least $300 to $400 a year. Those who make a special attempt to minimize their giving, especially if they are known to earn nicely by Satmar standards, are accorded especially low prestige.[3]

The fact that this generous giving is a continuous strain on most people is one reason for an increasing reliance on outside welfare structures. Satmarer who are gainfully occupied pay social security, and employees belong to unions. Most also purchase some form of medical insurance. In time this is bound to reduce both the permanent and emergency cases that warrant collection. In fact, even the values are in process of changing, as those who work and are in business, while priding themselves in giving, have also been acquiring the value of financial self-sufficiency and are thus doing their utmost to prevent the possibility that either they or their children should have to fall back on zedakah. In view of the emphasis on working, as well as the fact that individual welfare cases are mostly immigrants whose proportion to those born and bred in America is naturally decreasing with time, it is safe to predict a gradual shift toward using the larger society's resources to satisfy the community's welfare needs.

This completes the list of what are, at least in part, distinct institutions in Satmar. Many familiar American institutions are either completely absent—e.g., science—or diffused with the institutions described. An example of the latter type is leisure, which the Satmarer do not recognize as a distinct sphere of life. Whatever "entertainment" they seek is either within the framework of religion—singing and dancing, for example—or the family (weddings and similar festivities). Sports, movies, reading for pleasure, and so forth, are forbidden, though some women manage to evade the restrictions without severe sanctions. Our next task is to account for the vital processes of control and change, the forces and mechanisms that enable Satmarer to preserve their present way of life and the opposing factors that make for change or difficulty.

Little change has occurred in welfare related behavior during the past three decades. I did notice an increase in organized zedakah activity. Although synagogue collection by individuals continues, numerous special-purpose organizations sprung up. Alongside, one notices a huge increase in organized collection techniques. The most common is the "party", called usually by a rebbetzen (although many "commoners" also convene parties to help out an acquaintance, not unlike one arranges a shower for a bride-to-be), for the specific purpose of collecting for a given cause. While the technique was not unknown a generation ago, by now it has proliferated to a point that many informants admitted that it constitutes a burden on limited income individuals, who nevertheless feel they cannot absent themselves without loosing face and social standing.

When I first studied the Satmar community, there seemed to be an increasing movement toward reliance on resources from the surrounding society rather than sole reliance on those generated within the community. This movement has only partially been successful. Considerable outside sources have been increasingly used for answering internal needs. However, the need and drive to elicit contributions from private individuals and businesses within the community, not only failed to diminish, but visibly increased. The "villain" here is the familiar process of "rising expectations" which assumed a somewhat new twist in our case. As they became more affluent and learned to utilize available resources of U.S. society, Satmarer also became more ambitious in matters of welfare. They now want to do more for the needy than they did in more austere times. They also became aware that problematic phenomena such as various forms of mental deficiency once accepted by many with a degree of stoic fatalism, are actually amenable to at least some amelioration, given sufficient funds. The result is that, instead of needing less, they need more internal contributions and are thus investing greater effort to raise what they consider as necessary resources. Only time will tell whether this process will eventually reach a plateau from which it will then begin to decline. As of now, it does not seem likely to do so in the near future.

Notes

1 Young, healthy individuals who feel themselves unemployable, to the point of justifying their reliance on others, are few in number and not very respected, because the Rov specifically encourages working. Those who have a valid reason for not working, such as illness, will rarely collect for themselves but will have a relative or friend do it for them, thus preserving anonymity and dignity.

2 Education and welfare overlap in two ways. First, supporting a Torah school is in itself considered an act of zedakah. And, second, many schools house children from poor homes—especially in Israel—whom they may, in addition to teaching, also provide with food during the day and sometimes complete room and board.

3 Informants have pointed out several such cases to the writer. As a matter of fact, most of the individuals involved happen to come from families of high status and, furthermore, are at present successful businessmen—two characteristics that are considered definite assets in the culture. But their failure to contribute in accordance with their means largely cancels their desirable attributes.

PART FIVE

VITAL PROCESSES

HAVING examined the main elements in the structural fabric of Satmar, we are now ready to tackle the double-edged problem of control and change. We are, first, faced with the task of explaining how the community succeeds in preserving its core culture to the degree that it does; how it has managed to bring up a generation in this country that has remained within the fold, a generation from which literally less than a handful have deserted. We must then turn around to understand the external and internal forces that have caused some changes already and seem to threaten more. Without understanding these dynamics, we are left with the erroneous impression of a static situation, without even as much as a guess concerning the future.

XII

Insulation and Control

The Problem of Control: A Point of View

WIDELY differing views on the subject of social control include two polar stands. At one extreme is the thesis—best expressed in Freud's postulate of the *id* vs. the *superego*—that individual needs and interests are inherently opposed to those of society. To accept this assumption leads one to conclude that the problem of controlling individuals' tendency to seek personal gratification is all-pervasive; that imposing social bonds and cultural restrictions of any sort is ipso facto problematic. At the opposite pole is the position—formulated by C.H. Cooley[1] and more recently by M.E. Spiro[2]—that culture is basically geared to the satisfaction of individual needs, therefore culture and person constitute two sides of the same coin. Theoretically, in this view, social control should not be a problem at all.

Even casual reflection suggests that both extreme positions are untenable. The Freudian view not only fails to take account of numerous cultural norms that cater directly to the individual's needs, but overlooks the more fundamental fact that humans lack genuine instincts and would thus literally not survive without the guidance provided by cultural norms and social organization. On the other hand, the "two sides of the same coin" view neglects such well-known phenomena as combat anxiety, that clearly demonstrate the strains imposed on individuals by some sociocultural requirements.

My stand in approaching this subject is middle of the road. I assume, first, that any culture contains some elements satisfactory to the individual and others that clash with personal desires. The problem of control lies in the latter of these two, where cultural requirements produce individual strain, thus generating motivation to disobey. Further, I assume a great deal of variation among cultures. both in relative proportion of satisfaction and strain and in the specific institutional areas they are located. Hence a discussion of control within a given culture must be preceded by identifying the culture patterns that seem to present the problem.

The Genesis of Strain

In Satmar culture the regulation of sex behavior, work, food consumption, secular education, and outward appearance generates a variety of pressures. Since the rules have already been described in detail, a brief summary will suffice here before analyzing their effect.

Sex is undoubtedly the most tabooed subject in Satmar culture. Contact between members of the opposite sex outside marriage is limited to business, informal social visitation, and necessary verbal exchange between primary relatives. Any other conversation is suspect, and physical contact beyond infancy is strictly forbidden. Married partners are required to observe a post-menstrual taboo period of at least twelve days during which any physical contact must be avoided. In fact, any public mention of the topic meets with disapproval.

In the realm of work, we recall the strong proscriptions regarding work on Saturdays and major holidays, proscriptions that cannot be violated without automatic expulsion from the community. In addition, the culture encourages, though it does not strictly demand, full or partial refrain from work on numerous days of lesser significance.

Food regulations are equally extensive and strict. Not only are Satmarer—like all Orthodox Jews—required to follow certain procedures in the processing of meat and dairy products or Passover foods, but they follow these rules according to the strictest interpretations and hence limit their trust in these matters to members of their own or culturally similar communities.

Secular education beyond a rudimentary knowledge of the "three R's" is limited to occasional technical training, preferably outside the walls of institutes of higher learning. Colleges and universities constitute mysterious unknown territory and are thought to offer, along with some useful technical knowledge, instruction in heresy in an environment free of all moral restraints. A full college education is thus beyond the reach of any Satmar man or woman.

Finally, prestige in Satmar requires conformance to the semi-formal code governing outward appearance, which especially affects males. They wear beards, dangling sideburns, special hats, long dark coats, and, on Saturdays, a shtraamel and kaaf-tan. The result is, naturally, an unmistakable appearance which allows instant identification of a member of Satmar or a similar group.

The strains resulting from these regulations are numerous. In the case of sex life, it is rather obvious that from early child-hood one must curb temptation for any physical or social con-tact with a member of the opposite sex. Even in marital life, the post-menstrual taboo imposes heavy strains. While claiming that the end result is an overall satisfactory sex life, informants also verbalized the difficulties involved. As we shall see, several con-trol measures are directed against the temptation to transgress.

Another area of resulting strain is that of recreation. Several of the above rules, together with a few others, limit recreation to religious and family festivals. Television is banned for it affords a view of "half-naked women" and of violence. Radio is also discouraged, though not forbidden, because it transmits the voices of singing women to which men are not supposed to listen. Movie- and theater-going is tolerated but to an even lesser degree than radio: only women are known to attend occasionally. The fine arts, though not curbed by specific rules, are considered alien to the culture. Artistic creativity is con-fined to the religious sphere and does not appear to be very original or highly artistic. The same is true of its enjoyment: few Satmar members have ever seen an original painting or listened to a symphony. Strict regulations of modesty in dress render beaches and swimming pools "off limits", except where com-plete privacy for members of one sex can be assured. Finally, travel is curtailed by food restrictions and a peculiar outward appearance, as well as by a desire to have access to religious facilities such as ritual baths that are not readily available every-where.

A final sphere in which strain is visible is that of economic activity. Limitations on secular education, the ban on Saturday and holiday work, and the imposition of an exotic appearance, have the natural effect of limiting earning capacity. As seen from Table 3, Satmar Hasidim are not only excluded from the liberal professions (with the exception of teaching in their own school system) but are absent from the lower-order white-collar occupations. Although by no means a poverty-stricken community, strain is apparent due to the multiple factors that encourage high spending.[3]

The question is, therefore, how does Satmar manage to control its members and prevent them from seeking less burdensome ways of life? How does it succeed in keeping its American-born-and-bred youngsters from leaving the community for the opportunities that the New York City atmosphere seems to offer?

In Quest of an Explanation

Needless to say, the Satmar community has no power to coerce conformity. Attempts to force compliance would not only result in a head-on clash with the surrounding legal-political system—a clash which would have catastrophic consequences for the community—but would be doomed to rapid failure. The intended victim would be eagerly assisted by social service agencies located in Williamsburg. Aside from the old settlement-house zeal to Americanize that still pervades these agencies, most of their staff reputedly harbor no great love for Satmarer and their like. Thus, even in the unlikely case that a Satmarer would be inclined to use force,[4] he would feel obliged to control his temptation lest he incur incalculable damage to the community as a whole.

In the absence of outright coercion, one is tempted to seek an answer in the realm of economics. But the situation yields little support for the thesis that members stay within the community because it is costly to leave it. Table 6 indicates that the occupational sphere of most Satmar members includes non-Orthodox Jews or Gentiles. In the case of the self-employed, some 70 per cent cross their cultural boundaries in the process of earning their livelihood. As for the employees, among whom the percentage distribution is reversed, we ought to realize that the type of work in which most of this category engage could be easily carried outside the community. Of some 320 employees, the largest single block of 212 comes from category 6 of Table 5 (operatives, service workers, and kindred workers), which involves work that has nothing to do with Satmar. In fact, educators employed by Satmar and similar communities are the only category of employees who truly depend economically on Satmar or some of its allied groups. The others merely prefer to work in a familiar environment where they find certain advantages relating to their cultural norms. For example, one need not go to the trouble of convincing an employer who is himself an Orthodox Jew to allow the employee to observe religious holidays or to allow interruption of work when time comes for prayer. But these are advantages only for one who wishes to retain his culture. It would therefore be illogical to explain control against deviation in terms of advantages that cease to be such as soon as one leaves the community and its way of life.

Add to all this the facts that (1) in its past in Hungary, the community was not economically autonomous and, unlike such closed communities as the Amish, has never even tried to establish its own economic foundation; (2) in the United States, despite the fact that employment in a shop has become respectable, self-employment continues to be preferred; and (3) the leader himself continues to encourage his followers to seek work and business outside the community, and it becomes clear that economics is not likely to be at the root of Satmar's social control.

My own observation of Satmar life suggests four interrelated sources of control: (1) prevention, (2) the reward system, (3) the socialization process, especially its gaps, and (4) external reinforcement.

Prevention is the most deliberate of the techniques. Satmar Hasidim are aware that many rules are difficult to follow and thus try to remove the temptation to transgress. In the area of sex behavior, for example, the sexes are separated almost from birth; teenagers are answerable for their whereabouts around the clock; no adult is permitted complete privacy with a member of the opposite sex other than spouse or primary kin; and even married adults avoid any show of affection during the post-menstrual taboo period. Satmarer explain their distinct outward appearance partially in terms of its effect in keeping one away from undesirable places and people. A final example: the ban on wine and bread of Gentiles or non-Orthodox Jews aims specifically at avoidance of undesirable social contact.

Control is somewhat less conscious but nonetheless visible in the operation of the informal reward system. Membership in Satmar is accompanied by many satisfactions. First, the community offers a great deal of emotional support within its extensive network of social relationships both within and outside the family. Then, many opportunities are provided for expressive behavior within the complex of Hasidic behavior patterns. Of central importance here are the rewards emanating from the figure of the almost worshiped leader, who not only relieves the members of the burden to make important decisions but offers them rich emotional gratifications through his "performance" and often by his mere presence. These rewards are effectively withdrawn from the deviant, some of them automatically, by the simple fact that the rebel is reluctant to admit his dependence on the group or its leader.

The key to the social control system, however, lies in the socialization process in both its formal and informal aspects. Without it, the mechanisms of prevention and reward are not likely to be effective. Prevention alone, in the case of sex behavior for example, would hardly be sufficient were it not for the fact that at both home and school sex is surrounded with so much secrecy and embarrassment that one is bound to experience a high degree of uneasiness in any legitimate encounter with the subject, let alone in connection with illicit behavior.

Similarly, effectiveness of the reward system depends heavily on socialization. Many rewards are not inherent in the experience but are a result of having learned to perceive the behavior in question as satisfying. For example, in order to enjoy the Rov's chanting of prayers or his talks, it is necessary first to acquire some knowledge of these matters. Primarily, however, one must acquire intense awe and admiration for the person of the Rov in order to value as highly as Satmarer do everything he does.

Even more important are the negative aspects of Satmar socialization, i.e., what is *not* offered to a youngster in the process of upbringing. The surrounding American culture contains potential equivalents for many of the experiences Satmarer consider rewarding. But in order to avail oneself of these, one must possess skills that Satmar fails to inculcate. For example, one might find substitute primary relationships for the ones he/she would have to renounce in the community, except that such relationships depend on shared informal aspects of culture. A product of Satmar is not likely to be familiar with the more subtle aspects of American culture, because such items as sports, literature, and other arts are systematically excluded from the training process. The same may be said with regard to potential substitutes for the aesthetic rewards that involve the person of the Rov. Or consider the prospect of assuming responsibility for important personal decisions which would inevitably result from leaving the community. Whether or not this is perceived as a threat is a matter of socialization, as those who acquired the skill and habit to make their own decisions would welcome the opportunity to assume greater responsibility. But a Satmar youngster is not allowed the opportunity to decide important matters. Everything is decided for him by his parents up to the time of marriage, including the choice of a mate which is initiated by parents. Upon marriage, dependency is merely transferred to the person of the Rov. Hence a member of Satmar is likely to feel threatened by the need to make personal decisions. In fact, this very decision to leave the community and to change the entire mode of behavior is likely to present a major difficulty. The effectiveness of the socialization process may, in large degree, be attributed to the high level of consistency and seriousness among adults when it comes to matters they consider vital. In Satmar there are no double standards, so often observed and commented upon in the larger American culture. No significant adult reserves for himself the right to violate norms that he wishes to inculcate in the young. Likewise, matters of belief are discussed in a way that takes basic postulates for granted; theologizing that would tend to raise doubts is totally omitted. Thus a growing youngster encounters no contradiction in the behavior of significant adults to the world view that he is being taught.

Parents are given most of the responsibility to socialize the young and to erect preventive mechanisms. Many rewards are administered within the network of kinship. Similarly, the threats of withdrawing rewards and of ejecting one into a strange world owe much of their effectiveness to familial ties. This is true both for young and adult. Should a married man, for example, contemplate a break with the community, he would almost certainly be rejected not only by his friends, but also by his spouse, his children, and his family of orientation. The loss of spouse, may be especially keen, because it was in marriage that the man had most likely found the only outlet for sexual experience—within the framework of his culture and without recourse to courting techniques he has not mastered. All this renders it highly unlikely that our imaginary hero would seriously contemplate such an adventure. No wonder parents are eager to marry off their children at an early age, for in addition to naaches, fulfillment one expects from seeing perpetuation of family, one also feels that once his children are married they are securely lodged within the fold of the community.

Finally, many aspects and events of the surrounding world indirectly support Satmarer's social-control efforts. The nature of these may be understood in terms of values and goals that Satmar shares with outsiders, some of them with the other Orthodox Jews, others with all Jews, and still others with Western middle class. Whenever others with whom a value is shared visibly fail to achieve it, while Satmar seems to succeed, the effect is to confirm to Satmarer the validity of their definition of the situation. It is as if they engaged in a dialogue with outsiders about the relative merits of their different approaches toward the same end, and the failure of the others occasions a triumphant exclamation on the Satmarer's part: "You see? Your approach is failing and ours works!" Let us consider a few examples.

In the United States, commercialization has made deep inroads in Jewish Orthodox life. Some rabbis who are officially known as Orthodox prosper by sanctioning various evasions of

Jewish religious law. Some of the evasions—such as permitting mixed seating of men and women in the synagogue—are of necessity public, while justification is often sought by means of legalistic argumentation. Other evasions—such as ordaining unqualified candidates for a fee, or accepting responsibility that a product is kosher without actually supervising its production—are semi-clandestine in nature and occasionally assume racketeering dimensions. Control of these matters is, for reasons we need not go into, exceedingly difficult, but occasionally a scandal is exposed.[5] At such time Satmarer find confirmation of the suspicion that had caused them to create their own kosher food industry, which has yet to be compromised.

The State of Israel is another bone of contention between Satmar and most other Orthodox groups. Satmarer brand Israel an ally of Satan, whereas most Jews view it with various degrees of sympathy, some even going so far as to consider it a beginning of fulfillment of the Messianic promise. Occasionally, however, some Israelis behave in a fashion revolting to all Orthodox Jews who then unite in protest. The autopsy problem is a prime example. Israeli physicians have persistently been performing autopsies for research purposes on those who die in hospitals, without requesting the consent of the family. As we have seen, Jewish religious law forbids any tampering with a dead body, and protests against the unilateral action of physicians (sanctioned by Israeli law) have come from all Orthodox circles, occasioning in Satmar considerable mockery of those who read Messianic significance into the Jewish political state.

A good example of the values Satmar shares with all Jews is that regarding mixed marriages. Except for a small minority, Jews in this and other countries seek to maintain some kind of Jewish identity. Mixed marriages are hence regarded with apprehension among most Jews. Yet such marriages take place at an increasing rate,[6] not only among those who wish to shed their identity but also in families that have tried to maintain ties with Jewry on a basis other than Orthodox religion—proving to the Satmarer the futility of finding substitute frames of reference for Orthodox religiosity.

Finally, in the general area of middle-class values, subsumed in Satmar under mentshlichkeit, we can look at behavior patterns such as high crime rates, illegitimacy, premarital and extra-marital sexual relations, which are frequently reported and wailed-about in the general press. Their virtual absence in Satmar is frequently cited as proof that the Satmar way is conducive toward being not only a better Jew but a better human being.

To be sure, all three outside worlds—Orthodox Jews, Jews, and the rest of the perceived world—do not altogether match the Satmarer image of them. Not all kosher food produced outside Satmar lacks proper supervision; not all Zionists disregard religious sentiments; not all non-Orthodox Jews fail to create safeguards against intermarriage. Also, many aspects of the non-Jewish environment are positively valued in Satmar. However, Satmarer systematically ignore these elements of the environment and focus on those which validate their own view of the world in which they live.

In sum, Satmar safeguards its core culture and controls against deviation by minimizing opportunities to deviate, by offering the obedient rewards which are withheld from the deviant, by its socialization system that not only inculcates the "right" way of living but also teaches one how to enjoy its rewards and, more important, prevents the acquisition of mental tools that might enable one to seek and find alternative satisfactions. At the same time many aspects of the world without reinforce Satmarer's view of that world, thus diminishing the likelihood of their renouncing their own culture.

Two varieties of significant and potentially far-reaching developments have influenced the control process in Satmar during the years that have elapsed since my first research visit. One type originates in broad economic and demographic changes and the other, in the particular situation surrounding the succession and its aftermath. Specifically, we have mind, in the first case, occupational shifts (cf. Addenda to Chapter IX) that enable and require more movement into, and communication with the outside world, as well as demographic decentralization accommodating the new situation. On the leadership front, we focus here on the rise to the top position of a practical administrator who, on the one hand, modified the structure in recognition of the new demographic reality and on the other, exercises a leadership style characterized by reduced emotional grip on the rank-and-file. As a result of these two sets of forces Satmar control has been visibly transformed.

Primary relations within the family-community-leader triad, which once formed the backbone of Satmar control by generating rewards on which individuals so heavily depended, continue to operate under the new conditions, but with considerably reduced effectiveness, as both the extent of rewards and degree of dependence on them decreased. Many of today's more mobile Satmarer, especially among the younger ones, seem to have learned to enjoy occasional escape from round-the-clock supervision. They have also acquired the capability to find and enjoy some things the world without has to offer. In addition, the absence of Reb Yoel's electrifying presence seems to have increased many individuals' capacity and willingness to make important decisions, thus reinforcing personal autonomy and further decreasing dependence on the primary community.

As old techniques began fading, new ones appeared on the horizon. Coercion, almost non-existent as an internal control mechanism in yesteryear's Satmar, became of increasing impor tance in today's community. To understand it, we first have to realize what made it possible, as well as what rendered it attractive. The fact that today Satmar has a huge network of schools employing large numbers of teachers and an array of supporting personnel, has handed the leadership immense economic power. Then, the rise of an independent townlet which the new leaders consider to be, in a sense, their own, has created additional coercive means through the ability to control access to desirable community facilities and to other benefits (cemetery-related privileges, for example).

Alongside availability came the prolonged strife surrounding the not-entirely-completed succession process. Through the years, dissenters managed to publish and disseminate underground pamphlets, build and organize rival facilities (synagogues, ritual baths, and, especially, schools), organize rival banquets on community festive days, and, allegedly, threaten to or actually commit violent acts (setting fires, for example) against establishment leaders. Under the circumstances, the leadership decided to use its available powers against the rebels, considering the measures as the only means available to them for controlling against spread of opposition to sympathizers and fence-sitters. As mentioned, earlier (see updates to various chapters, especially Chapter VIII) schools and other community facilities were employed in an attempt to control dissenters. While no loyalty oath or its equivalent is required for employment (in fact, some close relatives of opponents are working for the system), open expression of opposition to or criticism of the establishment virtually assures dismissal. Other community facilities, particularly the gravesite of Reb Yoel, were also harnessed. The area surrounding the building containing the shrine was fenced in and guarded by loyalists who often deny access to open opponents. Some have on occasion not been admitted to the entire Kiryas Yoel cemetery. Opponents are also known to have been forced out of principal synagogues. There have also been allegations of physical violence, allegations dismissed by establishment spokesmen as fabrication, unauthorized acts by overzealous youths, or responses to provocation. In short, defining active opposition as unacceptable, the leadership (including the Rebbeh's family and his inner circle) decided that force is the only way to deal with the problem, if not to eliminate it altogether, at least to quarantine it and prevent its spread.

What is the net result of the shifts in techniques on effectiveness of control? Although lacking precise measures, numerous symptoms suggest that control today is considerably weaker than it once was. Aside from the persistence of internal division and conflict, psychiatrists, psychologists, social workers, and community knowledgeables I interviewed, all pointed to the existence of a growing set of problems, including drug abuse, mental breakdowns, even sexual deviance, virtually unknown in earlier Satmar. Informants, in this case professionals, outsiders who work with Satmarer affected by the problems, are virtually unanimous in attributing these to stress resulting from large families, especially when accompanied by financial difficulty. They also readily emphasize the role played by opportunities provided by geographic mobility, afforded by occupations involving frequent travel outside community boundaries. Insiders, admitting the phenomena, stress the relatively small numbers involved, while outsiders do not quite agree. Regardless of actual numbers, their relatively recent appearance indicates declining effectiveness of social control. We shall return to the subject in discussing Satmar's probable and possible future.

Notes

1 C.H. Cooley, *Social Organization* (New York: Charles Scribner's Sons, 1909), *passim*.

2 M.E. Spiro, "Culture and Personality: The Natural History of a False Dichotomy," *Psychiatry*, 14 (February 1951), 19-46.

3 More about the factor of economic strain in the next chapter.

4 A note of clarification: Satmarer do use physical punishment in child-rearing, mostly mild, in both home and school. What we are discussing here is the hypothetical use of coercion against a grownup or an advanced teenager who would wish to leave the community.

5 See, for example, *New York Times*, March 19, 1959, p. 28. Occasionally a grotesque, rather than a dishonest, episode occurs which reflects the shady character of the kosher food industry. For instance, at the time of the research a certain nightclub in New York City advertised itself as kosher. This in itself is grotesque enough, because nightclubs stand for behavior quite out of character with religious observance. But, in addition, New York City authorities underscored their questionable nature by requesting that all persons occupationally connected with nightclubs have their fingerprints taken by the police. *Life* (December 5, 1960, p. 138) carried a picture of the rabbi in charge of supervising the food at the club, as his fingerprints were being taken. The Satmar newspaper (*Der Yid*) utilized the incident as an illustration of the pitiful state of *kashrut* (regulation and manufacture of kosher food) in America and the low level to which a rabbi is willing to stoop for a few dollars.

6 *Cf.* E. Rosenthal, "Studies of Jewish Intermarriage in the United States," *American Jewish Yearbook* 1963, American Jewish Committee, pp. 3-53. One may question (as I do) both the representative nature of the Iowa and D.C. data and Rosenthal's conclusions, but this does not concern us at the moment. What is important here is (1) that extensive inter-marriage does occur and (2) that this is a matter of grave con-cern—especially to non-Orthodox Jews, for it is their children who are involved. In fact, the appearance of the above-mentioned article trig-gered, in Conservative and Reform circles, a rash of near-hysterical dis-course on the subject that lasted for several years.

XIII

Change and Strain

DESPITE the high degree of success of its insulating mechanisms, Satmar remains exposed to internal and external forces beyond its control. Most important are those dynamic processes that affect the heart of the culture, religion. For it is the preservation of this cultural core that Satmar is all about. We would not be interested, for example, in the changing trend toward job-holding by women, except for the fact that this economic phenomenon relates to behavior in sensitive focal areas of the culture.

Education of Females

The unsettled nature of Bais Ruchel, the Satmar girls' school, is a problem with these essential elements: State law demands that girls, like boys, attend school until the age of sixteen. But tradition has not only failed to provide guidance for an effective Jewish curriculum but has actually militated against such a program. As a result, the secular department has become quite effective, thus creating a gap in the anti-acculturation protective system. Abroad, women had also been more acculturated than men; but while the situation in Hungary seems not to have created problems, the danger is greater in the United States where women assume an increasing role in family decision-making and thus may have greater opportunity to make their views felt. At the time of my research, the situation at Bais Ruchel had been marked by frequent outbreaks of conflict, usually mended by the Rov's decisive word. Despite the acceptance of the Rov's decisions, residues of dissatisfaction have remained. Since strain seems to be built into the situation, the area of female education may be considered one of Satmar's standing problems.

Economic Pressures

Economic imbalance resulting from the clash between motivation for high spending, on the one hand, and limitations on earning, on the other, constitutes another unresolved dilemma in contemporary Satmar. True, at the moment the problem is not in the forefront of Satmarer's consciousness, and it would be a mistake to expect violation of major norms in the quest for higher income. Yet it would be equally erroneous to discount the problem altogether. In fact, several facts testify to the presence of the dilemma.

Most generally, one finds a high degree of money consciousness among Satmarer, which comes to the forefront in a variety of ways. In my many informal conversations, the subject turned up either directly in the form of complaints about artificially created wants, or, obliquely, in statements of pride about obligations being met despite modest incomes. This awareness appears to reduce the perceived rewards of membership in the community.

A more tangible and by far more serious result is the trend toward working wives, which stems from the necessity to make ends meet. This, in turn, gives rise to several potential threats. First, where both father and mother work, supervision of children is necessarily diminished. Youngsters often return from school before the arrival of either parent, remaining for hours without parental care or nurture. When the mother does come home, she must usually spend the evening cooking, serving food, washing dishes, sewing-and-mending clothes, and so forth, because even the combined earnings of both parents rarely permit employment of domestic help. The father is also occupied during the evening, helping out in the house, helping his sons with their Torah studies, or studying Torah himself. Neither parent is left with much time for developing a relaxed relationship with children, thus undermining one of the child's main sources of security—the home.[1]

Another consequence of working women is the changing balance of power within the family. To appreciate the threat inherent in this change we must recall that women are more acculturated than men, and that the girls' school seems to perpetuate this trend. Hence power may be gradually slipping into the hands of those who are penetrating the barrier that is designed to keep Satmar culturally insulated.[2]

Finally, economic pressures have begun to change even the attitude of fathers toward their sons' secular instruction. Many have begun to feel that mastering the language of the land is necessary for making a better living.[3] When the school was founded, many fathers tried to prevent their sons from attending the secular classes. A decade later such attempts all but vanished, and a few actually began to express open dissatisfaction with the inefficiency of Torah V'Yiroh's secular department. If this department should ever become effective, it might create even more severe problems than the girls' school now does. Presently, males hold the key to Satmar's cultural outlook, and their acculturation may necessitate radical changes in that outlook, which is presently focused on resistance to serious acculturating trends.

The Succession Problem

The absence of an heir apparent to the Reb Yoel, who was in his eighties and suffered a stroke a few years ago, is probably the most serious threat to the present structure of Satmar. To appreciate its scope we must remember some aspects of the community's history as well as the gigantic dimensions of the Rov's role.

Historically, the Rov has acquired his following by achievement rather than ascription. Most of the Rov's followers had actually abandoned other communities to join his. Consequently, Satmarer, unlike most other Hasidim, had a personal rather than a dynastic loyalty to the Reb Yoel. Consequently, many were disposed to be highly critical of any individual would-be-successor to whom they would consider transferring their intense feeling of trust and admiration.[4]

Socioculturally, any individual who aspired to fill the Rov's role would have to possess more or less the following attributes. He would have to be a descendant of a Hasidic dynasty, probably either the one of Sighet (the Teitelbaums) or the one of Sanz (the Halberstams). He would have to enjoy the reputation of one who has been "holy from the womb," i.e., of having an impeccable past without which it would be impossible to bestow on him the necessary hallowed image. He would also have to be a recognized Torah scholar so that the Hasidim would be able to accept his decisions as law. Then, in order to be suited for the role of a Hasidic rebbeh, he would have to project an image of a wise man who is able to descend to the level of the common man, whom he would need to advise in practical matters. Finally, he would need to possess a forceful personality and master numerous skills—such as public speaking—in order to lead the community effectively. Quite an order, to say the least.

Not only was it difficult to find an individual who possesses all these qualities, but the emotional attachment of Satmarer to the Rov prevented them from even thinking about a possible heir. Whenever I tried to broach the subject, I met with anxiety and a refusal to discuss it. "The Rov will live to see the Messiah," would be the normal abrupt reply. Reluctance to search naturally reduced the likelihood of finding a suitable successor. In view of their intense individual and communal dependency on the leader, it seemed certain that without one Satmar would not survive in its present form for very long.

Population Increase

Finally, Satmar's rapid natural demographic growth,[5] poses a potential threat to the present form of interpersonal relations, which might not be possible with an enlarged membership. Especially the system of control, which depends to a large degree on close personal ties, would seem to be threatened by the inevitable loosening of these ties as a result of numerical increase.

As in the case of other problems, a solution is not impossible, for some cultures that are equally dependent on informal inter personal control mechanisms have solved the problem of growth.[6] But as yet, Satmar has no safeguards against this or other threats.

These four sets of threatening forces are not isolated but closely interwoven. The ascendance to greater power of the more acculturated female results from her increasing assumption of responsibility for the family income, which, in turn, results from economic pressures. It may also lead to increased acculturation in general, making it easier to find substitute satisfactions for those now offered within the community. This, together with the reduction of rewards that seems to result both directly and indirectly from economic pressures, may provide further incentive for leaving the community. If, in addition, the rewarding and unifying figure of the Rov should be absent from the scene for a prolonged period of time, the growing population may not be able to maintain Satmar as the closed community it now is.

The sources generating strain and causing unanticipated change discussed in this chapter continue to operate in present-day Satmar. We have already indicated most of the results to date. However, as in all human societies, the dynamic dimension in this community is ubiquitous. There seems little doubt that further changes are on the way.

As already noted, female education remains an unresolved problem. To be sure, Satmarer have managed to retain virtually all of their American born-and-bred daughters within the fold. These young women appear to be culturally indistinguishable from their mothers. At the same time, differences are apparent. For one, today's young women are more outspoken, openly expressing criticism of internal occurrences they dislike. I found this to be true even of ones most loyal to the present regime. Beyond mere criticism, these young women organize and push for changes they deem important. By doing so, they keep the change-process alive and moving. For example, by pushing for new improvements in their daughters' secular education (cf. addendum to Chapter VII), they help increase the gap between the two arms of Bais Ruchel's educational system, thus perpetuating women's increasing superiority over men when it comes to familiarity with and mastery of many important features of the surrounding American culture. Ultimately, this spells still more power. Signs of restlessness with the traditional stay-at-home role, already observed in the new tendency to seek work for the sole purpose of getting out of the house (other indicators point in the same direction), could be understood in this context.

Similarly, the economic factor continues to be a dynamic force. True, today's Satmarer seem to be more comfortable than those of a generation ago. The greater affluence is clearly manifest in the large numbers who have managed to leave (and still do so) their original enclave in Williamsburg. In the new subcommunities, especially Borough Park and Kiryas Yoel (I did not have a chance to visit Monsey), the houses are newer, better, more expensive, and better equipped. In fact, even in Williamsburg significant improvements are visible. As one example we may take the fact that new housing now in the process of being built is not at all cheap. In one instance, a figure of $130,000 with a required $70,000 downpayment was quoted for a modest three-bedroom condominium under construction. While still considerably lower than, say, in Borough Park, both the size of the initial sum and of mortgage payments for the balance are not exactly affordable by the impoverished.

At the same time, however, needs and ambitions have also been rising. The already-mentioned community needs for maintenance and expansion of its huge and growing institutional networks and consequent continuous pressure for ever larger contributions, is an excellent example. The more affluent one is reputed to be, the more one feels these pressures, many emanating from outside Satmar's formal boundaries. Refusal is difficult. It may spell loss of status and for those in business, these may actually constitute necessary business expenses. Add to this the continuous quest for more and more expensive possessions. Again, women play a significant role, as agents of both stimulus and response. They, more than their husbands, arrange and partake in fund-raising affairs. They also play a major role in the push for more material comfort. At the same time, women are both capable and willing to lend a hand, if necessary, in order to meet the ever rising demand for more income. The old process thus continues and only time will tell exactly to what changes it will eventually lead.

Finally, the succession problem looms larger than ever as a potential source of future strain. Granted, for the time being the problem seems to have been solved. The overwhelming majority seems to have accepted Reb Moshe as the legitimate heir and leader. From the community's perspective this was no doubt a wise decision. A vacuum at the top would most likely have resulted in a virtual collapse of the institutional structure. By all accounts, things were in disarray at the time of Reb Yoel's departure, largely as a result of the fact that during the last eleven years of his life, the old Rebbeh was paralyzed and functioned more as a symbolic than as an actual leader. His wife and a number of her friends unofficially ran the show and while each local leader tried to keep things going, no one assumed the role of centrally supervising and coordinating the multi-faceted structure. Reb Moshe reorganized and tightened matters. While introducing a great deal of operational decentralization, he has managed to remain in charge and to prevent chaos. In other words, despite the existing internal strife between the new leadership and the dissidents, Satmar has, by and large, remained a single community.

Nevertheless, dissent continues and so does conflict. Together they may prove in the future to be more disruptive than the apparent small number of open opponents would suggest. The existence of many more hidden sympathizers is conceded by the present leadership. When the time comes for the helm to pass again, it is not at all clear (though not totally excluded as a possibility) that a single heir will manage to keep the community united, even to the extent that it presently is. There are clear indications of a potential split, possibly into even more than two parts. For, aside from the already open conflict, there is the additional factor presented by the sub-communities, who may at the time of a new transitional crisis be ready for full independence. Interestingly (and significantly), unlike a generation ago, Satmarer today readily talk about the possibility of future fission. While one cannot predict with absolute certainty that this is what will actually occur, it does appear to be a plausible scenario. If the community does eventually break up, new and more significant changes seem inevitable. What are now different tendencies will undoubtedly develop into full-fledged differences under conditions of organizational independence. In such a case, the only common bond between the kin communities may well be the memory of Reb Yoel which all will continue to hold sacred, coupled with at least some degree of commitment to the anti-zionist norm which is so closely associated with the memory of Satmar's founder.

Notes

1 In addition, few parents recognize any need for a child to have free spending money. Youngsters are thus deprived of the emotional security emanating from parents and the feeling of independence that most American youngsters associate with having a suitable allowance. It may well be that the observed aggressiveness of contemporary Satmar youngsters relates to this deprivation. Incidentally, one of my most rewarding experiences was corroboration of this observation from an independent source. C. Henoch, a psychologist from Yeshiva University, made a comparative study of several groups of children, one of which was Satmar. His conclusion, which he shared in a personal conversation with me in 1961 (after the above observations had been formulated), indicated, among other things, that Satmar children reveal statistically significantly higher sibling rivalry, desire for parental love, and craving for money than did the other two groups.

2 Several observations led me to believe that a slight trend in the direction of women's acting as acculturating agents may have already begun. One young mother made a few sarcastic remarks about the quality of the English department in the boys' school, concluding, "If I did not go over the lesson with my son every evening, he would not even know the few words he does!" This woman was, then, not only concerned with her son's progress in secular subjects, but was powerful enough in the home to make her son spend his free evening time on the English lesson rather than, in accordance with the accepted ideal, on study of Torah.

3 Some knowledge of the English language is needed in most occupations in which Satmarer are engaged. Storekeepers, even the ones in Williamsburg, have out-group customers. Manufacturers not only employ non-Jewish workers but must also interact with retailers and other manufacturers who do not speak Yiddish and whose association is essential. Even factory workers employed in the community must work with English-speaking individuals. In addition, they belong to unions, in which they take an interest but have a difficult time communicating with the leaders or reading the literature. Besides, a factory worker who cannot communicate with an outsider lacks the secure feeling that he will be able to seek employment elsewhere, should the need arise.

4 As we have seen in Chapter 2, one core group actually had not accepted an heir for long years before it joined Satmar.

5 In 1961, the 860 households already had a population of over 4,500. The rate of increase appears very high, if judged from the only figure available to the writer—the ratio of living children to adult females.

When corrected to females over twenty, the figure is 3.95 living children per female—one of the highest in the world. (The correction was necessary because in World War II virtually all children were killed by the Germans and new births began only after 1945. As a result, Satmar had an extremely small number of youngsters aged fifteen to twenty.) See *Demographic Yearbook 1969*, United Nations, Department of Economic and Social Affairs, pp.235-240.

6 The Amish, for example, have a system whereby a unit is subdivided when it reaches a certain size. See W. M. Kollmorgen, *The Culture of a Contemporary Rural Community: The Old Order Amish of Lancaster County, Pennsylvania*, U.S. Department of Agriculture, Rural Life Studies, No.4 (September 1942).

XIV

Attraction and Repulsion: A Few Illustrations

THE Strengths and weaknesses of Satmar culture may be best illustrated by three cases which differ in nature. One involves a former stranger who joined the community, the second is an instance of departure, and the third portrays a rather rare case of simultaneous flight and gravitation. Together they illustrate at least some of the forces of reward and strain at work within the Satmar community.[1]

In Quest of the Authentic

Mosheh was born in the United States between the two world wars to East European immigrants, who were determined to remain Orthodox Jews despite numerous obstacles that lay in the path of that stubborn minority. When Mosheh reached school age he was sent to yeshivah for an Orthodox education. He developed into a withdrawn, serious boy. Disinterested in sports, he devoted his time and energy to study and meditation. The New York City climate of that period was anything but encouraging. The overwhelming majority of even the immigrant generation plunged head-on into the hustle and bustle of the big city. With the goal of moving ahead economically, they rapidly shed all that appeared to be obstacles in the way, including religious beliefs and practices. Those few who moved against the stream were disorganized and fragmented, providing no real community to which a growing youngster could escape from the dissonant environment. Hence, withdrawal into oneself was a logical solution.

The Rov's arrival to this country in 1946 found Mosheh a restless teenager in search of an environment he could accept while adhering to the way of life he was taught at home and in school. His father remembered Hasidic rebbehs from abroad, but he had become reconciled to the pre-World War II pattern of encountering in the United States only minor rebbeyic scions who came here for the one purpose of collecting money. He thought of the Satmarer Rov as being just another one of those insignificant characters, and he told his son so. Mosheh, however, refused to accept the verdict and on one holiday decided to join the Satmarer in prayer. He became so attracted that he entered the Satmar yeshivah, then married and settled in Williamsburg, remaining a member of Satmar.

What was it that attracted Mosheh to a community that was strange even to his immigrant father? It was, in his own words, the first time in his life that he found a group of Orthodox Jews who were serious, consistent, uncompromising, and possessed a high degree of integrity to boot. Above all, he found a community in which "he felt at home," something he always needed, sought, but lacked before he found Satmar.

Mosheh's case clearly illustrates the effectiveness of the integrative control forces discussed in Chapter XII. These forces not only retain individuals who were born and bred within the community, but also attract to Satmar outsiders whose upbringing and personal makeup render them responsive to the appeal of this culture.

Although Mosheh was not brought up within the community, his early experience prepared him for the embrace of Satmar. Obviously he had not accumulated much strength to cope with the strains built into the complex culture of the larger society, with its ambiguous, often conflicting value system. From his parents, who struggled and sacrificed for the ideal of Orthodoxy, he seems to have acquired a yearning for purity. Thus when he went to yeshivah he took the idealism of Jewish Orthodoxy more seriously than his age-mates and, in the absence of congenial peers, became a withdrawn loner.

This brings us to the role of the environment. What we termed "external reinforcements" in the case of native Sat marer, served in Mosheh's case as preconditioners. Loneliness at school may be bearable when one can fall back on an encouraging environment or community. But neither the general climate of the American thirties and forties, nor much of what passed as Orthodoxy during that period, provided a setting for young Mosheh to validate his expectations of reality.

Thus the attraction of Satmar. The Rov, a person with integrity, who is unwilling to compromise for purposes of popularity or personal gain, was a concrete example of the ideal. At the same time the community provided a setting in which, for the first time, Mosheh did not feel alienated. Interestingly, while he claimed to feel at home, Mosheh also admitted that with the exception of a limited circle of friends and acquaintances he remained in part a stranger within Satmar, something he attributed to the fact that he is not of Hungarian background. Apparently the circle to which he belongs suffices to assuage the feeling of alienation he experienced before his arrival in Satmar.

Departure, Almost

Velvel grew up in a cultural environment similar, in fact physically adjacent to, Satmar. His father respected the Rov highly, yet he was not a Hasid in the sense of accepting the Rov's judgment as infallible. This was the extent of the difference; the rest was virtually the same. The home atmosphere, the Eastern European small-room private school in which Velvel received his education which consisted of studying religious subjects exclusively, the general theory and practice of religion were no different from those experienced by the typical Satmarer in Eastern Hungary.

As a teenager, however, Velvel began to grow restless. Several factors were responsible. The years were the turbulent thirties when the German menace developed into a constantly rising threat to European Jewry. Youngsters aware of the danger began feeling locked into a narrow trap from which they wished to escape to parts of the world beyond the reach of the Germans, where people—including Jews—breathed freely. Then there was the matter of reading. The townlet in which Velvel

lived had a profusion of secular Yiddish-language reading materials—books, newspapers, journals—imported from Poland and
the United States. Although forbidden by the Jewish "establishment," this literature was widely read, especially by the young.
Velvel was no exception. He devoured virtually tons of the forbidden fruit, which served the dual purpose of providing, on
the one hand, a vicarious experience of a reality beyond reach
and of increasing, on the other hand, the desire to break out
from both his physical and cultural boundaries.

Then came the crisis years of the early forties: struggle for
sheer physical survival, uprooting, destruction, concentration
camp; then the anti-climax of liberation which brought a realization of the thoroughness of the destruction process. Velvel now
confronted a strange world, a world annoyed with those who
managed to survive and had the nerve to kick up a fuss about "a
few wartime casualties." During these years Velvel went through
a variety of attitudinal and behavioral convulsions. He gradually
departed from his native culture, flirted with several popular
ideologies, and upon liberation, went to Western Europe where
he partook in the mode of life about which he used to dream as
a teenager. He was disappointed, dissatisfied, and began yearning for certain qualities of his childhood culture—interpersonal
warmth, marital and general family fidelity, the Jewish holiday
atmosphere, absence of gross violence, and, above all, faith and
hope—qualities he missed in the culture of the West, at least in
the part of that culture he experienced and observed.

Velvel thus opted for Orthodoxy, realizing at the same time
that he had reached a point beyond complete return. Despite
his disappointment, the fling with Western culture left him with
a love for free inquiry and openmindedness. He thus could not
bring himself to reaccept censorship, complete insulation, or
narrow dogmatism as part of his existence.

Upon migrating to Canada, Velvel married an Orthodox girl,
established an Orthodox home in which children are brought
up likewise, and is known as an Orthodox Jew but not as a
Hasid. He has a marginal, occasionally strained relationship
with the Hasidim of both the city where he lives and New York
City where he often visits. He remains friendly with the Satmarer Rov, even has a degree of reverence for him, but does

not pretend to be a follower. Satmarer know that he "departed," that he is not "one of theirs." Yet they also recognize that his departure is not complete, that he not only remains an Orthodox Jew but retains respect for Satmar. This pleases them, and they take it as an indication of their strength and ability to command recognition from outsiders.

In Velvel's case, sharp edges are absent at both ends of his metamorphosis. Velvel was never a Satmarer, in fact not even a true Hasid in the full sense of the term. Nor did he abandon or oppose Orthodoxy. These details suggest that absence at the outset of the element of complete dependency may have been a factor in Velvel's desire to explore and examine, something he retained even after his partial return. In other words, Velvel may confirm the view that conditioning for dependence in childhood, coupled with the Rov's role as decision maker, are important control factors, elimination of which considerably weakens the control structure. At the same time, Velvel's clinging to Orthodoxy suggests that other factors do play a role. He seems to have been ill-equipped to find satisfactory equivalents in Western culture, in which he missed a number of ingredients that he had learned to need. The Hasidic culture of the Satmar variety may thus not be a "take it or leave it" proposition, a suggestion to which we shall return.

On the other side of the coin, Velvel's desire to break out of his cultural isolation was the chief reason for his departure, and his "unauthorized" reading furthered that desire. This accords with our speculation that if women, who presently read a great deal of forbidden literature, win more power and if, in addition, the Rov departs from the scene, cases similar to Velvel's may mushroom within Satmar.

"Flight"

Sender's parents, Satmarer Hasidim from long ago and part of the core group that came here at the end of World War II, brought him to this country as an infant. He thus belongs to the first "American" generation of Satmarer. An active and vivacious youngster, Sender pursued a variety of activities and interests (wood-carving, gossiping, politicking). Even though these were not deviant in nature, they nevertheless distracted him from what was supposed to be his main interest—the study of Torah. These "extracurricular" excursions often dismayed his parents, who, while proud of their good-looking, lively son, responded nervously whenever Sender did something unpredictable or showed up where he was not expected to be. Thus the parents, though they loved their son and continued to praise him in front of others, gradually began treating Sender as something of a black sheep. The parents' attitude was inevitably communicated to other adults, especially teachers and principals, who had some dealings with or authority over the youngster.

Sender was about fourteen, attending the yeshivah division of Torah V'Yiroh, when several outside distractions kept him away from school for several days. The supervisor, angry and indignant, suspended Sender for an indefinite period and threatened him with complete dismissal. This was a harsh punishment. Suspension from school carries a stigma which a youngster from a respected family finds especially difficult to bear. Without saying a word to anyone, Sender disappeared.

When he failed to return home in the evening, his parents grew restless. They waited till the next day to investigate what happened and to establish whether they were dealing with an accident or a deliberate escape. In the morning they checked with the bank where their son saved his earnings from occasional odd jobs, and discovered that all his money had been withdrawn the previous day. There was no doubt that Sender had run away from home. The question was, What next? To whom does one turn?

The father, as an oldtime Hasid of the Rov, would take no important step in any matter without first consulting his rebbeh. The Rov was in a resort town where he was spending the summer. Quickly a long-distance call was placed with an emergency request for advice. The Rov calmed the anxious father: "It is a typical youth act. Don't worry, he will turn up soon!"

Sure enough, a day later Sender arrived at the Rov's summer residence. He brought complaints against the harsh treatment accorded him by the yeshivah supervisor (and, according to an unconfirmed report, against severe treatment at home), claiming innocence of any wrongdoing and expressing his wish to be reinstated at school.

Not only was Sender's wish granted, but the Rov's personal secretary immediately flew to New York where, in addition to arranging for reinstatement, conveyed to all yeshivah students a strict order from the Rov not to talk of the incident. Violation of the order would result in expulsion.

This was the end of it. Sender returned to the yeshivah. Within a few years he married and joined the adult community of which he is a bonafide member. The incident is as good as forgotten.

Two aspects of Sender's case are especially illuminating. First, we see the absolute trust in the Rov that a Satmar youngster acquires early in his life, a feeling that anything that goes wrong is to be blamed on malicious or incompetent individuals whose wrongdoings may be set straight by the Rov. This complete trust, which is readily observable among all strata of the Satmar population, acts as a powerful cohesive force, preventing the emergence of feelings of alienation when Satmarer are faced with irritating situations. The fact that the Rov did set matters straight no doubt reinforced Sender's original faith, which he then carried into adulthood.

Even more significant is the confidence of the Rov in Sender's speedy "return" to the community. What the Rov displayed was a deep conviction that one who is brought up in Satmar simply does not flee, even if he feels wronged and frustrated. The Rov's remarkable intelligence, together with his extensive experience, have apparently sensitized him to the fact that it is extremely difficult for a Satmar youngster to find solace in the strange outside world and that one is therefore bound to return and seek rectification from within. Again, the fact that the expectation materialized and Sender returned served to reinforce the Rov's conviction that the socialization of Satmar is an effective deterrent against deviance, that as long as the system remains intact one can safely assume that "once a Satmarer, always a Satmarer."

These cases illustrate some, though obviously not all, of the forces of attraction and repulsion that operate in Satmar. What does it all amount to, as far as the future is concerned? What are Satmar's prospects for survival in this country? These, together with other questions raised in the Introduction, are the subject of the next and final part of the book.

How do attraction-repulsion work today in Satmar? Most noteworthy here is the already-mentioned virtual cessation of influx from without. Apparently, the change in the perception of the leader, from that of possessing high charisma in the case of Reb Yoel, to that of being an effective administrator in Reb Moshe's case, combined with the tense internal situation, left the community with few, if any, attractions to offer outsiders.

Moreover, one can also observe a beginning measure of repulsion (not counting and not to be confused with opposition and deviance mentioned in the update to Chapter XII). One hears nowadays expression of sentiments by loyal insiders, including some employees, to the effect that some outside communities (whose orthodoxy is beyond question even within Satmar) look more attractive than their own. At the moment it is impossible to establish the extent of this feeling. However, it is a novelty for non-opposition individuals to verbalize such attitudinal tendencies, openly and without hesitation. At the moment this does not seem to be a serious threat; however, in the context of speculation on Satmar's future, it should be kept in mind.

Notes

1 The cases cited are authentic. The heroes themselves supplied most of
the information, while other informants filled in a few details. The
names and a few irrelevant data were changed in order to protect the
privacy of the persons involved.

PART SIX

IMPLICATIONS AND CONCLUSIONS

WHAT does it all add up to? What do we gain from studying this relatively insignificant community of a few thousand souls? Unfortunately, examination of a single case does not, by its very nature, permit any "conclusions". A study of this kind may, however, yield suggestions about various levels of problems. These suggestions form the subject of the concluding chapters. The first of these chapters contains a few clues of a sociological nature—what the case of Satmar suggests to the student of human social behavior. The second and final chapter comprises reactions of a broader character, ranging in scope from problems associated with Satmar's future to overall majority-minority relations in a pluralistic setting.

XV

Statics and Dynamics:
Some Implications

HAVING described and explained the life and culture of this insular community, what are the wider implications of its vital processes? What does Satmar suggest about these universal social processes that might enhance our understanding of them?

Social Control

To begin with, a rather safe conclusion may be made regarding the role of economics. If economic control does not play a role in Satmar's ability to command the loyalty of its members, then we are justified in proposing that economics is not universally at the root of social control and may not even be a necessary control mechanism of any society. It would appear that, at least in this realm, we have been too enthusiastic in accepting theories of economic determinism, either the variety proposed by Adam Smith, or the one advocated by Karl Marx.

On the other hand, we see that a society may effectively control against deviance and defection through skillful manipulation of resources that are not economic in nature and are, furthermore, amply available in every society. In particular, the capacity to lend social response to, and psychic support of, the individual is a resource that all interpersonal networks possess. That all individuals depend heavily on positive primary-level human response is one of the firmly established principles of contemporary social science and need not be elaborated. There is no apparent reason why any society cannot, as Satmar does, manipulate this dependence and put it to use for control purposes.

A point to be made, however, is that one cannot assume that a society will use this potential control factor. What seems indicated in the Satmar experience is that effective use of human relations for this purpose involves some skillful maneuvering, avoiding the extremes of quick rejection for a minor offense and of intense personal loyalty on the part of parents and friends which would result in frequent disregard of major deviant acts. Effective use of human relations also requires a seriousness among adults, the absence of double standards when it comes to the major values and norms that a society wishes to guard. All this, so readily observable in Satmar, would seem to be universal because it is fully congruent with established learning theory. Furthermore, what clinical and educational psychology has been suggesting for effective control in the more limited spheres of home and school might be logically extended to the higher level of society as a whole. Our case furnishes at least one concrete illustration of effective "application" of principles that might otherwise be regarded as mere theoretical speculation.

As for specific techniques, the lessons of Satmar are, of course, of more limited scope, since they are geared to the preservation of particular values in a peculiar setting. Of special interest, though, is the contribution to control made by negative aspects of socialization, by omission in the socialization process to inculcate capabilities that might enable individuals to adjust to the informal side of life outside the community, and especially the absence of training for independent decision-making. To be sure, the limited applicability of this purposeful omission is obvious. It is difficult to imagine that, say, Swedish society would have much use for such a strategy. But collectivities facing threats of defection may well need to resort to some variant of this technique, whether they maintain border guards or not. Such seems to be the case in the Soviet Union, where the drive to eliminate Western art forms has often reached hysterical dimensions. To a lesser extent the phenomenon is visible in the United States, where insecure elements (e.g., the American Legion) feel threatened whenever they realize that high school students (occasionally those in college) are exposed to a definition of reality that clashes with their own "patriotic"

view. The same may be said for training in independent decision-making, as—to use the same examples—both totalitarian
regimes and threatened segments in our midst seem to have little use for encouraging independent thinking, especially among
the young.

Cultural and Social Change

Examining the role of economic and technological factors in
the process of change, we see a different picture. Unlike in the
case of control, we cannot disregard economics as an independent dynamic force. For example, the highly important change
in attitude toward job-holding by women is motivated exclusively by a desire for more family income. The notions that
keeping house is boring and that women need more interesting
outlets for their energy are alien to Satmar, at least at this
moment.

Nonetheless, economics is not alone in generating pressures
for social and cultural change. If we look, for example, at the
educational scene, we find that the major changes there,
namely, bureaucratization and the creation of a girls' school,
have their origin in the legal-political sphere. The law demanding a secular department in private schools dictated the consol-
idation of schooling into a larger organization which, in turn,
had to be bureaucratized; whereas compulsory education laws
necessitated the formation of Bais Ruchel. Political reality is the
precipitant here. The fact that Satmar is not an autonomous
polity forces adaptation to the requirements of the outside
political structure.[1]

Then, even where economics appears to be the prime mover
of change, the process is different from that suggested by Marxians, who regard the social relationships that govern a given system of production as most crucial. M.J. Levy, for example, has
argued that once a society accepts industry as a mode of production, it will eventually evolve a system of social relations
based on what one can do, rather than on what one is. The reason for the inevitability of such a development is, according to
Levy, the fact that industrial work must be governed by impersonality. The risks are too high to evaluate personnel on criteria

other than ability to perform, and it is only a matter of time before impersonality spreads to social relationships outside the shop.[2]

In Satmar this does not seem to be the case. After two decades of working and dealing in an impersonal setting, Satmarer seem, if anything, more appreciative of the primary community to which they return after work. True, this is not an autonomous society, and one may ask whether the pattern described by Levy may not be more characteristic of economically autonomous societies where (1) one is forced to relate to fellow members of his own culture both at work and outside of it, and (2) the motivation to escape into one's own community after working in a strange environment is lacking. Data from other sources, however, lead us to believe that the tendency not to allow impersonality to permeate all social life is not confined to special cases of unassimilated minorities.[3]

Rather than the social structure of work, what has influenced the acceptance of working wives in Satmar seems to have been the value of conspicuous consumption. When translated into ever-rising aspirations, this value made it difficult to accept the limitations imposed by the culture. The quest for new sources of income led the majority to send their wives to work, which, in turn, created further strains on the traditional system.

How typical is the above sequence? This is a question that cannot be answered at the moment; only cross-cultural data could eventually provide an answer. What does seem clear is that even changes originating in the economic sphere do not universally follow the sequence proposed by Marx and his followers.

A related theoretical problem on which the case of Satmar may shed some light involves the sequence of change as it relates to the core or "focus" of the culture. This question was tackled years ago by Melville Herskovits, whose "cultural focus" theory of change is built around it.[4] Herskovits proposes that change tends to begin at the focus, the institutional area that lies at the very heart of a given culture, and spreads from there to the outlying regions where change is resisted to a greater degree. The reason given by Herskovits is psychological in nature. The things that matter most to a given group—so the argument goes—are in the forefront of thought and attention. Intensive attention also involves a search for improvement, which, in turn, produces variety and change. Conversely, people tend to think less of those areas of existence they consider to be of lesser importance, and therefore tend to be less motivated to change the customary way of fringe activities.

In Satmar there is little doubt that whatever change has occurred has followed a path diametrically opposite from the one claimed by Herskovits. Very little has been changing at the focal area of religious belief and practice; the dynamics described clearly originate in regions such as economics, politics, and some facets of socialization, regions peripheral to the culture and unguarded by its specific norms. From there, the pressure moves toward the inner spheres.

Some students of change have for various reasons either neglected or rejected Herskovits' theory.[5] Yet, the notion of "focus" does seem to have merit. We may not wish to go to Herskovits' extreme of disregarding the nature of the institutional area and concentrating exclusively on the position that a given area occupies within a given culture. At the same time, in our search for pattern in change it seems equally unreasonable to disregard position altogether. It would seem plausible to suggest that, for example, changes in religious practice would have wider ramifications in societies such as those of Medieval Western Europe where religion occupied a central position, than in contemporary United States in which religion is of marginal importance.

One possibility is to offer a modified hypothesis, introducing another variable, namely, existing norms and attitudes toward change in the focal area. Not only do Americans—one of Herskovits' illustrations—focus on technology, but they also value technological change positively. (Advertisers are well aware that in the case of a technological product, "new" means "better.") Similarly, for Israelis (another example cited by Herskovits), especially Zionists, revival of Hebrew as a living language is an essential component of the ideal to reclaim the ancient homeland and its transformation from a relic to a settlement of working and living people. Change in the language is therefore taken as testimony that the language is again alive, not a petrified medium for esoteric study. Conversely, Satmar culture contains strict anti-change norms vis-à-vis its focal area, religion. Anything that resembles innovation here is suspect and automatically rejected. In cases of this kind, change may have to intrude through the margins, where receptivity is greater and caution against change is weak or altogether absent.

Of course, this begs the further question of what determines whether a given culture will welcome or reject change in its central region. While a full discussion of this question would lead us further afield than we could reasonably venture within the framework of this study, one observation seems warranted. The determining factor does not appear to be whether or not economics and technology are of central importance. The buffalo cult in Toda[6] is tied to the economic activity of buffalo herding; yet the norms against change in the cult seem every bit as stringent as those in Satmar when it comes to religion. On the other hand, Israelis appear no less eager to change the noneconomic sphere of language than Americans delight in changing automobile models. The world of reality just appears to be more complex than monocausal theorists would have us believe.

Summary of Propositions

To summarize this discussion we may abstract a set of propositions concerning the universal processes of control and change.

1. Control of a society over its members can be accomplished without controlling economic resources.

2. Similarly, effective control does not require use or threat of coercive force.

3. A high degree of conformity may be achieved through the rewarding mechanism of informal relationships that would be denied the deviant, provided (a) judicious use in which both extremes of quick rejection and rare or selective application are avoided, and (b) serious adult attitude toward norms in question is reflected in absence of double standards for adults and the young. In other words, judicious socialization plus absence of double standards are prerequisites for (though not absolutely assurance of) effective informal-relations-based control.

4. Where defection is a serious threat, effective control may require that the socialization process carefully avoid equipping members with skills enabling facile adaption to reward systems of other cultures.

5. Change may originate in any cultural sphere, including economic activity.

6. Where acceptance of and involvement in a given economic/technological system seems to generate wider change, social relations governing production may not be the decisive factor. The sequence may well begin, especially in the case of modernized systems, with acceptance of aspirations for high consumption, which may then strain those elements of the culture that limit earning capacity.

7. In searching for a sequence of change, it is advisable to pay attention not only to the nature of the institutional area where change originates, but also to the position that the area in question occupies vis-à-vis the entire culture. When change begins at the focus it is likely to have wider and quicker consequences for the remainder of the culture than when it originates at the periphery.

8. Receptivity to change at the focus of the culture is likely to accelerate sociocultural innovation. Where change is welcomed in the focal area, innovation is likely to proceed from the center to the periphery; whereas in cultures containing anti-change norms in their central regions, dynamics are likely to follow an opposite course, from margin to center. In the first case we may observe a rapid pace of change and in the second, a much slower one.

9. Whether or not economic activity is focal to a culture does not seem to determine the degree of receptivity to change at the focus, since we find cases of both receptivity and resistance to change at the focus in both situations.

These are mere suggestions, hypotheses which need to be further tested in larger quantities of data. The problems raised here, however, are basic to a better understanding of our times. Maintaining a reasonable balance between preservation and change is at the root of most national and international dilemmas today.

Although the basic nature of both control and change described above still exist in today's Satmar, significant changes have occurred on both fronts. Control now includes a generous portion of coercion, including economic measures, denial of access to community facilities, denial of other membership privileges, and alleged violence. At the same time, what is left of the once exclusive primary-reward techniques, have undergone modification and weakening. A new, more acculturated generation emerges which finds it easier to escape insulation and to find substitutes for family-and-community-based rewards.

As control changes and tensions increase, the old dynamic forces, still at work, are bolstered by the changing balance between reward and cost of Satmar membership. Understandably, the result is the acceleration of the change process, most significantly manifested in internal conflict and in various forms of deviance, both virtually non-existent a generation ago.

It bears repeating that in spite of all this, the basic culture of Satmar has, to this point in time, been preserved. Desertion is still being kept at a minimum and even those who do leave, wind up in culturally similar settings, thus reflecting a high degree of success of Satmar control when it comes to basics. At the moment, the manifest threat is to the nature of the top of the social pyramid. What we notice at the lower reaches are attempts to escape tension, rather than to rebel against the culture as such.

Turning now to the process of change, we again observe both continuity and discontinuity. We have seen the continued role of the economic factor, which remains in the marginal region of Satmar culture. The faint beginnings of feminism also encounter no resistance from well-established core norms. On the other hand, internal strife around the issue of leadership definitely does touch a central nerve. If this situation lingers on without a peaceful resolution, it may well trigger basic changes in community organization and in the role of the leader, even though the daily life style may remain virtually intact for a considerable period of time. Even so, we see here the possibility of at least some changes emanating at what Herskovits called the cultural core, a development new at Satmar.

Finally, examining the theoretical propositions arrived—at three decades ago, One finds it necessary to suggest a few amendments: 1-3. Regarding the first three propositions—the possibility of sociocultural control via human relations, without economic or other coercion—the recent injection of sanctions into the Satmar control system does not negate the possibility of their omission. In fact, this has been demonstrated for a period of over three decades of Satmar's existence in the United States, not an insignificant time span for an immigrant population in this country. The question which the history of the last decade raises is whether the changed conditions created by the passing of the Old Rebbeh necessitated resort to these mechanisms. One could argue (as I am inclined to) that the necessity has not been demonstrated. On the contrary, there seems to be room for claiming that control-effectiveness might have been greater had the leadership refrained from use of coercion. Since dissidents have appeared in all branches of Satmar, a close inspection—with an eye on comparison and contrast—of the situation in the three locations examined yields some interesting and instructive details. In Borough Park we find least use of force. A small group rebelled, separated and moved into a separate location without being disturbed in any fashion. A logical explanation for the leadership's failure to react harshly seems to be that this is the most pluralistic scene. A number of Hasidic communities basically acceptable to, some even admired by Satmarer can be found in this part of Brooklyn. They all have full private school facilities. Satmar apparently recognizes that its leverage there is quite limited. Regardless of the reason involved, it is a fact that failure to react to local dissidents coincides with virtually no damage or threat to the Borough Park Satmar establishment. In Williamsburg, where Satmar headquarters are presently located, dissidents receive a much sharper rebuke from the leadership than do their counterparts in Borough Park. Again, the explanation seems to lie in the degree of dominance. Williamsburg also has a few other Hasidic groups, whose school facilities are, however, not quite complete, especially lacking in the area of girls' education. Thus sensing greater dominance, Satmar has been reacting more harshly to opponents. The latter counterattacked and established a girls' school of their own which, in turn Satmar sharply condemned and ordered sanctions against parents and children connected with dissident schools. However, the degree of turmoil and damage to Satmar still seems to be minor. It is Kiryas Yoel, where Satmar is actually the only extant community and where, as noticed, it claims exclusive legitimacy, that the struggle is fiercest. The full establishment arsenal is being deployed in the war against the "rebels." It is in the same location where we find the most significant countermeasures by the dissidents in the form of founding a complete school network for both genders, building several independent ritual baths and establishing an underground religious court which issues pamphlets attacking official acts, as well as their claimed justification by Jewish religious law. It is also there that, as the election figures of January 17, 1991 suggest, the challenge to Satmar seems to be most serious. One may thus plausibly posit the existence of an inverse relationship between utilization of punitive measures and degree of effectiveness of the control system.

4. In the light of what has been happening in Satmar and in the world since the demolition of the Iron Curtain, one is led to doubt the long-term possibility in our high-tech world of insulation against even informal elements of rival, especially neighboring, cultures. Thus, proposition 4 may have to be rephrased to read: *societies which feel threatened by rival cultures will attempt to avoid equipping youngsters with skills that enable informal communication with members of those strange cultures.* This way we avoid both the claim of necessity and the implication of ability to have long-term success in this endeavor.

5-6. I see no need for any alterations in these two. As seen in much we have discussed till now, their validity does not seem to be challenged by recent developments.

7-8. Our observation regarding the current conflict around the issue of leadership, no doubt a focal area in Satmar, seems to necessitate amending the notion that change at the center is likely to have quick consequences in the culture as a whole. For, in spite of the conflict, Satmar is not in imminent danger of collapse as a culture. What seems to be warranted is a distinction between focal changes straining continuity of culture patterns affecting daily life and between those challenging some structural elements. It is in the first case that spread of change throughout the cultural web may be rapid; whereas in the latter case, the possibility might exist that while some restructuring in the affected social sphere may be necessary, the rest of the culture may escape radical surgery.

9. As with propositions five and six, I see no need for alteration in this proposition.

Notes

1 It is, of course, possible to argue that the American political and educational systems are themselves products of modern technology. But this is an unproved thesis. It is doubtful, to say the least, whether the Soviet Union will eventually develop patterns similar to those of the United States. Should Satmar have wound up within the Soviet orbit, it would no doubt have been forced to make changes of a completely different nature—changes that would, again, have been forced by the Soviet political, not technological, system.

2 M.J. Levy, "Some Sources of the Vulnerability of the Structures of Relatively Non-Industrialized Societies to Those of Highly Industrialized Societies," in B. F. Hoselitz, ed., *The Progress of Underdeveloped Areas* (Chicago: University of Chicago Press, 1952), pp. 113-125.

3 *Cf.*, for example, W. Bell and M. D. Boat, "Urban Neighborhood and Informal Social Relations," *American Journal of Sociology*, 62:4 (January 1957), 391-398.

4 M.J. Herskovits, *Man and His Works* (New York: Alfred A. Knopf, 1948), pp. 542-560.

5 See, for example, H.I. Hogbin, *Social Change* (London: C.A. Watts & Co., 1958), pp. 89-95.

6 The case of the Toda is mentioned by Herskovits in his discussion of cultural focus. For the original report, see D.G. Mandelbaum, "Culture Change Among the Nilgiri Tribes," *American Anthropologist*, 43:1 (January-March 1941), 19-26.

XVI

Conclusion: Some Thoughts On Insular Existence

BEYOND the generic problems discussed in the last chapter, Satmar elicits responses to dilemmas associated with insular existence—dilemmas from the perspective of Satmar proper, from that of other minorities, and from that of the overall pluralistic society.

Whither Satmar?

All things considered, how viable does Satmar's social fabric appear to be at present, and what may one venture to predict concerning its chances for future survival?

Satmar's structure is basically sound, but it contains flaws which, if not corrected, may one day undermine the community's health and pose serious obstacles to its continued existence. Of the problems discussed in Chapter 13, two appear to be the most serious: the discrepancy between economic aspiration and limitations on earning imposed by cultural restrictions, and the absence of an heir to the Rov. It is difficult to see how several thousand adults with ever-expanding middle class desires will continue for long to accept the fact that they must earn their livelihood within the constantly shrinking range of occupations open to individuals with a high school education or less. Within a megalopolis the size of New York City, even this narrow range may be sufficiently large to support thousands of families. But living in the midst of New York City only accentuates Satmar's predicament. Aside from the need to maintain insulation against cultural currents with which one is in daily contact, there is the more difficult problem of safeguarding peace and security while residing next door to disliked and hostile ethnic aggregates. In addition, the climate of the big city is perhaps one of the main factors in nurturing the desire for conspicuous consumption, the desire that is at the root of the economic problem. Satmarer are thus caught in a vicious cycle. In fact, during the late fifties and early sixties a community-wide movement had been under way in Satmar to move into an isolated development away from the metropolitan area, precisely to escape undesirable contact and to build an autonomous setting where the quest for luxury could be more easily tamed. The movement failed due to the resistance of large numbers who felt that their and their wives' employment depended upon New York City's economic diversity. Thus the community remained in the city, and so did its unresolved economic dilemma.

The second and most serious immediate problem is that of finding a successor to the Rov. Beyond doubt, failure to do so will force thoroughgoing adjustments in the system that may alter it beyond recognition. For the individual, inability to turn to the Rov for guidance will require adjustment to a new reality in which one must make and accept responsibility for one's own decisions. On the community level, the absence of a unifying leader will inevitably spell fragmentation. The common sentiment of past loyalty will probably not be strong enough to prevent large numbers from drifting away. And even though most of them will in all likelihood retain the main elements of Hasidic culture for some time to come, Satmar as a distinct powerful unit may cease to exist.

Jewish Orthodoxy

The phenomenon of Satmar must also be considered within the wider context of Jewish Orthodoxy, for the United States phase of this community coincides with the remarkable renascence of Jewish Orthodoxy in this country. While many Orthodox Jews have looked askance at extremes, most have looked at Satmar with respect and admiration. It has become a symbol of Orthodoxy's tenacity and ability to defy the melting-pot ethos. Thus it is proper to ask what Satmar's experience over two decades suggests about the prospects and problems of Orthodox Judaism in the Western environment.

On the one hand, there is little doubt that Satmar offers encouragement to Orthodox Jews in the West, for it has done away with many earlier shibboleths. Some thousand families have demonstrated that one can exist in the United States while adhering to such fundamentals as the observance of the Sabbath and the holidays, and the dietary restrictions of kashrut. Above all, one can even bring up his children as Orthodox Jews. In fact, Satmarer have done much more than this. They have brought to New York City their way of life by wearing exotic garb and celebrating weddings and holidays in the streets, frequently obstructing traffic while doing so. What is more, the surrounding population has come to accept all this as normal. This contrasts sharply to the pessimism that pervaded the Orthodox camp a few decades earlier when the air in America was considered nonkosher, when adhering to Orthodoxy was believed to require enormous sacrifices which only a scattered few were likely to accept, and when the chances for educating large numbers of the American-born children as Orthodox Jews appeared slim indeed. As for open observance of customs on any scale, that was unthinkable. In the United States before World War II, even Orthodox Jews seem to have accepted the slogan of the nineteenth-century Russian Enlightenment: "Be a Jew in your house and a human being in the street!" That Satmar has been considered a guiding force in the change of mood is obvious to all who are acquainted with the Orthodox scene—and legitimately so.

On the other side of the coin, Satmar has also brought into sharp relief two genuine problems with which Orthodox Jews here have barely grappled, and with less than a clear appreciation of their magnitude.

Zionism presents a complex and many-faceted dilemma for Orthodoxy. Some rudiments of the problem appeared, as we have already seen, at the beginnings of Zionism. The thrill provided by the prospect of an age-old dream materializing was marred by reluctance to accept redemption initiated by man— and spearheaded by secular Jews at that. The three-quarters of a century that have since passed have not only failed to solve this original rift but have widened and deepened it. Orthodoxy has not worked out a satisfactory reconciliation between the realization of Jewish secular statehood and Messianic belief. Even the extreme Zionist wing of Orthodoxy, which insists on viewing Israel as a "beginning of the Redemption," often finds it difficult to defend an anti-religious (not merely religiously neutral) majority in Israel and public policy that frequently reflects that majority's antagonism toward the religious minority.

At the same time, the solution adopted by the extreme Orthodox wing represented by Satmar, namely, complete rejection of Zionism and Israel, does not seem correct either. This is not merely a question of practicality and feasibility; it touches on vital Orthodox principles. Most Orthodox Jews think it impossible to dissociate completely from the movement that counts among its accomplishments restoration of Jewish sovereignty in the Holy Land, accommodation for persecuted Jews anywhere in the world, and restoration of a degree of self-esteem to Jews everywhere. Then, too, it is difficult from an Orthodox religious point of view to justify rejection of Jews—any kind of Jews. The mechanism of excommunication, never used too frequently, has been discontinued during the last few hundred years. Even Satmar has not advocated its restoration, despite the fact that its attitude and behavior vis-a-vis Zionists has often been as if the latter were indeed excommunicated. Perhaps most dangerous is the risk of being allied with international anti-Semitism, an agonizing prospect for any Jew.

To date no satisfactory solution to this dilemma has been worked out within the Orthodox camp. The prevailing attitude seems to be that it is wiser to deal with each detail of the problem as it arises, and to hope that time will somehow take care of the matter. To what degree this hope is justified remains to be seen. All we note is that the problem is a serious one, and that Satmarer, by acting as chief spokesmen for the extreme wing that rejects Zionism completely, have kept this problem in full view of Orthodox Jewry.

Equally serious is the second problem, that of maintaining an appropriate balance between insulation from and participation in the surrounding society. Satmar's advocacy of a high degree of insulation, especially in matters of higher education, has an even wider following within Orthodoxy than its stand vis-à-vis Zionism. For example, many Orthodox institutes of higher learning have adopted during the last few decades a policy that forbids their students to attend college. The difficulty is that during the same two decades a college degree has become a prerequisite for decent employment. Can Orthodox Jews continue to ignore this reality? Aside from the occupational factor, can Orthodoxy allow itself to ignore developments in the world of Western learning at a time and in a place where Jews have become full citizens and presumably do not wish to return to a ghetto? One could even argue that the fear of being exposed to what others have to say is in itself an admission of lack of confidence in one's own views. He who feels confident in his stance should logically not seek to avoid confrontation with challenging alternatives.

A final aspect of this problem is a concomitant of insulation, partly a justification for it—the need to maintain internally a negative image of the outside world. This frequently results in joining hands, implicitly, with radicals (both right and left, but especially on the right) who have an equally vested interest, albeit for different reasons, in maintaining such an image of contemporary Western society. Such an alliance is, to say the least, precarious, for these same elements have traditionally been the main carriers of anti-Semitism.

Opponents of insulation have not yet worked out a formula for an acceptable mode of full participation. After all, a college environment is not exactly an Orthodox Jew's dream. To mention just one example, sexual freedom is incompatible with Orthodox Jewish living, and no one has yet figured out how to insulate orthodox college students from the strong temptations available on campus. Nor has anyone found a way to reconcile the attitude of free inquiry with the Orthodox demand for a degree of doctrinal rigidity. At least such reconciliation has not taken place on a wide scale. As in the case of Zionism, Orthodox Jews have dealt with this problem on a stop-gap basis rather than attempting to work out a long-range solution. One doubts whether the stop-gap approach will prove adequate, whether Orthodox Jews will be able to delay much longer the painful process of meeting head-on this admittedly difficult problem which Satmar, among others, has kept in the forefront of Orthodox consciousness.

Jewish Existence

Satmar is an atypical minority among contemporary Jews. But its experience is not without significance for Jews everywhere. Far from being a curious sect that tore away from the mainstream of Jewish history, Satmar is an extreme expression of the commitment to Orthodox Jewish living according to a pattern formed before the modern era. Unless one chooses to dismiss all of Orthodoxy as a temporary nuisance, a mere vestige of the past that has no significance for the present, one would do well not to ignore such phenomena as Satmar.

To recall some pertinent history, during the nineteenth and twentieth centuries distinctly different patterns of relationship between Orthodox and non-Orthodox developed in Eastern and Western Europe. In the East, external pressure prevented a definite split, while in the freer atmosphere of the West, the Orthodox and non-Orthodox parted company. In the United States a curious situation emerged. On the one hand, the climate is Western in character, so that on the basis of the European experience one might expect Orthodoxy to go its own way. But this has not happened. Several factors are responsible. First, after the waves of mass migration of the late nineteenth and twentieth centuries, East European Jews came to dominate the Jewish scene, and they tended to continue their habit of cooperation. Then Jews developed a congregational religious structure, which had the effect of rendering a split between Orthodox and non-Orthodox unnecessary. Motivation to separate had originated in the tensions that developed from the need to cooperate in a tightly knit community structure. The absence of such an umbrella allowed each group to form its own independent congregation without resorting to large-scale separation between denominations. Finally, the holocaust that descended on European Jewry during World War II and the emergence of a Jewish state soon thereafter created a common focus for all Jews and discouraged internal fragmentation.

This common focus also created a form of community orga- nization—the Federations—which, loose as they may be, have brought back the importance of cooperating within a single structural framework. At the same time, the tensions inherent in such cooperation have also begun to reemerge, and they are especially acute in the Orthodox camp. Orthodox Jews are not only a numerical minority but tend to be the less affluent sector of the Jewish scene. In the Federations, where power is corre- lated with levels of financial contribution, Orthodox Jews inevitably wield little power. Tension is visible when it comes to such problems as allocating funds for the needs of American Jewry. Orthodox Jews who have built a large network of all-day schools throughout the United States would like the Federations to finance these schools. The Federations have, with few excep- tions, refused to heed this request, causing a great deal of frus- tration and dissatisfaction in the Orthodox camp.

Now Satmar has presented a concrete alternative. As in many other matters, Satmarer refused to join most American Ortho- dox Jews in cooperating with the non-Orthodox. As soon as they arrived in the United States, Satmarer decided to continue the separate organization to which they were accustomed abroad. This way they became also financially independent. During the time of my research, for example, Satmarer them- selves managed to provide some 90 per cent of their million- dollar school budget. Many Orthodox Jews have come to envy Satmar's independence. Lately one hears voices within the Orthodox camp that Orthodoxy should follow the example of Central and Western Europe before World War II and create its own organizational framework. Although it is premature to predict a genuine movement in this direction, such a possibility does exist. If this should come about, the American Jewish community might experience a serious split resulting in the emergence of two distinctly separate patterns of development. This possibility demands caution by those who would attempt to generalize about American Jewry as a single entity.

On a broader level, Satmar is a reminder, though in extreme form, to all Jews that one day they may be forced to come to terms with the problem of what constitutes Jewishness beyond living in or sympathizing with an independent Jewish polity.

Whether one rejects, accepts, or is neutral to the idea of Jewish statehood, one may not be able to avoid explaining the huge investment necessary to preserve a Jewish identity.[1]

Thus, whatever one's opinion about Satmar, the questions it raises about Jewish unity and Jewish identity are vital problems for Jews, wherever they live. Jews of all persuasions ought to look more closely at their exotic brethren.

Preservation of Minority Culture

As a minority that has succeeded until now in preventing absorption by the majority, Satmar also contains a few lessons for the general problem of preserving minority culture.

If Satmar demonstrates the possibility for survival of Jewish Orthodoxy in this country, there is no reason why this lesson should be confined to Orthodox Jews. Satmar may also provide some insight into the requirements for successful survival of other minority cultures. It seems reasonable to suggest that, first, there must be strong motivation for the desire to hold on to one's culture. Nostalgic longing for sausage, goulash, or gefilte fish is not likely to constitute sufficient motivation. More important and deep-seated values seem necessary, values to which the members of the minority cling in the conviction that these are superior to those held by the majority and are thus worthwhile preserving.

Even so, this deep-seated motivation may not be a sufficient guarantee for successful preservation. Social scientists, in their reluctance to deal with such concepts as "free will," have traditionally played down the importance of conscious effort.[2] In analyzing minority survival, they have instead searched for impersonal sociocultural variables.[3] It may be time to take a second look at the importance played by conscious decision-making and willingness to invest money and effort for the achievement of a given goal. The fact is that hundreds of thousands of Orthodox Jews who had similar values to those found in Satmar failed to survive merely because they did not translate their desire into concrete action. In contrast, Satmar decided at the very beginning that it would not follow in the footsteps of earlier immigrants; that it would build schools and a community structure at considerable sacrifice in order to preserve its way of life. That it has succeeded until now suggests that others might do likewise.

The Pluralist Society

Let us, finally, turn our attention to the other side of the fence and consider our case and its implications from the perspective of the larger society within which the minority is situated.

The change of mood in the United States during recent years —from an erstwhile emphasis on melting the minorities into a culturally homogenous nation, toward acceptance of the idea of cultural pluralism—is well known. The reasons underlying the change are obvious. As the pace of immigration diminished and the proportion of immigrants to natives became smaller, the anxiety of the "establishment" naturally subsided. In addition, international events during and after World War II projected the United States into a role of world leadership that made it difficult to continue at home a policy of de facto intolerance of cultural differences.

It would, however, be a mistake to assume that the change-over toward cultural pluralism has been complete. Public schools in minority areas still tend to consider it as one of their chief legacies to Americanize immigrant children, usually in the name of opening the path toward upward mobility. Public officials still display uneasiness when confronted with unassimilated minorities, especially those whose value systems prevent them from fully participating in the larger society.

Regardless of one's opinion about the survival of the melting-pot zeal, one should admit the existence of a problem: cultural pluralism versus national unity. The case for cultural pluralism can be made not only in the name of humanistic value but on the basis of realistic analysis. First, we recognize today that by their very nature complex societies are pluralistic. A society may have the option of outlawing ethnic or religious differences, but it cannot possibly eliminate the cultural pluralism that accompanies occupational and class differentiation. If one accepts this realistic nucleus, it is difficult to limit pluralism to occupation and class, and not include ethnicity or religion. One could

argue further that from a purely practical point of view, pluralism is beneficial. A society that allows the coexistence of many
alternatives should have more flexibility and viability than one
committed to the narrow path of one "right" alternative. For
example, Americans may discover from the Satmar educational
system that schools can be viable without emphasizing occupational values. This would indeed be a strange idea for
Americans who are so used to thinking of schools in terms of
jobs; but when faced with a crisis, as American education
currently is, it could not hurt to reexamine this premise.
Americans might also learn something from Satmar about
social control. Some may ask themselves, in view of Satmar's
success, whether adult cynicism may have something to do with
juvenile transgression. One could, no doubt, cite similar
examples from other cases such as the Amish or Hutterites.

Nevertheless, the problem of working out a formula for unity
in spite of diversity remains. There is no question that when a
minority retains a value system significantly different from that
of the majority, it is not likely to participate fully in the majority
society. Satmarer, for example, will not contribute their share of
physicians, lawyers, or any professionals, not only in the United
States, but wherever they may settle. If one accepts the legitimacy or even the inevitability of less than full participation, the
question still remains, what constitutes minimally acceptable
participation?

On the societal level, this dilemma appears within every society with a degree of complexity and heterogeneity. On a higher
plan, the question of how to achieve peaceful coexistence
despite cultural diversity is world-wide. A generation ago,
anthropologists, under the impact of the Nazi horrors, hotly
debated the issue, arguing whether recognition of difference
(cultural relativism) or emphasis on similarity was the proper
road to peace. Today, a generation later, the debate has subsided but the problem remains and, with a world constantly
shrinking, begs more than ever for solution.

The relationship between the micro problem of fitting an
exotic cultural type such as a Satmarer Hasid into American
society and the macro problem of world peace may seem far-
fetched. Yet they do appear to be related. If we are to believe

Hitler, his raging Judaeophobia had some rather modest beginnings. He used to look upon Jews as Germans, until

> One day when I was walking through the inner city [of Vienna] I suddenly came upon a being clad in a long caftan, with black curls.
> Is this also a Jew? was my first thought.
> ... Secretly and cautiously I watched the man, but the longer I stared at this strange face and scrutinized one feature after the other, the more my mind reshaped the first question into another form: Is this also a German?[4]

How many times Hitler's "revelation" has been experienced with less tragic consequences we shall never know. But surely we have reached a point of civilization when such an attitude is no longer tolerable. Diverse cultures *can* coexist peacefully, this much we know. Is it outlandish to suggest that how a Satmarer Hasid makes his way within American society may tell us a great deal about how to approach larger problems of life between peoples?

Notes

1 Observing the current Jewish scene, one cannot fail to be impressed with the curious shift of roles between Orthodox and non-Orthodox Jews when it comes to the questions about the nature of Jewish identity and continued existence. The Orthodox, who otherwise accept a mystical definition of reality, are in this case very mundane and practical. They see Jewishness as consisting of concrete behavior, and existence as depending on practical contingencies. The worldly "liberal" Jews tend to define Jewishness in terms of some theoretical values, unrelated to any concrete behavior, and to see existence as guaranteed by some mythical historic force.

2 For an illustration of the dogmatic nature of the assumption that rational action plays no significant role in human behavior, cf. E. H. Wolf's review of S. N. Eisenstadt, *The Political System of Empires* in *American Anthropologist*, 67:1 (February 1965), 172-176. The reviewer asks: "What sort of phenomena are explained by saying that rulers might or might not develop autonomous goals? What kind of sociological concept is the human will?" (p. 175). The debate over the recent vogue for some sociologists to return to an action orientation has centered mostly on such problems as the possibility of a value-free sociology, or the compatibility of action with scientific research. The question concerning the theoretical place of rational action in human behavior, which would seem to relate to the very heart of the action problem, has been largely ignored (at least in the literature that has reached the writer to this date).

3 See, for example, S. A. Freed, "Suggested Type Societies in Acculturation Studies," *American Anthropologist*, 59:1 (February 1957), 55-67.

4 Adolf Hitler, *Mein Kampf* (New York: Reynal and Hitchcock, 1939), p. 73.

XVII

Conclusion II

The opportunity to revisit a field a quarter of a century after originally studying it, is a rare privilege indeed. Finding a new generation under new leadership, alongside a good portion of the old population, including many erstwhile informants; as well as beholding a culture which is basically the same one observed decades ago, yet one that has undergone important changes, all provide a unique perspective for reflection. It affords the possibility to compare and contrast the old with the new, as well as to assess, against a new background, the validity and adequacy of ideas and conclusions reached analyzing a bygone reality. The addenda to the foregoing chapters are intended to share with the reader at least some of these. In addition, an investigation of this sort, an originally unplanned longitudinal study, tends to yield new insights in theoretical/conceptual areas beyond the boundaries set for the first study or even the restudy. In order to accomplish both tasks—evaluation of old ideas and forwarding of fresh ones—it seemed appropriate to deviate from the updating pattern utilized in previous chapters and, instead, add a second Conclusion.

Comparing Notes with the Past

We shall first examine the diagnoses/prognoses offered a generation ago, to see how they stand up in light of what has actually happened in the last few decades.

Continuity of Community and Culture
In the sixties and early seventies it seemed that even though Satmar culture did not face immediate disintegrative threats, its

continued existence as a significant community hinged on 1) satisfactory resolution of the succession problem; 2) finding a degree of equilibrium between an increasing level of economic/financial aspiration, on the one hand, and indigenous norms which tended to limit opportunities, on the other; and 3) adjustment to rapid population growth resulting from high birth-rate. Looking at the current scene, it seems that the community has so far managed to partially resolve all three problems and has, correspondingly, been fairly successful in remaining a significant sociocultural entity on American soil, especially the Jewish scene. They did settle on a successor who has been keeping the Satmar ship on course, albeit not without difficulty. The fact that the difficulties are internal, thus unprecedented and novel in character, keeps one from regarding the succession as an unqualified success.

On the economic front, new technological development, especially in electronics, has opened new opportunities, creating a cluster of trades that are clean, have no history of stigmatized hard physical labor or dirty unhealthy shops, and thus appeal to this basically middle-class population. Most significant has been the advent of the computer. Readjustment of virtually the entire American economic scene to the advantages presented by the dazzling spread of this field, has made it possible for capable individuals to get on board without formal college degrees. Many Satmarer, both men and women, have done just that; some have managed to beat a path to the employment offices of large corporations, a feat their forebears a generation ago could not have envisioned in their wildest dreams. However, the problem does not seem to be resolved completely. Aside from the fact that not all individuals have the talent or inclination to enter high tech occupations, the rapidity with which new developments in electronics render older systems obsolete, places increasing limits on those with mere technical training. Thus, the new opportunities may prove not to be sufficient in the future. This is especially so in view of the clear fact (indicated in the update to Chapter X) that the upward push on the aspirational side of the equation not only continues, but appears to be accelerating. Even that part of the population which managed to escape the Big Apple has not experienced

the hoped-for relief. Kiryas Yoel is not really as isolated from
New York City as the planners of the exurban settlement had
hoped. A few visits convinced the writer that the middle-class
push for material possessions is as strong there as it is in the
metropolitan enclaves, if not stronger.

Finally, the emergence of four autonomous sub-units may be
considered to constitute a partial solution to the population
explosion in this prolific community. Again, however, it does
not resolve the growth problem in its entirety, for a number of
reasons. First, the growth is so rapid that by now some of the
subunits are already too large for the type of primary informal
control on which the community depends so much. Second, the
autonomous nature of the parts contain the possibility (some
claim, the probability) of an eventual complete split (a topic to
which we shall return). Last (certainly not least), the developed
internal conflict (to the genesis of which the increased population has, no doubt, been a contributing factor), is likely to
aggravate the process of dealing with the inevitable problems
resulting from numerical growth.

Thus, the following sketch of the future of Satmar as it looks
today is not that much different from that of a generation ago,
but does show some new wrinkles, which is natural since we are
now standing three decades later.

As mentioned before, numerous insiders expressed the opinion that a generation hence the community is likely to divide.
The present autonomy of the sub-units may be transformed
into complete independence. Additional splits may occur along
ideological and loyalty lines, following an age-old Hasidic pattern to bypass geographic boundaries (Cf. Chapter II). If fission
eventually occurs, it may bring about some unanticipated nor
mative change and may further weaken Satmar's already
reduced stature outside its boundaries.

It should be reemphasized, however, that the earlier predic-
tion regarding cultural continuity may justifiably be repeated
three decades later without any qualification whatsoever. Satmar has retained its basic way of life virtually intact and has
managed to bring up a generation in the middle of the nation's
largest metropolis and to imbue it with its culture, thus quintu-
pling the population in a matter of a single generation. Even

the prospect of eventual internal division(s) does not necessarily constitute a threat to the culture as such. It is tempting to argue that such a process may actually have the opposite effect. The emergence of more than one leader and the resulting absence of a central authority figure, may facilitate adaptive normative adjustments, thus obviating the necessity for radical change and the possibility of mass desertion. In other words, fission may turn out to have a positive net functional balance with regard to cultural preservation. Therefore, all considered, Satmar's daring effort to become established in the United States while resisting cultural assimilation, has so far been highly successful. One may thus arrive at the theoretical conclusion that the inevitability of assimilation envisioned by Robert E. Park and his students, has not been born out by reality, not if one beholds Satmar and related Orthodox Jewish scenes in the waning years of the Twentieth Century.

Orthodox Jewry, Zionism, and Higher Secular Education

To avoid ambiguity, terminological clarification is necessary. The designation "Orthodox Jew" is used to denote one who is generally committed to an officially unreformed Torah-based ideology and behavioral code. However, the Jewish Orthodox population, while sharing this basic commitment, at the same time displays a wide variety of shades. At the extreme left of the continuum we find religious Zionists (often called Modern Orthodox) for whom Yeshiva University serves as the academic base in this country. They at least claim to have solved problems associated with Zionism and higher education. Whether they actually did, is another question, which we shall raise soon. However, our main concern is with those to the right of the Zionist variant. It is this category that has struggled with these problems and on whom Satmar was seen to have had a significant influence.

For this Orthodox Jewish population, the dilemmas do not seem nearer to solution today than they appeared to be a generation ago. In spite of differences among sub-segments, the issues readily surface in conversation with both leaders and followers. Recognition of Satmar's role in challenging the pre-

World War II established acceptance of both Zionism and college-level education, is readily acknowledged by those right of center. So is its role in the post-World-War II resurgence of traditional Orthodoxy, here and world wide. However, compared to a generation ago, there is a marked shift to the past tense. With few exceptions, informants, both within and outside the Satmar community, display a great deal of ambiguity when assessing the role played by present-day Satmar. Outsiders are particularly outspoken on the subject. A sympathizer with the Satmar position on the subject of Zionism, put it this way: "The zealotry of present-day Satmar just doesn't have the ring of authenticity." This sentiment is widely echoed. Virtually all outsiders I contacted offered their opinion that this central ideological earmark does not possess its original luster. To a large degree this may well be a function of time. A glance at history clearly indicates that once they pass their pioneer stage, all utopian and quasi-utopian ideologies (e.g., Reformation, Enlightenment, Socialism) tend to lose a large portion of their early electrifying appeal.

In sum, Satmar's problems envisioned a generation ago have been partially resolved and, consequently, the community survived in modified form. However, life there, as anywhere else, is constantly evolving. Further adaptive modification will be necessary for survival into the next generation. Not surprisingly, the necessary adaptations, seem to lie in the same general areas; succession, population growth, and synchronization of normative guidelines with economic aspiration will continue to present basic challenges to the dual task of cultural survival and Americanization. Details will, of course, differ; however, just as I wrote three decades ago, I envision changes, but not imminent collapse. In addition to practical experience, today's Satmar has in its favor a changed cultural climate in this country, a climate in which different cultures existing in their own "islands" within the larger society are looked upon with increasing acceptance. This new climate, resulting from an increased popularity of multiculturalism, contrasts sharply with the atmosphere in the nineteen fifties when being different was regarded as being clannish and, worst of all, "Un-American."

More General Implications

Continuing my reexamination of earlier conclusions, a few words need to be said regarding the implications of Satmar for the wider subjects of continued Jewish existence as a distinct sub-culture and the still broader problems of a true pluralist society. Actually there is very little to add or modify here beyond the observation that in both areas the problems involved have not merely failed to disappear, but have actually become more acute and recognized for what they are.

Among Jews, intermarriage with non-Jews is steadily rising. The vague perception of what constitutes Jewishness when stripped of a tangible code of cultural behavior regulating daily life, no doubt lies at the root of this obnoxious bellwether problem which seems to defy solution. Thus, whether one likes or hates Satmar and other varieties of Orthodoxy, a Jew who wishes to keep a distinct identity cannot avoid facing the problem of what it is one wishes to preserve and at what price. Even the Modern Orthodox Jews, who do adhere to the Torah-based behavior code, cannot entirely avoid the problem. Their intense Zionist commitment raises the question of being Jewish outside the Jewish homeland. Furthermore, considering that in these circles commitment to Jewish political independence has been elevated to centrality, even in a religious sense, of being Jewish, one may ask a question (the mere mention of which is considered heresy): what would Jewishness be in the absence of a Jewish polity? or in a world in which nationalism would play a considerably reduced role in human affairs? In searching for an answer to these and related questions, one may have to engage in closer examination of "right wing" Orthodoxy, to see what one can learn from the latter's rather unexpected success during the post-World-War-II era.

On the still broader issue of pluralism within a larger society such as ours, the last few decades have witnessed the emergence of Black (or African American), Hispanic, Native American, and a variety of other ethnic identities once thought to have disappeared in the great American melting pot. Whether one accepts or rejects the legitimacy of bilingual education or of Black English, few maintain nowadays the illusion that all these are temporary phenomena and that one day Americans will accept a single homogeneous culture. The question of how unity is to be maintained alongside diversity, is more clearly recognized than it was a generation ago.

Moreover, the problem is not confined to the United States. As these lines are written (July, 1992), search for a viable E PLURIBUS UNUM formula has become global, but is especially visible on the European continent where recognition of the fact that technological development has made it more difficult even for relatively large nations to remain locked into narrow national boundaries, than it first appeared. Soon after World War II, Western Europe embarked on a path of regional cooperation. At first rather slow, the movement has gained momentum during the last few years. Not only was there no parallel movement toward cultural homogenization, but as the ideal of a European community draws closer to realization, anxiety about losing cultural identity surfaced in such areas as the British Isles and, of all places, Denmark, where a majority voted against joining the proposed tightening of the regional bond. Recently, the phenomenon and its attendant problems have moved East where it suddenly assumed critical dimensions. Collapse of the Soviet Union, Yugoslavia, and the rest of the former communist block has unleashed nationalist forces throughout formerly federated regions, despite recognition that none of the provinces crying out for independence can actually remain viable without some form of larger federation. What they seem to say (at least, we hope so) is that they agree with the idea of federation, as long as each unit is recognized as legitimately sovereign within its own boundaries, unlike the Soviet and Yugoslav pseudo-federations that were abused for the purpose of, respectively, Russian and Serbian colonization and domination. The process of reconciling the centrifugal and centripetal tendencies is likely to be difficult and costly, but inevitable. The point is that in this rapidly shrinking world, micro-level examination of islands such as Satmar, merit close scrutiny. These microcosms attempting cultural preservation without illusions of political independence and U.N. membership and simultaneously seeking integration within a larger society, while not providing models to follow, may at least help us behold the nature of problems involved, anticipate at least some difficulties, and indicate possible avenues of solution. Faced with the problem, we might do well to dust off the concept of "organic solidarity" proposed a century ago by Emile Durkheim and to relearn his lesson that as units increase in size, solidarity once based on similarity of parts, must now rest on interpendence of vastly dissimilar ones —pluralism instead of melting pots.

Returning to the case at hand, it seems that the analysis of Satmar and the prognosis offered at the conclusion of the original study seems to have more than withstood the test of time, both in regard to internal community dynamics and with respect to implications for the various worlds without.

Extending the Horizon

A restudy inevitably yields new ideas, new speculations. A new reality is not merely a revision of an earlier one, but contains elements that are actually new or almost so, elements that could hardly have been predicted before they appeared. For example, while it was possible to envision some problems accompanying the Satmar succession process, one could not have imagined their exact nature or the shape of the resulting internal conflict. New realities provide new vistas which enable the viewer to form fresh impressions, to draw new inferences. It is to the latter task that the final portion is devoted.

Routinization of Charisma

In earlier writings[1], I dwelt on the community aspect of Hasidism, on the fact that early in Hasidic history a new *type* of community emerged which I saw as the key to understanding Hasidism's survival for over two centuries in a variety of cultural settings. This form of community, I further argued, which is independent of geographic location, proved to be highly adaptive, not only for Jews whose geographic instability accelerated in the modern era, but, inadvertently became a highly adaptive community-type for modern man in general, due to industry's tendency to weaken and occasionally totally eliminate neighborhoods' and small towns' capacity to function as meaningful communities.

It is time now to look at another facet of the phenomenon. Granted, a variety of mobile communities have emerged during the last century-and-a-half which, instead of centering on a village or neighborhood, focus on occupation, ethnicity, religious organization and a variety of other communalities.[2] However, not many have organized around charismatic leaders; few have become dedicated followers of an individual they accepted as an extraordinarily gifted person whose decisions they unequivocally follow. In fact, not all Jews have become Hasidim. Of those who did, many left these fellowships, others joined them, and still others remained formal members, supporting and occasionally visiting the rebbeh and his court, but only partially following the path indicated by the "holy man." To understand this part of the movement, we need to turn to the subject of charismatic leadership, especially its routinization. This requires a brief review of the literature dealing with the subject.

Max Weber laid the foundation for the study of charisma basing his sketch (as we would expect from a grand theorist) on cases that appear in sharp relief on the global historical map. He left the tasks of examining parochial specimen and of filling-in details to future micro diggers[3]. Weber defines a charismatic leader as one who claims to possess some extraordinary gift(s) that sets him apart from, and above ordinary individuals. He stresses that the target population's acceptance of the person's claim is what makes for effectiveness, not the individual's actual possession of that superordinary talent[4].

If we assume this to be so, then the question arises under what conditions are people likely to accept such an individual's claim to superiority? Weber does not deal with the subject directly. However, in Talcott Parsons' words, "a good deal of evidence has accumulated on this subject . . . [that] where an established institutional order has to a considerable extent become disorganized, where established routines, expectations, and symbols are broken up or are under attack is a favorable situation for such a movement to occur."[5] Anthony F. C. Wallace in his "Revitalization Movements" offers what is probably the most elaborate and specific statement on the situation during the period when an individual claiming superhuman powers is likely to appear, as well as on the basis of his acceptance by a sizable following:

> "Over a number of years, individual members of a population . . . experience increasingly severe stress as a result of the decreasing efficiency of certain stress-reduction techniques. . . . While the individual can tolerate a moderate degree of increased stress and still maintain the habitual way of behavior, a point is reached at which some alternative way must be considered."
>
> "This process of deterioration can, if not checked, lead to the death of the society . . .; the society may be defeated in war, invaded, its population dispersed and its customs suppressed . . . But these dire events are not infrequently forstalled . . . by a revitalization movement."
>
> "Whether the movement is religious or secular . . ., [solution] seems to depend on a restructuring of elements and subsystems which have already attained currency in the society . . . . *The reformulation also seems normally to occur in its initial form in the mind of a single person* (my italics) . . . ."
>
> "The dreamer undertakes to preach his revelations to people . . .; he becomes a prophet. . . . As he gathers disciples, these assume much of the responsibility for communicating the "good word," and communication remains one of the primary activities of the movement . . . ."
>
> "A small clique of special disciples . . . clusters about the prophet and an embryonic campaign organization develops with three orders of personnel: the prophet; the disciples; and the followers."
>
> "It would appear that the emotional appeal of the new doctrine to both the prophet and his followers is in considerable part based in its immediate satisfaction of *a need to find a supremely powerful and potentially benevolent leader.*" (my italics)[6]

What Wallace suggests, in other words, is that following a prolonged crisis which the established culture fails to resolve by conventional means, a charismatic "prophet" who brings an unconventional message promising to resolve the problems, has a chance to get a hearing and to be accepted as a leader. Acceptance is thus based on the followers' "need to find a powerful . . . leader."

We now arrive at what is, for our purpose, the critical issue, that of routinization, the question of whether and under what conditions can charismatic leadership continue after the original leader's demise. Clearly, Weber had a difficult problem at hand, one virtually impossible to solve completely within the boundaries of his own framework. On the one hand, if charismatic leadership is to become more than a passing curiosity (and many among his followers are likely to develop strong interests in continuity), a formula for succession must be worked out. On the other hand, routinization means establishment of some kind, whereas a true charismatic leader represents, by definition, the very antithesis of established routine. His leadership is based on acceptance of the claim that extraordinary *personal* character justifies disregard of established ways of dealing with problems, substituting personal will for so-called conventional wisdom[7].

Looking at the grand historical picture, Weber saw the solution as involving a switch from personal charisma to that of the "office." Instead of personal super-human quality, it is the crown or the papal throne which accounts for whatever charismatic quality remains in, respectively, royalty and the papacy.[8]

Thus, we get what amounts to a solution, but only a partial one, if that. What emerges is a routinized system which involves presence of a distant leader at the top, often a mediocre individual who, surrounded by a gilded facade and assisted by elaborate ceremonial and pageantry, keeps alive the illusion of extraordinariness. What maintains such system may be raw power and/or an appeal to the desire for some form of relief from the boredom of day-to-day exlstence. (It may be more than sheer chance that the dramatic decline in our century of monarchy as a meaningful leadership form coincides with the meteoric rise of the entertainment industry with its ability to provide much more effective amusement than changing of guards and royal weddings can offer.) This is a far cry from truly charismatic leadership which, though rarely free of pageantry, involves a potent leader believed to be capable of solving critical problems by virtue of superhuman qualities. Before returning to our case, let us take another look at the routinization problem, extending our view beyond those of Weber and Wallace, while retaining their respective premises regarding the nature of charisma and the conditions creating a propensity for its acceptance.

The problem Weber encountered applies to charismatic leadership appearing in response to large-scale crises affecting large populations of entire regions. Here, routinization seems to run into a "catch 22" problem. Original leaders who fail in their promised missions, loose their charisma and wind up on the historical heap of the forgotten. (Huey Long, George Wallace, Eldridge Clever, and Huey Newton quickly come to mind as contemporary examples). Conversely, when they do succeed in restoring a satisfactory state, there is no further need for superhuman leaders. (Sensing the problem, Hitler, after his astonishing original success, artificially created a series of crises, which eventually buried him). It is in cases of the latter variety that holders of charismatic offices will suffice, as, for that matter, would leaders without any charismatic pretense. Witness what occurred with the advent of the modern era. Science with its demythologizing tendency, combined with technology that brought the promise of establishing human control over the environment, challenged whatever charismatically-colored rule existed in the West. In Sixteenth-Century Europe, a large portion of its population opted for existence without a pope. In the Eighteenth Century, North American settlers not merely overthrew their crowned ruler, but wrote into their constitution a prohibition against issuance of nobility titles. During the next few centuries, as modernization raised the level of optimism, all Western crowned heads of any significance were gradually transported to museums.

However, modernization failed to produce unilinear or uniform progress. While science and technology increased confidence by enabling mass-production of daily necessities, undreamed-of speed in global communication, or escape from terrestrial gravity and landing on the moon, the modern period also lessened human control in other matters, producing new types of crises. Industrialization shrunk the world, creating an unprecedented level of economic and political interdependence which, at this moment, nobody seems to be able to control. Nowadays, Americans are worried about goods produced in the Far East, about jungles cleared in Brazil, and about Japan's emergence as a global economic superpower. National independence of the kind that once made a Monroe Doctrine seem realistic, is a bygone ideal, while effective world government seems to lie in the nebulous future. Macro-level crises, now much larger in scope, continue to appear, producing matching-level charismatic leaders, which, when a normal state returns, are replaced by other types. In our century, the economic collapse in the 20's brought forth Hitler in Germany, where the crisis was gravest. Less-worshipped, but ultimately more effective figures—Roosevelt, Churchill—surfaced in countries where the somewhat cooler hell allowed a measure of rationality to survive. As soon as the crisis subsided, however, all these once highly-valued leaders were gone. In earlier periods, similar aftermaths might have given rise to a process leading to charismatic offices. In our age, one pope is apparently enough for the entire West. Yesterday's giants were replaced by such lack-luster heads of state as Adenauer, Truman, and Attlee.

It is a different, and for our purpose a more interesting story, when we lower our sights and look at micro-level crises, confined to a limited population and potentially of longer duration. Here we are likely to find persistent need for superior leaders regarded as capable of solving, or at least mitigating nagging problems that refuse to go away. These needs are not likely to be answered by someone at the top surrounded by the glitter of pomp and circumstance. What is called-for are accessible real-life persons from whom the troubled and insecure expect, and receive comfort and hope. It is within these population-pockets that we are likely to find localized "revitalization movements," both religious and secular varieties. It is here that we must look for successful routinization of true charisma. With the above in mind, we shall reexamine the Hasidic case. In doing so, we retain Weber's definition of charisma, as well as Wallace's premise that it is severe crises which create the propensity for accepting charisma.

Hasidism provides us with a first-rate example of a micro-level situation. Its emergence, though, resembles that of a large-scale occurrence. It came in an atmosphere of desperation affecting virtually all East European Jews, except those in the northern part of the region (Lithuania, Bielorussia; see Chapter II). However, while the new formula succeeded in restoring a sufficient degree of confidence to start the process of rebuilding, a heavy residue of economic and political problems persisted. These became aggravated under the reign of Catherine the Great, when Jewish residence became confined to the infamous Pale, causing large-scale dislocations and new levels of poverty. Under these conditions, aggravated every few years for the remainder of Czarism's life-span, Hasidism not only failed to disappear after its initial success, but developed the already-mentioned ageographic community type which proved to be so widely adaptive. However, community structure is an empty shell, unable to function without some cementing focus. Unable to resort to options utilized later by other uprooted populations (trade and professional associations, for example) and plagued by persisting internal and external problems, East European Jews built their communities around a rebbeh, a Hasidic master they regarded as having reached a level of holiness and purity that qualifies him[9] to offer hope and advice—a charismatic leader. Yes, most Hasidic communities did offer pageantry which helped sweeten an unattractive daily reality. They also developed inner circles (administrative staff, in Weber's terminology) deriving benefit, economic and other, from the community's continued existence. They, finally, also developed a hereditary system of succession. All of these make them resemble feudal systems; it makes them look like another traditionalized situation of the variety treated by Weber, in which charisma of the office replaced that of the person. Due to continuation of crises, however, presence of a truly charismatic person remained to this day an essential ingredient, without which a Hasidic community, by definition, does not exist. Given their characteristic independence and the resulting capacity for adaptive diversification and change (cf. Chapter II), Hasidic communities maintained this essential form of rulership by developing a variety of succession techniques, still to be found among contemporary Hasidic units. Some (e.g. Belz and for most of its history, Lubavitch) opted for single succession, successfully fighting off any aspiring rival. Others (e.g. Viznitz) subdivided the rebbeyic patrimony among several aspirants virtually every generation. Still others (including Sighet-Satmar) wound up somewhere between the two extremes. The freedom to vary techniques enabled a community to install eventually an acceptable charismatic leader. Given the fact that communities have retained their ageographic structure, automatically means voluntary membership, which has reinforced the imperative of personal charisma; without one, the dissatisfied may leave and there is very little the establishment can do to prevent it. At this point, a word of caution is needed.

We should not end with the mistaken notion that Hasidism's appeal has been confined to the poor and needy. The clientele has been wide and varied. While drawing its basic sustenance from crises, the term should not be taken too literally. The rich and successful had insecurities of their own. After all, unless they converted (even that did not solve the problem entirely, especially in the Twentieth Century), external hatred and discrimination affected them no less, often more, than it did their less-fortunate brethren. True, many of the upper-middle-class left the communities and others maintained mere marginal affiliation. However, still others, often attributing their very success to the holy man's benediction, have retained, through generations, strong loyalty to their rebbeyim. They contributed large sums to help maintain the court, which reciprocated and rewarded their generosity by according them public honor (a front seat in the synagogue, a place near the rebbeh at "the table", verbal recognition by the rebbeh, etc.), thus reinforcing continued affiliation. In fact, independence of each community eventually resulted (not unlike it did in the case of Protestant denominations) in stratification of communities. Some (e.g., Nadvurna and its offshoots) catered mainly to the lower-class, while in others (Rizhin and its descendants) the successful laid their stamp on the entire community; the rebbeh's court came to resemble a royal palace, which occasionally aroused the ire of the authorities who accused them of autonomous state-building and treason. We noticed in Chapter II that middle-class-based Hungarian Hasidism was visibly less "Dionysian" than most Hasidic courts further East. The same applies to the upper-class communities in Eastern Europe, where the higher exuberance exhibited in less affluent fellowships was often scorned as being "barbaric" and "primitive."

The case of Satmar also draws attention to a few additional details regarding succession of charismatic leadership. I have in mind the circumstances generated by a departing leader's magnitude of charisma and duration-of-tenure. Both seem to influence the degree of ease or difficulty surrounding a given succession process. The higher the charismatic strength of a leader and the longer his reign, the more difficult the succession is likely to be. The confluence of both—i.e., when, as in our case, a highly magnetic individual stays at the helm for a long period— succession is likely to be extremely painful. In addition to Satmar, we find this confirmed in a number of cases in Hasidism's history. To mention a few well-known examples, legendary eighteenth and nineteenth century Hasidic giants, e.g., Lizhensk, Annipoli, Lublin, Apta, left no noteworthy descendants to continue their courts. There were also disciples who created communities and dynasties of their own (the founder of the Teitelbaum dynasty [see Figure 2] was a disciple of "The Seer" in Lublin), rather than claiming to be successors of their masters. In the Nineteenth Century, the founders of the Halberstam dynasty left comparatively minor successors. With the exception of a very weak formal successor in Shinyeveh, none of their numerous descendants, even the most capable of them who set up shop in other towns where they drew their own followers, never even attempted to assume the title "Sanzer Rebbeh" or "Shinyever Rebbeh." For generations, numerous individuals continued to regard themselves as Sanzer and Shinyever Hasidim (see Chapter II for more on these "orphans"), without accepting a rebbeh; the preserved memory of the founders was just too overwhelming. Will some similar "orphans" emerge in Satmar? Only time will tell.

This brings us to a final point, before we turn to theoretical speculation. During the last few decades, Hasidic communities worldwide have been reverting to new techniques for assuring continuity and control, techniques that may eventually result in significant modification of both individual and community character. Specifically, I have in mind two developments: bureaucratization, by now almost universal among communities of significant size, and the creation of geographic centers, for the time being limited to a few.

Bureaucratization relates to another process, namely, school-system development. With the exception of an early start in this direction by Lubavitch, Hasidic communities did not have their own systems prior to World War II. They sent their children where other Orthodox Jews did, mostly to a so-called *heder*, a small-room single-level school operated by a private teacher who

earned his livelihood from it; or, to community schools, where
such were available. After the mass-migration which followed
the Holocaust, conditions, especially in the United States, man-
dated that private schools be large enough to accommodate
state requirements, and each Hasidic community took the
opportunity to build its own system. In addition to following
the American congregationalist pattern which discourages centralization, Hasidic rebbeyim and community leaders had their
own calculations. They saw in separate community schools an
opportunity for rebuilding and for maintaining their followings
shattered by the War. They succeeded beyond the wildest
expectation. Fellowships such as Bobov, Spinka, or Square,
which began from scratch, are by now counted among the most
viable Hasidic communities.

With school systems, bureaucracy became an absolute necessity. The need to include state-required general-studies departments and the quest for having a full community system which
covers the entire range, from kindergarten through graduate
study, required bureaucratic organization and management.
The influence of these specialized managers, however, reaches
beyond the school walls. They now constitute a professional
class, indispensable for a community arm regarded as vital to its
very existence. Most (nearly all) Hasidim who were used to deal
directly with people they knew personally and with whom they
could argue and negotiate, now find themselves forced to
accept dicta based on expertise claimed by bureaucrats. These
specialists then need to develop specialized knowledge. As of
now, Hasidic bureaucrats (at least the ones I encountered
within and outside Satmar) are self-taught, not graduates of
management schools. Even they, despite the fact that most are
members of the community and thus still on informal terms
with their clients, are jealous of their professional prerogatives,
to which the rebbeh himself must occasionally yield. As administration becomes more complex, some form of professional
training will likely enter into the picture. When it does, the
trend toward professional class-consciousness will no doubt
intensify.

The twin developments of community school-systems and
bureaucratization have many unanticipated consequences. For

one, we see gradual acceptance of expert knowledge as both important for the community and as desirable for individual careers. It further means increasing appreciation of secular knowledge, at least the applied variety. Perhaps most important for the long-run is a visible trend toward declining dependence and corresponding rise of self-reliance, thus eating away at the underlying motivation for being part of a Hasidic fellowship. This goes a lot further than in the case of the above-mentioned more-affluent communities. Here we are not dealing with successful main-street traders who are surrounded by an envious hostile majority. Successful merchants continue to exist and are also on the rise. In addition, however, we observe the emergence of a new class of people whose independence is based on possession of skills, vital internally, but also marketable outside community boundaries (see addenda to chapters VIII and IX). The implications are not confined to those directly involved, but are community wide. Aside from constituting a well-regarded category of individuals who may serve as models to be emulated, the entire phenomenon of community-operated school systems is gradually changing the nature and motivation for belonging, which is coming to be based on the necessity to utilize the schools, rather than on the charisma of the rebbeh. The new foundation is a rather tenuous one. The fact is that all Orthodox communities, Hasidic as well as yeshivah types, offer similar curricula in their educational systems and are, furthermore, eagerly accepting clients from without. Which means that it is not necessary to join any organization in order to get an Orthodox Jewish education for one's children. One could even argue that the non-affiliated have the advantage of choice; they can shop for the best schools available, without being restricted by community ties. There is, of course, an exception: locations that offer no choice. This turns our attention to the second novel technique, namely, the trend among contemporary Hasidim toward building geographically-bounded control centers.

While creation of community owned-and-operated schools is by now universal among contemporary Hasidim (also, among non-Hasidic groups), building of culturally-homogeneous villages and townlets is a rather slowly-spreading trend. In the

United States, we have some half-dozen of such locations
(which, as we know, includes Satmar's Kiryas Yoel), all located
north of New York City, within commuting distance from the
city. The explicit reason given for the enterprise is a desire to
get away from the crowded big city, from its strange, often hostile neighbors, and from its multiple temptations for Hasidic
youngsters (e.g., half-dressed women). In addition, they also
acquired the (in most cases latent) functions of providing
secure operating centers for communities and of elimination of
competition.

Most seem to work well, except that they lack the traditional
choice-of-belonging that resulted from absence of geographic
boundaries. In these townlets, the inhabitants are expected to
accept the "party line" and the institutionalized services offered
from above. The official position is that choice still exists,
because one who cannot accept the system should not move
there to begin with, while those who discovered their dislike
later should move out. However, as time passes, populations
tend to grow, especially considering current encouragement by
cultural norms to do so. With growth comes the potential for
differences in opinion which, in the absence of choice other
than moving which is both upsetting and costly, may develop
into serious conflict, as it did in Satmar's Kiryas Yoel. Underlying this potential threat is the fact that Diaspora Jews in general
have become adapted to situations where "others" run the civic
part of life and, thus, lack experience in managing polities
which inevitably involves some coordination of diversity.
Hasidim have the additional difficulty that their historical
strength has been based on their communities' facile mobility,
unhampered by geographic confinement. Potential for conflict
is magnified by the just-mentioned shift in the loyalty- base from
devotion to a charismatic rebbeh toward dependence on services offered by bureaucratically-managed organizations. If
these trends continue, today's larger Hasidic communities may,
after all, come to resemble monarchies in decline; i.e., they
may, in essence, cease to be true Hasidic units. (In the section
which follows, we shall look at additional factors reinforcing
this trend). If this scenario holds, true Hasidism is likely to
continue via smaller units, catering, as usual, to crisis-ridden

populations in need of genuine charismatic leaders [10], and the cycle will probably start anew.

At this point we are ready to glance at theoretical implications of what was said on the subject of routinization of charisma. To repeat, there is no apparent need for questioning or modifying Weber's position on the nature of charisma, or of Wallace's view that crises prepare the ground for its acceptance. What the case of Satmar and the general phenomenon of Hasidism suggest is the need to attach the following propositions regarding routinization of charismatic leadership:

1. *While large-scale crises tend to be resolved after a while, those smaller in scale affecting limited populations may persist over longer periods of time.*

2. *While eventual modification of charisma by traditionalization and from-person-to-office transfer seems inevitable in large-scale cases, this is not necessarily so in more limited fields where serious difficulty persists. On the contrary, continuation of crisis is likely to create continuous dependence on persons regarded as possessing superhuman ability to offer solutions and hope.*

3. *Even in smaller populations, crises do not last forever. Neither does population size remain constant. Changed conditions and increased size are likely to alter the nature of extant needs, consequently modifying leadership character in a direction reminiscent of situations in larger settings treated by Weber.*

4. *However, short of worldwide utopia, some population pockets are bound to experience unmanageable problems. Thus, for the predictable future, true charismatic figures are likely to be found in problem-ridden human islands.*

Ubiquity and Inevitability of Sociocultural Change

Finally, the Satmar case provides a clear theoretical lesson that in spite of the manifest possibility to resist some change in areas of culture once thought to be impossible to preserve in the modern world, it is virtually impossible to successfully ward off any and all change, regardless of effort exerted and of price paid. While generations of Anthropologists have emphasized the universality of change, even in so-called primitive societies once regarded as static, our case, in addition to providing a concrete field of observation of how the process actually occurs, also brings to light both the potential and limit of purposive effort on behalf of continuity. The discussion which follows includes (albeit in expanded fashion) factors treated earlier, alongside additional ones suggested by observation during the restudy.

1.   Economic-technological factors. In addition to the desire for expanding consumption dwelt-upon earlier, the new reality forces reconsideration of the role played by new technology, especially computers. By mastering this new futuristic field, Satmar men and women are now able to communicate with virtually the entire world, without as much as leaving their homes. Therein lies a possibility for broadening horizons, as well as additional potential for reducing dependence on the narrow confines of the community which, we have seen, plays such an important role in the Hasidic ethos. While this is still a long way from the process visualized by Marxians, it does not entirely contradict the latter, not if one is willing to expand the concept of "social relations" accompanying a given technology to include relations beyond the confines of the work environment. The more general proposition emerging here is that *acceptance of and involvement with boundary-widening high technology, is likely to create more exposure to outside culture, as well as greater autonomy among individuals and, hence, increased receptivity to outside influence, thereby counteracting insulating mechanisms intended to create dependence on the supportive environment within a community.* Together with developments leading to bureaucratization, the ultimate effect may well be one of weakening, though not entirely eliminating, sociocultural systems relying on effectiveness of insulating efforts.

This is apparent in both large and small systems; in China as well as in Satmar.

2.   Conflict, change, and continuity. In addition to examining the influence exerted by structural (e.g., bureaucratization) and high tech on the process of change, we shall also look at the relationship between conflict and change, as well as the oft-assumed opposites of change and continuity. Notions about the relationship of these three are not new. Decades ago, Coser[11],

drew our attention to the positive functions of conflict, pointing to its relationship to adaptive change and its function of channeling dissatisfaction into evolutionary change *within* the system, thus preventing violent revolutionary change *of* the system[12]. Today, these propositions are well established in social science. However, Satmar not merely provides an opportunity for direct observation of Coser's principles in action, but suggests going a step further. It seems that successful adaptive change is actually part and parcel of cultural continuity[13]. It seems that unless some structural changes occur in the Satmar system to accommodate the dissatisfactions underlying the current conflict, Satmar as a distinct system may not survive. Most of its members may well (in fact are likely to) remain strictly Orthodox Jews for the near future, but are not likely to remain members of the community's direct structural successor. Again, wider applicability seems warranted. For example, historians generally agree that the changes of the New Deal have saved capitalism in the United States. Developments in post-communist Russia and Eastern Europe are too recent for meaningful historiography, let alone agreement. However, the confusion is in itself instructive; leftover communist hard-liners are referred-to as conservatives, if not outright reactionaries. Perhaps, when this history is eventually written, it may be necessary to discard these and other concepts rendered non-functional by end-of-our-century processes. Thus, speculation on the relationship between sub-division and continuity within a small obscure community like Satmar, may, once again, point to related developments in the universe at large.

A Personal Postscript

I take this opportunity to air a few comments on subjects which have held my attention during much of the three decades since I have first studied the Satmar community. The first relates to the general value of community studies. When I originally planned the study, I was, curiously, encouraged by anthropologists and discouraged by sociologists. This was 1960, when the trend in sociology was well under way toward technically sophisticated quantitative investigation of limited subjects in fields deemed to be of immediate relevance. I decided to heed the advice of anthropologists, rather than that of my formal reference group, a decision I never regretted.

The experience of beholding a total society proved invaluable. Professionally, it enhanced my qualification as a teacher, not only of introductory course in which one is required to survey all the main components of the field, but of a variety of advanced courses I occasionally accepted outside my chosen area of concentration. Moreover, even when working within my area, I felt more comfortable being familiar with adjacent regions interacting with the central focus of my work. In addition, I reaped numerous benefits in my private life. As an Orthodox Jew, my work in Satmar shed light for me on a variety of problems and issues one must confront as a result of consciously embracing any ideology and attempt to live accordingly. An Orthodox Jew cannot, for example, pursue a career in classical music or the military, without encountering awesome, virtually insurmountable obstacles attempting to observe one's Sabbath and holidays. There is, in other words, a price exacted for any ethnic or religious affiliation. Confronting the nature of the price and willingness to pay it is as valid an indicator as any of how important a given ideological social choice is to those who profess it. I also came to realize that some change to accommodate changing circumstances is unavoidable and that, therefore, all aspirations and claims to absolute immutability belong to the world of fantasy, not reality. I do not wish to bore you with a long list of personal pet peeves, beyond reiterating that having reached the home stretch of my professional career, I have few regrets and a lot to be grateful for; I do not harbor hatred for distractors and critics, but am forever grateful to all those who offered support and encouragement.

Notes

1 Israel Rubin, "Chassidic Community Behavior," *Anthropological Quarterly* 37:3 (July, 1964), 138-148. "Function and Structure of Community: Conceptual and Theoretical Analysis," *International Review of Community Development* n. 21-22 (1969), 111-122.

2 For what may be the earliest statement on the subject, see Emile Durkheim, *The Division of Labor in Society* tr. George Simpson. The Free Press of Glencoe Collier-Macmillan New York-London: 1933. Preface to the Second Edition: Some Notes on Occupational Groups. pp. 1-31.

3 Max Weber, *The Theory of Social and Economic Organization* tr. A.M. Henderson and Talcott Parsons. Edited with an Introduction by Talcott Parsons. The Free Press of Glencoe Collier-Macmillan, New York-London 1947, pp.363-373, 386-392.

4 *Ibid.*, pp.358-359.

5 Talcott Parsons, Introduction To Max Weber, *op. cit.*, p.71.

6 Anthony F. C. Wallace, "Revitalization Movements," *American Anthropologist* 58 (April, 1956), 264-281.

7 Max Weber, *Op.cit.*, pp. 363 and ff.

8 *Ibid.*, pp. 364.

9 With two or three exceptions, it were men who occupied the status of rebbeh. The known exceptions—The Founder's daughter, the daughter of Reb Hayim Halberstam of Sanz, [and a third with a nebulous history]—were apparently tolerated on account of their lustrous fathers, but not really accepted. In contemporary Satmar, loyal followers of the present Rebbeh often accuse the Old Rebbetzen (around whom Reb Moshe's opponents tend to cluster) of wanting to occupy her late husband's position, something (they point out) generally regarded as inappropriate for a women. Thus, "him" expresses an historical fact.

10 Among Hasidim, decline of some communities and rise of new ones is not new; only details differ. The question of whether the current novel set of circumstances is of different quality, will only be answered by time. My projection is in the affirmative.

11 Lewis A. Coser, *The Functions of Social Conflict*. New York: The Free Press, 1956, and especially his "Social Conflict and the Theory of Social Change," *British Journal of Sociology* VIII (1957), 197-207.

12 The latter theme is also forwarded by Bernard Barber in his *Social Stratification*. New York: Harcourt, Brace & World, 1957. See his comparison and contrast of stratification systems in Chapter 17, pp.478-502.

13 This is obviously implied, though not clearly formulated by Coser in his *British Journal of Sociology* article cited in n. 11.

Index

Abraham, 59
Acculturation, 173–174, 283–284;
    of men, 235–236;
    resistance to, 68, 173–174,
    201–202, 219–232, 275–
    276, 282–283; of women,
    235–238
Adam, 58
Adolescence, 145. *See also*
    Courtship; Education
Affection, display of, to children,
    144
Aged, 146
Age of reason, 19
Aggressiveness, among children,
    143–144. *See also* Conflict
Agudath Israel, 36, 174
Americans, Satmarer's view of,
    203
Amish, 224, 277
Amulets, 21
Anti-Semitism, 35; after World
    War I, 36; and
    anti-Zionism, 201–202,
    204–205, 270–271; and
    insulation, 271–272; in
    Russia, 36; in the United
    States, 201–202
Anti-Zionism. *See* Anti-Semitism;
    Zionism
Arab Golden Age, 17–18
Arad, Rumania, 47
Arts, 222
Ashkenazim, 17–18. *See also*
    Hasidim; Satmarer;
    divisions among, 29–30; in
    Hungary, 33–35; in
    Satmar, 44, 46
Atonement, premarital, 134–135
Attire, Satmarer, 222; of adult
    males, 107; for burial, 147;
    of females, 107; of married

adults, 134–135, 137;
    occupations related to,
    192; for prayer, 89; rules
    of, 191; Sabbath and
    holiday, 94–95, 104, 137;
    for weddings, 134–135
Aufreef, 133–134
Auschwitz. *See*
    Birkenau-Auschwitz
Autonomy, of institutions, 121
Autopsy, opposition to, 147, 228

Baal Shem Tov, 22, 24, 60
Baal-tefilah, 89
Babylonian Talmud, 60–61, 168.
    See also Talmud
Badhan, 134
Bais Ruchel, 164–166, 174–175,
    179, 234, 258. *See also*
    Girls, education of
Bar-mizvah, 140
Basht. *See* Baal Shem Tov
Baths, ritual. *See Mikveh*
Bavaarfen, 133–134
Behavior. *See also* Control, social;
    effect of employment on,
    194–196; religious, in
    Satmar, 88–114; standards
    for, 121
Behr, Reb Dob, 24
Bet-din, 200
Beth Jacob (girls' schools), 174
Bet-midrash, 89
Bible, Jewish, 55. *See also* Torah
Bikkur holim, 207
Birkenau-Auschwitz, 47
Birth control, 69, 139
Blacks, 202
Body, human, Satmarer opinions
    of, 56–57. *See also*
    Purification; Sex

Boys, education of, 142, 144–145,
    161–163, 167–173, 182
Bread, handling of, 191, 225
Budapest, Hungary, 47
Bylaws, of Satmar, 77

Calendar, Jewish, 93. *See also* Hol-
    idays
Camps, 165–166, 170
Censorship, 191; of textbooks,
    173, 176
Central Rabbinical Congress of
    the United States and
    Canada, 78–80, 84, 203,
    206–207
Ceremonies, religious. *See also*
    Holidays; Religion; Wed-
    dings; for male children,
    139–140
Change. *See also* Acculturation;
    Control, social; adaptation
    to, 150; causes of, 234–
    241, 258, 261–266; effects
    of, 260–261; historical
    unimportance of, 57; resis-
    tance to, in education,
    174–176; theories of, 258–
    261
Charity, 211–214
Children: attitude toward, 145;
    desirability of, 139, 162;
    education of. *See* Educa-
    tion; independence of,
    143–144; lack of, 122; lack
    of time for, 235; of mixed
    marriage, 129; naming of,
    149; obligations of, after
    death of parents, 149;
    preference of male, 139;
    responsibility of parents
    toward, 124; segregation
    of, by sex, 138, 142, 144–
    145, 224; training of, 140–
    145
Chimmish, 168
Chmielnicki, Bogdan, 21
Christianity, 19
Circumcision, 59, 107, 139

Code, religious. *See* Religion,
    Satmarer behavior regard-
    ing
Collection for charity, 211–212
Commentary, 4
Community: decision-making, 68;
    participation, Hasidic, 26–
    27, 32, 46; structure,
    Hasidic, 24–27, 45–46;
    structure, Hungarian
    Orthodox, 28, 31–33
"Conditions," 132, 134
Conflict: avoidance of, 200, 202,
    204–205; in Bais Ruchel,
    258; over financial
    matters, 203, 230–232
Congregation Yetev Lev
    D'Satmar, 3, 47, 78–79. *See
    also* Satmar
Conservative Jews, 20
Conservatives, in Satmar, 80–82
Consumption: conspicuous, 192–
    194, 259, 269; habits of,
    192
Control, social, 220–221; sources
    of, 223–232, 256–258;
    strain produced by, 12,
    221–223
Cooley, C.H., 220
Coser, Lewis A., 300–301
Cosmology, Satmarer conception
    of, 57–61
Cossacks, 21–23
Cossack wars, 22, 27
Courts, Hasidic, 33, 42. *See also
    Din-Torah*
Courtship, 131–133
Cousins, marriage among, 129
Creation of the human race, 57–
    58
Crime: absence of, 200, 203, 229;
    among dissenters, 230–231
Crusades, 18
Culture, Satmarer, preservation
    of, 5, 220–232. *See also*
    Acculturation, resistance
    to

Dairy products, 190–191, 193–194

Dating, 150–151

Days of Awe, 69–70, 96, 112

Death, 146–150. *See also* Inheritance

Decision-making: lack of, in children, 143–144; in religious matters, 77–79; role of, in preserving culture, 275; role of Rov in, 67, 69, 80, 111–112, 225–226; Satmarer's lack of, 67–73, 143–144, 226, 257–258; strategy for limiting, 257

Demonstrations, anti-Zionist, 81, 202

Dibrey Hayim, 32

Dibrey Yehezkel, 32

Diets, of infants, 141. *See also* Food, kosher

Din-Torah, 200, 203

Discipline: of children, 141; Hasidic, 27–28; of Hungarian Orthodoxy, 31; of Jews, by God, 60–61; in Satmar schools, 169, 173, 249

Dishes, for kosher food, 193 194

Divorce, 123, 146; grounds for, 136; remarriage after, 123, 146–147

Dowries, 133

Durkheim, Emile, 287

Economic activities, 5, 190–199; effect of, on social control, 223–224, 256, 258, 262; in Hungary, 224; limitations on, 223, 269; pressures of, 235–239, 258–259; role of religion in determining, 190–193

Education, 67, 141–142, 161–184. *See also* Schools; of boys. *See* Boys, education of; changes in, 161–162, 178–184, 234–235, 258; of girls. *See* Girls, education of; higher, 195–196, 221–222, 271–272, 283–284; in

Hungary, 161; implications for Satmarer, for America, 277; occupational, 163, 177, 180, 183; Orthodox, 270–273; problems of higher, for Orthodox Jews, 272–273; religion in, 162; secular, 162–163, 166–167, 171–173, 175–176, 179–183, 221–222, 236

Eineklach, 76, 212

Elijah's Cup, 105

Endogamy, community, 128

Engagement, 131–132; ring for, 194

English, in the schools, 171, 176–177

Enlightenment movement, 19

Entertainment, 213; effects of control on, 222

Equality, in Satmar, 76–77

Esau, 59

Europe, history of Jews in, 17–36. *See also* Satmar, history of

Excommunication, 271

Exodus, as theme of Passover, 104–105

Extermination, of Jews, 61, 146, 273; by Cossacks, 21–22

Family, Satmarer, 122–152; behavior within, 131–152, consciousness of, 162; importance of, in determining status, 122, 124; male-female roles in, 124–125, 139–140, 142, 144, 152, 234–236, 238–239; responsibilities toward, 125; size of, 139, 282; structure of, 125–131, 149–152, 282; ties with, after marriage, 145–146

Farming, absence of Satmarer in, 196

Federations, 274

Food. *See also* Meals; kosher, 108, 190–191, 193–194, 221; in the synagogue, 91

Freedom: dangers of, 31; lack of, in Europe, 201; political. *See* Zionism
Freud, Sigmund, 220
Funerals, 148–149
Furniture, purchase of, 194

Gabaim, 78
Galicia: anti-Zionism in, 36; Hasidism in, 32
Gentiles: Jewish conception of, 57; Satmarer conception of, 59
Germany. *See also* Nazis; Jews in, 27–28; Orthodoxy in, 20
Ghettos, Jewish, 19, 46–47
Girls, education of, 68, 144–145, 161–164, 166, 173–184, 234–235, 238; in Hungary, 173–174; Jewish studies, 162–163
God: attainment of, 23; Satmarer concept of, 54–61
Gossiping, in the synagogue, 91
Government: regard for, 200–201, 203–204; suspicion of, 200–202
Graduation: for girls, 177; lack of, for boys, 171

Habdalah, 96
Halah, 95
Halberstam, House of, 32, 42, 44, 129, 237, 295
Hamez, 191, 194
Handwashing, 110
Hasidim. *See also* Satmarer; behavior patterns of, 12–13, 24–27, 113–114; history of, 24–36, 292–293; in Hungary, 31–32; ideology of, 23–26; immigration of, 3
Hatam Sofer, 28, 31–33; descendants of, 33
Hazakah, 33
Hebrew: modern, 169, 260; study of, in schools, 167–169, 175–177
Herskovits, Melville, 259–260

Hevra-Kadisha, 78. *See also* Holy Association
Hilul Hashem, 57, 205
Hirsch, Rabbi Samson Raphael, 20
Historical Jews, 20
History: Jewish. *See* Jews, history of; as part of Passover, 104–105; Satmarer concept of, 57–61
Hitler, Adolf, 277–278, 291
Holidays, 93–106; community, 93; major, 93, 96–105; minor, 93, 105–106; table of, 97–103
Holy Association, 78, 147
Holy Land. *See also* Zionism; burial in, 148; Satmarer history of, 57–61
Holy Tongue, use of, in Satmar, 108
Homes, characteristics of, 138–139
Honeymoons, 136–137
Horovitz, House of, 42
Horthy regime, 46
Human relations, as form of social control, 256
Humash. *See* Chimmish
Hungarian, spoken in Williamsburg, 174
Hungary: deportation of Jews from, 46–47; Jews in, 28–36, 83
Hutterites, 277

Identity: preservation of, 275; symbols of, 106–109
Ikvey Hatzon, 184
Illness: charity during, 211; consultation with the Rov during, 113
Immigrants: acculturation of, 68. *See also* Acculturation; Orthodox Jewish, 3; and welfare, 212–213
Incest, 123, 126–127
Independence, training of children for, 143–144

Industry: absence of Satmarer in, 195 196; and change, 258–259

Inheritance: of estate of diseased, 149–150; of rabbinical position, 33, 42, 44, 236–237; of zadik's position, 25–26

In-laws, 125

Innovation. *See* Change

Institutions, autonomy of, 121

Insulation, of Satmar, 268–273

Insurance, medical, 212

Intercourse. *See also* Sex; after childbirth, 139; purification after, 109; on the Sabbath, 95–96; thoughts during, 122

Interferers, 135

Isaac, 59

Jerusalem, Satmarer in, 48

Jews, 93, 196; arguments among. *See* Moderates; Orthodoxy; Zionism; execution of, 21–22, 61, 213; German, 27 28; history of, 273–274; history of, in Eastern Europe, 21–28, 292–294; history of, in Hungary, 28–36, 83; history of, in Western Europe, 19–20, 28–30; Polish-Lithuanian, 18; Polish-Ukrainian, 21, 23; possible future split among, 274. *See also* Hasidim; Orthodoxy; Satmar

Joy, Hasidim's emphasis on, 23–25

Judaism: authentic, claimed by Satmarer, 80, 82, 107, 205; essence of, 20. *See also* Hasidim; Orthodoxy; Satmar

Kabalah, 21

Kadish, 149

Kelal Yisrael, 25

Keley-kodesh, 75

Ketubah, 135

Kidush, 96

Kiryas Yoel, 71, 178, 198, 231, 239

Kohanim, 128

Kollel, 151, 182

Krooleh, Hungary, 46

Kvittel, 112

Lactation, 141

Laws: civil, regard for, 200–201; religious, 88. *See also* Religion

Learning, importance of, 23, 44–45, 91–92, 145. *See also* Education; Schools; Torah, study of

Leaven, riddance of, for Passover, 104

Leaving the community: effects of, 227; incentives for, 238, 245–248; prevention of, 258, 261–262

Leisure. *See* Entertainment

Levirate, 126

Leviyim, 128 129

Levy, M.J., 258

Leyl shimurim, 105

Libraries, opposition to, 176

Life, Satmarer concept of, 56–57

Literature, Jewish, 4–7. *See also* Talmud; Torah

Lithuania, Jews in, 18, 23

Lower class, in Satmar, 77

Males. *See also* Boys, education of; Family, male-female roles in; appearance of, 93, 107; dominance of, in religious matters, 77

Marriage: age of, 131; consummation of, 136; customs accompanying, 133–138, 213; desirability of, 227; division of responsibilities in. *See* Family, male-female roles in; mixed, 129, 228; preparation for, 145–146; Satmarer attitude toward, 123; second, 123, 126, 128,

146. *See also* Mate,
selection of
Masturbation, 142
Matchmaking, 131–132, 150–151.
See also Mate, selection of;
consultation
with the Rov during, 112–113
Mate, selection of, 124, 128, 131–
132, 144. *See also* Incest
Mazah (unleavened bread), 191,
194
"McCarthyites," in Satmar, 76, 80
Meals, "conduct of, Food; Seder;"
Tables; for *Rosh Hodesh*,
106; Sabbath, 93–95
Meat, kosher, 190–191, 194
Mechittonim, 126
Mendelssohn, Moses, 19
Mengele, Dr. (German selector),
47
Menstruation, restrictions on
intercourse after, 133,
137–138, 142, 221 222
Mentshlichkeit, 121, 228
Messianic belief, 21–22, 36, 61,
105, 109, 202, 205. *See also*
Zionism, Satmarer
opposition to, and
Orthodoxy, 271
Mezuzah, 107, 138
Mikveh, 109–110, 133, 136, 138,
183; for the dead, 148
Militancy, of Satmarer, 46, 60,
80–81
Minorities. *See also* Pluralism,
cultural; implications of
Satmar for, 275;
preservation of culture,
275–276
Minyan, 90, 140
Mitnagdim, 23
Mizrahi, 36
Mizvah dance, 136
Mizvot, 57, 107; number of, for
Gentiles, 57, 59
Moderates, in Satmar, 80–82
Monogamy, 123
Moonkatsh, 45
Moses, 58–59
Mourning, 147–149

Movies, ban on, 191, 213

Naaches, 145, 227
Names, importance of, 107
Nationalism. *See* Zionism
Nazis, 277–278; in Hungary, 46–
47
Neologues, 31
Neturey Karta, 48, 204
Noah, 58
Nusah Sepharad, 89

Occupations, 4, 145, 192–193,
195–198, 281. *See also*
Work; education for, 163,
281; selection of, 193
Oppression, Jewish, 18, 46–47; as
theme of Passover, 104–
105
Optimism, Hasidim's emphasis
on, 23–25
Orshovah, Hungary, 44
Orthodoxy. *See also* Hasidim;
Satmarer; effects of
commercialism on, 227–
228; in Hungary, 28, 31
33; opposition of
American Jews to, 4; of
Reb Yoel Teitelbaum, 44;
relation of Satmar to, 269
273; relaxation of, in
Europe, 20; of Satmarer,
3–4; split in, 273–274;
survival of, 6; in Western
Europe, 20
Outsiders. *See also* Gentiles;
attraction of, to Satmar,
244–248, 251; desire to
escape contact with, 268;
and social control, 227–
228

Parsons, Talcott, 288
Passover, 93, 96, 104–105, 169;
cost of, 197; food for, 191,
194
Peace, world, 277
Pentateuch, 55, 60, 88–89, 93. *See
also* Torah
Pidyon, 112

Pilgrim Holidays, 93, 96
Pluralism, cultural, 6, 276–277.
    See also Acculturation,
    resistance to
Poland: Jews in, 18, 21–22;
    Messianic movement in,
    22
Policemen, Satmarer attitude
    toward, 201–202
Political activity, 200–209;
    guidelines for, 200–202; in
    the synagogue, 91
Population, growth of, 237–238
Prayer, 88–91; for Sabbath, 93–
    96; of the zadik, 25
Pressburg, Hungary, 31–33
Prevention, as source of social
    control, 224
Profanity, 57
Professionals, absence of, among
    Satmarer, 195–196, 223
Puerto Ricans, 202
Purification, 109–110. *See also*
    Mikveh; after intercourse,
    109, 136; of the dead, 148;
    premarital, 133
Purim, 105–106; collection of
    money during, 212

Rabbinical Congress. *See* Central
    Rabbinical Congress of the
    United States and Canada
Rabbis. *See also* Rebbeh; Rov;
    decline in number of, 193;
    inheritance of position,
    33, 42, 236–237; training
    for, 170–171
Radicals, relations with, 272
Rashi, 168
Reading: restrictions on, 213; as
    taught in schools, 167–168
Rebbeh: descendants of, 75–76;
    role of, 25, 67–73, 82–83,
    110–111
Rebbetzen (Reb Yoel's widow),
    71–72, 113
Rebellion, of schoolgirls, 177
"Reception of the Sabbath," 96
Recreation. *See* Entertainment

Reform, Jewish, 19–20, 31;
    opposition to, in Hungary,
    32–33
Relatives. *See also* Family;
    marriage of, 131. *See also*
    Incest; responsibilities
    toward, 125–126
Religion: effect of, on education,
    162, 167–168, 173–174;
    effect of, on organization
    of Satmar, 77–84;
    opposition to change in,
    260–261; role of, in
    economic behavior, 192–
    193; Satmarer behavior
    regarding, 88–114;
    Satmarer beliefs regarding,
    54–61; study of, in schools,
    162–163, 167–170, 175–
    176
Religious articles, purchase of,
    193
Residence, selection of, 128, 146.
    See also Homes
Reward system, 224–225, 256–257
Rosh Hashanah, 106, 169–170
Rosh Hodesh, 106
Rov. *See also* Teitelbaum, Reb
    Yoel; qualifications for,
    236–237; role of, 33, 67–
    73, 75
Ruah-hakodesh, 55
Rumania, Satmarer in, 47
Russia, anti-Semitism in, 36

Sabbath: observance of, 94–95,
    192; symbols of identity
    during, 107
Sabbatian movement, 22
Safed, Palestine, 21
Sanz, Galicia, 32, 44. *See also*
    Halberstam, House of
Satan, 56
Satmar: anti-Zionism in. *See*
    Zionism, Satmarer
    opposition to; attraction
    of outsiders to, 244–246,
    251; as authentic Judaism,
    80, 82, 107, 205; changes

in, 234–241, 263, 287; conservative/moderate split in, 80, 230–231; demographic changes in, 229–230, 282; effect of, on other Jews, 273–275; effects of leaving, 227; establishment of, in New York, 47–49; financial independence of, 274; formal religious structure of, 77–79; history of, 42–49; as an ideology, 80; implications of, for society, 275–278, 282; informal religious structure of, 79–84; insularity of, 268 269; location of, 3, 84, 178, 231, 298. *See also* Kiryas Yoel; Williamsburg; preservation of culture in, 220–232; problems of, 230–232, 240–241, 269; social structure of, 75–84

Satmar, Hungary, 42–47, 224

Satmarer: definition of, 3; execution of, 47; family relations of, 122–125, 230–232; misconceptions of, 4–5; orthodoxy of, 12–13, 283–285; outside the United States, 48, 286; population explosion and, 282; religious behavior of, 88–114; religious beliefs of, 54–61. *See also* Religion

Schools. *See also* Education; administration of, 164–166, 178–184; centralization of, 161–162; establishment of, 68; schedule of, 169–170; social structure of, 164–166; summer, 169–170

Science, absence of, in Satmar, 213

Seafood, 191

"Second Diaspora day," 93

Secularism: in education. *See* Education, secular; of European Jews, 19–20

Security, provision for, 69–70

Seder, 104–105

Sefirah, 105

"Sephardic Style," 89

Sephardim, 17–19; Palestinian, 21

"Seven Blessings feast," 135–136

Sex: effects of control on, 222; instruction in, 136, 142; premarital, 142–143; Satmarer attitude toward, 122–123, 137–138, 221, 224–225

Shabatai Zevi, 22

Shabuot, 105

Sheyneh yidden, 75–76, 212

Shiduhin, 151. *See also* Matchmaking; Mate, selection of

Shinyeveh, Galicia, 32, 44. *See also* Halberstam, House of

Shohatim, 75

Shohet, 33, 190

Shteebel, 27

Shteeblach, 89

Sighet, Hungary, 32, 44–45

Sigheter Hasidim, 45–46, 48. *See also* Teitelbaum, House of

Sin, 56–57

Sinai, 60

Slavery: retention of Jewish identity during, 106–107; as theme of Passover, 104

Socialization process: as a form of social control, 224–226, 250; negative aspects of, 226, 257–258; parents' role in, 140 145

Sofer, Reb Mosheh. *See* Hatam Sofer

Soferim, 75

Sororate, 126

Soul: "extra," on Sabbath, 94, 96; Satmarer concept of, 56–57, 60

Spain, early Jews in, 17. *See also* Sephardim

Spiro, M.E., 220
Sports, ban on, 213
Status: based on contributions,
    211–212, 294;
    determinants of, in
    Satmar, 75–77, 79–82, 91–
    92, 122–123, 144–145; of
    family, 122–124; related to
    occupation, 195; of
    women. *See* Family,
    male-female roles in
Status Quo Jews, 31
Strain: as a result of change, 234
    241; as a result of social
    control, 221–223
Sukot, 96
Swaddling, 141
Synagogue attendance, 89–90. *See
    also* Religion

Tabernacles, 93
"Tables," conduct of, 69–70, 111–
    112
Talmud, 55, 60–61, 168. *See also*
    Torah, study of; and
    funerals, 148; restrictions
    on incest in, 126; study of,
    in schools, 169–170
Taub, Reb Levi Yitzchok, 32
Teachers: religious, 75–76; in
    Satmar schools, 169, 171–
    173
Teitelbaum, House of, 32, 36, 43,
    129–130, 237
Teitelbaum, Reb Hananya
    Yom-Tov Lipa, 42
Teitelbaum, Reb Hayim Hersch,
    42, 44–45
Teitelbaum, Reb Moshe, 11, 32,
    49, 70–73, 206;
    accessibility of, 12;
    opposition to, by the
    Rebbetzen, 71–72; role of,
    73, 178–179; as successor
    of Reb Yoel, 49, 71–72,
    240
Teitelbaum, Reb Yoel, 3, 113;
    accessibility of, 4–5;
    allegiance to, 108, 111–
    114; anti-Zionism of, 66;

death of, 11, 49, 231, 240;
    as decision maker, 67–72,
    112–114, 226–227, 230;
    effects of absence of, 231,
    238; as head of schools,
    164; lack of heir for, 236–
    237, 269; liberation of,
    113–114; life of, 42–49;
    personal traits of, 65–67,
    251; power of, 80–84;
    private visits to, 112–114;
    rewards from, 225–226;
    roles of, in Satmar, 68–72;
    successor of. *See*
    Teitelbaum, Reb Moshe;
    trust in, 249–250
Teitelbaum, Reb Zalmen Leib, 45
Teleology, Satmarer concept of,
    57–61
Television, ban on, 191, 222
Temeshvahr, Rumania, 47
Temptation, 56–57
Thereafter, Satmarer concept of,
    56–61
Tikun, 91
Tishah Beab, 105
Torah: and crime, 200; decisions
    regarding, 69; forbidden
    as subject for girls, 173–
    174, 181; history of, 59–
    60; Satmarer concept of,
    54–56; study of, 91–93;
    study of, at home, 169;
    study of, in schools, 162–
    163, 169 170, 172; study
    of, in summer camp, 169–
    170; study of, in the
    synagogue, 91; technique
    for studying, 91–92
Torah V'Yiroh, 169–170, 172,
    236. *See also* Boys,
    education of
Tower of Babel, 58
Training, occupational, 144–145
Transylvania, 47
Travel, curtailment of, 222

Ujhely, Hungary, 32
Unemployment, charity during,
    211–212

Unions, membership in, 212

Values, preservation of. *See*
        Acculturation, resistance
        to; Control, social
Vandalism, 143
Violence. *See* Conflict; Crime
Voting habits, 203–204

Wage earning. *See* Occupations;
        Women, working; Work
Wallace, Anthony F.C., 288–289
Weber, Max, 288–290, 293
Weddings, 133–136. *See also*
        Marriage; the Rov's role
        in, 70
Welfare, 211–214
Well-being, spiritual, 110–114
Williamsburg, 3, 11, 264. *See also*
        Satmar; migration of
        Satmarer to, 47–48
Wills, 149–150
Wine, handling of, 191, 225
Women: changing role of, 124,
        152, 234, 238–239, 258
        260, 263. *See also* Family,
        male-female roles in;
        working, 140–141, 152,
        193, 235, 258
Work. *See also* Occupations;
        absence of, on Sabbath,
        93–94, 192; choice of
        locale for, 192–193, 195
        196, 223–224; Satmarer
        control of, 221; women
        and, 140–141, 152, 193,
        235, 258, 281

Worship. *See* Prayer; Religion
Writing, as taught in the schools,
        168–169

Yeled Sha'ashuim, 152
Yeshivah, 170. *See also* Education;
        Schools; in Hungary, 44–
        46
Yezer Hara, 56
Yezer Tov, 56
Yiddish: in the schools, 168; use
        of, in Satmar, 108
Yiddishkeit, 121
Yismah Mosheh. *See* Teitelbaum,
        Reb Moshe
Yisroel, Reb. *See* Baal Shem Tov
Yizhoki, Rabbi Shelomoh, 168
Yoortzaat, 149

Zudik, 24 26
Zealots, in Satmar, 76, 80, 83
Zedakah, 211, 213
Zekut-abot, 57
Zionism: and change, 260–261,
        287; emergence of, 35;
        opposition to, in Europe,
        55–56; and Orthodoxy,
        269–270, 272; problems
        caused by opposition to,
        205–206; Reb Yoel
        Teitelbaum's opposition
        to, 66; Satmarer
        opposition to, 4, 36, 44–
        46, 48, 60, 76, 80–82, 109,
        143, 174, 202, 204–206,
        228; and the study of
        modern Hebrew, 169

Satmar, a Hasidic community of Jews originating in an area that once belonged to Hungary, parts of which are incorporated in neighboring countries. They have settled in the United States in the '40s and '50s. Determined to resist assimilation, they succeeded, not only for themselves, but managed to retain virtually all their offspring within the fold. Changes nevertheless occurred especially since the change of leadership. In this book, the author dicusses both the continuity and change offering a sociological analysis of both vital processes. The new edition brings their story up to date, projecting some prospects for the future.

Israel Rubin, an immigrant from Rumania, received his Ph.D. from the University of Pittsburgh and taught at Northwestern University, University of Minnesota, and Cleveland State University. He is now Professor Emeritus of Sociology. His writings include the first edition of *Satmar: An Island in the City*, and a variety of articles and reviews in social science journals.